Tilghman

The Legendary Lawman and the Woman Who Inspired Him

Howard Kazanjian and Chris Enss

TWODOT®

ESSEX, CONNECTICUT
HELENA, MONTANA

A · TWODOT® · BOOK
An imprint of The Globe Pequot Publishing Group, Inc.
64 South Main Street
Essex, CT 06426
www.globepequot.com

Distributed by NATIONAL BOOK NETWORK

British Library Cataloguing in Publication Information available

Library of Congress Cataloging-in-Publication Data available

ISBN 978-1-4930-4606-5 (paper: alk. paper)
ISBN 978-1-4930-8018-2 (ebook)

∞™ The paper used in this publication meets the minimum requirements of American National Standard for Information Sciences—Permanence of Paper for Printed Library Materials, ANSI/NISO Z39.48-1992.

Contents

Acknowledgments

The ability to tell this story would not have been possible without the Tilghmans' granddaughter, Suzie. She was kind and graciously provided boxes of Zoe and Bill Tilghman's mementos, cards, letters, poems, and journals to do the necessary research. Much of the material used in this book is being seen by the public for the first time, and that's due to the generosity of Suzie.

Others who contributed to the completion of this book were Jackie Reese at the University of Oklahoma Libraries, Western History Collection; the staff at the University of Tulsa, McFarlin Library, Department of Special Collections; Abigail Dairaghi at the University of Tulsa in the Department of Special Collections and University Archives; and Jon May, photograph archives specialist at the Oklahoma Historical Society.

Introduction

When Bill Tilghman was killed in the line of duty in the fall of 1924, his widow, Zoe Stratton Tilghman, had eighty dollars to her name. That money would have to last until she could earn enough to adequately care for herself and the three sons she shared with her late husband. An accomplished author, Zoe had supplemented the family's income as a regular contributor to the Oklahoma City newspaper *Harlow's Weekly* and through the sales of her books of poetry and nonfiction titles on the history of the Old West.

Married for more than twenty years to the well-known and respected lawman Bill Tilghman, Zoe was shattered when he was gunned down outside a café in Cromwell, Oklahoma. Forced to carry on without him, she decided the best way to bring in money and honor Tilghman's memory was to write a book about his life and work. She began the task in early 1925, but wasn't able to complete the job until late 1948. Zoe suffered through numerous highs and lows on the way to finishing the manuscript. Those heartaches and triumphs are key elements in the tale of the stalwart wife writing a biography of her heroic husband.

Zoe Tilghman's book *Marshal of the Last Frontier* not only did justice to her husband but also to the times and circumstances involved. Oklahoma's early years were marked with a desperate struggle to settle the territory, hostility toward the settlers who encroached on Native American lands, and lawlessness. For anyone who thought crime was romantic, Zoe's factual telling of Tilghman's life was a potent antidote. Crime is sordid, and the Wild West prefix didn't actually better its reputation. *Marshal of the Last Frontier* served as a cure for the delusion that crime is romantic. Zoe believed the history of the outlaw should be minimized and more attention and respect paid to the influential, law-abiding population and the valiant men who purposefully held the criminals in check and, in a gratifying large number of cases, extinguished them.

The early-day hunters and exterminators of the most violent desperados of a rousing frontier were, as a rule, quiet, plain, hardworking, determined, and skillful men. They took on the tough jobs and performed their duties the best they could.

Among the enforcement agents Zoe covered in the biography of Tilghman who worked with the marshal were Chris Madsen, Heck Thomas, Bud Ledbetter, and Bat Masterson. All had their fair share of trouble performing their sworn duties and acquired some fame along the way.

For more than fifty years, Tilghman was known by his peers and politicians as one of the West's outstanding peace officers. In addition to his importance as a law enforcement agent, Zoe highlighted the prominent part he played in helping to build the railroad, his relationship with the Native Americans in the region, and ranching in the early days of Oklahoma.

The story of Zoe Tilghman writing the story of Bill Tilghman is a firsthand picture of the many phases of life in the Sooner State. The events in their lives are set against a brief background of national happenings. Details about the daily life of a pioneer, the many people the Tilghmans knew, and the outlaws the marshal encountered are featured. Many sources were used in writing this biography within a biography. Among those sources are official records from the various sheriff and marshal offices where Tilghman was employed, Zoe's diaries and published works about Tilghman, and Tilghman's own letters and journals.

In recent years, reviewers and self-proclaimed historians have criticized Zoe for only writing about the most glowing aspects of her husband's life and career. They claim Tilghman was a horse thief and an embezzler and was guilty of attacking the corrupt Prohibition agent who murdered him. Not only is it unrealistic to think a devoted wife, crafting a book about a man she loved and who was revered by many, would include such information in the biography, but also claims like those noted ultimately proved to be untrue. Further documentation explaining the false allegation of horse theft, claims of misappropriation of funds, and the insinuation that Tilghman, not Wiley Lynn, was unscrupulous are addressed in the chapters to come.

Bat Masterson called Bill Tilghman "the finest of us all" and added, "He was everything you would want in a hero. His sense of justice and fairness separated him from all the other lawmen like night and day." In 1949, the editor of *Tulsa Daily World* boasted, "All Oklahomans need to remember the daring accomplishments of Bill Tilghman and his life for we would not be here today without them." In an article in the May 29, 1949, edition of the *Tulsa Daily World* about Zoe Tilghman's biography of her husband, the writer noted that he believed Bill was sacrificed to the lawless Prohibition era.

"It was a sorry finish for Bill's matter-of-fact and useful life. And an awful commentary on the times," the article concluded. Zoe Tilghman agreed with the statement. "Bill, who had much to do with stopping the era of vulgar and daring outlawry, was a victim of neo-barbarism, an insidious infliction of semi-sanctified gangsterism," she wrote in her memoirs.

In November 1924, newspapers across Oklahoma reported on Bill Tilghman's demise and called him the "bravest of the brave." After her husband's death, Zoe recalled that Bill had always been "a good man who was short on talk and long on work." The only monument Marshal Tilghman ever hoped for was that he would be remembered fondly by the men and women whose lives and property were made safe by his honesty and courage.

What follows is the biography of a devoted author's struggle to write the biography of a notable lawman.

Prologue

Deputy Marshal Bill Tilghman nudged his galloping horse in the side with his spurs to encourage the animal to run faster. The lawman was after a fugitive who had gotten a bit of a head start and whose ride was swift and agile. The horse's ability to keep up with the outlaw's mount had a great deal to do with the rider in the saddle. Tilghman was a solid, broad-shouldered man in his early forties and the desperado he was pursuing was a petite, seventeen-year-old woman. Jennie Metcalf, known in the Oklahoma Territory as Little Breeches, led her horse across the prairie around the town of Pawnee with ease. The ride was so fluid she managed to remove her Colt six-shooter from the waistband of the oversized trousers she was wearing, turn around in her seat, and fire a volley of shots at Tilghman.[1]

The marshal grimaced as he spurred his horse on and lifted his Winchester out of the saddle holster. It was August 18, 1895, and the sun was a ball of fire. The wind at his face was like the breath of a furnace. He was hot and tired and in no mood to take part in a gun battle with a teenager. Tilghman hadn't anticipated the young woman would make a run for it when he set out to arrest her and her cohort, Annie McDoulet—alias Cattle Annie—for stealing horses.[2]

The pair's misdeeds extended far beyond horse thievery. For several months, the women had been working with the Doolin Gang. In 1895, William "Bill" Doolin organized a group comprised of some of the most ruthless criminals in the region. They robbed banks, stagecoaches, and trains. Marshal Tilghman and two other deputy marshals, Heck Thomas and Chris Madsen, had been on their trail for years, but the gang was always one step ahead of them. It was clear someone was helping them to navigate around law enforcement's efforts to apprehend the felons. After the Doolin Gang robbed the US Army payroll near Woodward, Oklahoma, in March 1894, the three officers discussed what they knew about each crime and what dubious characters seemed to always be in the general vicinity. Little Breeches and Cattle Annie were the prime suspects. The three men believed the women had been scouting for the gang, acting as their lookout, and keeping them in supplies. Tilghman was convinced the key to the Doolin Gang's demise was to capture the misguided youth who were aiding and abetting them.[3]

Acting on a tip Tilghman received in the summer of 1895, he and Deputy Steve Burke traveled to a farm outside of Pawnee where Cattle Annie and Little Breeches were rumored to be staying. The lawmen were less than three hundred yards from a crude cabin on the property when Little Breeches raced out of the structure, vaulted onto a nearby horse, and headed into the prairie. Tilghman gave chase after instructing his deputy to grab Cattle Annie, who was watching the action from a busted window next to the front door.[4]

Little Breeches's gun roared spitefully, but her aim was wild. It was difficult to hit a moving target on a horse at full gallop—a fact for which Tilghman was sincerely grateful. The marshal fired his shotgun over the young woman's head in hopes her ride would spook and lose its footing. The animal reared and Little Breeches almost dropped her pistol. She swayed in her saddle like a drunken man, regained her composure, and then spurred the horse back into a gallop. The distance between the marshal and the desperado widened. Tilghman's patience was stretched to the limit. He lifted his shotgun, took careful aim, and shot Little Breeches' horse out from under her.[5] The animal jerked and toppled over.

The rider was tossed hard from the saddle and before hitting the ground Little Breeches dropped her gun. When she caught sight of the weapon, she quickly crawled toward it. Tilghman reached the spot where the gun rested before the woman did and kicked it out of the way. Furious, Little Breeches grabbed a handful of dirt and threw it in the marshal's face. While trying to rub the dust out of his eyes, the runaway scratched his face with her nails. Still struggling to see, Tilghman tried to take hold of her flailing arms and her fists that were contacting his chin and torso. In the process he tripped and fell, and the cornered woman kicked him in his head and neck. The lawman batted her legs away from him while managing to get back on his feet. Little Breeches was relentless. She continued to hit and scratch Tilghman after he stood up.[6]

At last, the lawman pulled his revolver from his holster and leveled it at the woman. Startled, she took a step back and carefully eyed the marshal. Tilghman's nose and mouth were bleeding, and his face was riddled with claw marks. Little Breeches studied the battered man, trying to determine if he would shoot her. The seasoned marshal sensed her dilemma and, in answer to her unspoken question, pulled the hammer back on his gun. They stood staring at one another for a tense moment and then Little Breeches turned to run. Tilghman stiffened his jaw and fired his six-shooter.[7]

Ka-blamm!

* * *

A typewriter key punctuated the description of the sound of Bill Tilghman's gun, and the pristine white paper on which it appeared was then quickly pulled from the roller. Zoe Tilghman, an attractive, dark-haired woman in her early forties, read over what she'd written about the marshal's arrest of Little Breeches, comparing the telling with the lawman's notes he had jotted down on a worn Big Chief tablet. Satisfied she'd gotten the facts correct, Zoe sat back in her chair, stared out the window at a cold February morning in 1925, and studied the gray sky blanketing the Oklahoma City landscape. A strong wind scattered the falling snow around the wintry trees standing like ballet dancers poised to show how graceful they were in the bitter gusts that eddied and swirled.

The makeshift office in the modest three-bedroom home on Twelfth Street was cluttered with bulging file folders, notebooks, letters, cards of condolence, several past due bills, film canisters, photographs, and various guns, including a Winchester rifle. Everywhere Zoe looked she saw reminders of her late husband.

William Matthew Tilghman was born on July 4, 1854, at Fort Dodge, Iowa. He entered the field of law enforcement in 1874 and remained in the profession for more than fifty years. He rode with such well-known peace officers as Wyatt Earp and Bat Masterson and was referred to by his closest lawmen friends as the "greatest of all of us." Tilghman was celebrated by city officials and territorial politicians for his work. In 1905, he was honored by President Theodore Roosevelt for his dedication to law and order on the frontier. At a public tribute to the officer, the president remarked that Bill Tilghman was the kind of man who would "charge hell with a bucket."

In addition to being a legendary marshal, Tilghman was a father of seven children and a faithful companion to his second wife Zoe for more than two decades. His violent death in November 1924 devastated Zoe and the three boys they had together. Tilghman had encountered numerous criminals over the course of his career and had come through the gun battles relatively unscathed. When he took the job of bringing about stability in the untamed oil town of Cromwell, Zoe anticipated he'd take care of the work and return home to live out his days with her and their boys. She never imagined he would be gunned down in the line of duty. Now a widow at forty-three, Zoe was faced with how to continue without the man she cherished and admired. Not only would she be responsible to make sure nineteen-year-old Tench, seventeen-year-old Richard, and twelve-year-old Woodie were cared for on her own, but the debts the couple had accumulated fell solely to her to pay. Tilghman was buried on November 5, 1924, and on November 10, 1924, creditors came calling.

Zoe was the literary editor of the newspaper *Harlow's Weekly*. Her salary alone would not cover the family's needs and outstanding bills. She had been pondering the situation for weeks, in between reading Tilghman's detailed memoirs of the various manhunts, posse rides, shootouts, and arrests in which he participated over the course of his life as a sheriff or marshal. She reviewed with considerable pride the newspaper clippings he had kept about the outlaws he apprehended. Although he'd stayed on the job longer than any of his colleagues and squared off against more renegades than lawmen such as James Butler Hickok, Seth Bullock, or Virgil Earp, Tilghman's name wasn't as recognizable as most of the others in the field.

Among the correspondence Zoe had received from men and women expressing their sorrow over Tilghman's death were newspaper articles about Wyatt Earp's work in motion pictures, his friendship with film star William S. Hart, and the biography in the works about the lawman and his gunfighter life. Zoe had never personally met Earp but knew of him from her husband. She believed Tilghman's experiences were at least as daring and exciting as anything Wyatt Earp had done, and spanned a far greater number of years. The idea to write a book about Tilghman's adventures wearing a badge began forming in Zoe's mind a month after his passing and was rekindled after reading of a possible volume on Earp. She was convinced readers would appreciate the tales of Marshal Tilghman's efforts to tame the territory beyond the Mississippi. According to Zoe, "My husband was one of the West's greatest peace officers. He hunted down famous outlaws and killed when he had to. But Tilghman was more than an expert gunman who fought on the side of the law. He and other men who held dangerous jobs as sheriffs and marshals did the work of civilization along the whole frontier."[8]

Inspired by the women who had penned books about their accomplished husbands such as Elizabeth Custer, who was married to General George Armstrong Custer, and Jessie Benton Fremont, who was married to explorer John Fremont, Zoe hoped a tome written about Tilghman would bring him the recognition she felt he deserved and provide necessary revenue. Zoe was a respected author who had written several published articles and poems for various magazines. Her first book, *The Dugout*, about the life of early Oklahoma pioneers, was scheduled to be printed by Harlow's Publishing Company, a subsidiary of the newspaper where she was employed, in the fall after Tilghman was killed. She was hopeful she could persuade Victor Harlow, the founder of the publishing firm, to invest in a manuscript based on the life and services of the slain marshal.

Bill Tilghman meticulously chronicled his time wearing a badge. Oklahoma and Indian Territories were the last of the frontier, and it was there that the bad men of the nation congregated before the country was opened to settlement. Tilghman got his early training in law enforcement in Kansas, beside his good friend Sheriff Bat Masterson. Zoe would begin the story of Marshal Tilghman at the place known as one of the "wickedest towns of the Wild West." She was still grieving her loss when she sat down at her typewriter to pen Tilghman's story. With her fingers poised over the keys, she watched flurries of white cascading from the clouds above. She pulled the shawl she was wearing tight around her shoulders, and the frigid temperature on the other side of the glass crispened her resolve to do what needed to be done. As her fingers began the work, she no longer saw the frost-laced country beyond her back yard; instead, she was with her husband at his office in Dodge City.

* * *

In the early morning hours of July 6, 1884, Marshal Tilghman sat behind a distressed oak desk reviewing the paperwork he had completed on the latest arrests, information on inmates in custody including their charges, and the final judgment of the court on the cases. The sparsely furnished room was dimly lit by a bracket lamp that revealed a gun rack filled with rifles. Stacked on a shelf underneath the wooden case were several boxes of ammunition. The clock on the wall quietly chimed 1 a.m. Tilghman was so focused on the reports he didn't acknowledge the time. He didn't look away from the task at hand until he heard the muffled sound of gunfire reverberating from somewhere in the near distance. He eased himself out of his chair, grabbed a loaded weapon from the rack, and left the office to investigate.[9]

The lawman walked briskly down the main thoroughfare of town toward where he had heard the shots fired. Another round exploded and a river of customers poured out of Webster's Saloon and found their places in the street a safe distance from the entrance of the establishment. When Tilghman reached the scene, he was informed that the shooter inside the business was a gambler named Dave St. Clair. The marshal nodded his thanks for the warning, pushed open the batwing doors leading into the saloon, and slowly stepped inside.[10]

The tavern was in disarray—tables overturned, chairs tossed about, and chunks of broken glass and liquor bottles scattered around. The body of Bing Choate, a cattleman from Goliad, Texas, lay crumpled on the floor in front of the bar. A wide-eyed, visibly shaken Dave St. Clair was standing over the dead man with his gun leveled at him. When he caught sight of Bill, he turned his gun from the direction of the cowboy and aimed it at the lawman. Sheriff's Deputy Bill Bowles was across the room near the piano trying to protect a half dozen men and women seeking refuge from any more bullets. "It was a fair fight," Bowles announced to the marshal.[11]

Bill Tilghman and Dave St. Clair stared at each other across the room. Bowles sensed the tension between the men and chattered on hoping to diffuse any gunplay. "Choate said he was cheated in the card game," Bowles explained quickly. "He started waving his gun around and claiming that he was the fastest son-of-a-bitch in town. Choate called St. Clair a cowardly son-of-a-bitch then punched him in his face and head with a cane and said, 'I'll teach you a lesson. I'll kill you, you son-of-a-bitch.' St. Clair tried to explain himself then Choate jumped up and headed to the door acting like he was going to leave with the three other cowboys who were with him."[12]

St. Clair's expression didn't soften. He eyed Tilghman closely as the lawman contemplated his next move. Bowles continued talking. "Choate stopped when he was about eight feet from the door and faced toward the bar," the deputy expounded. "St. Clair knew, we all knew, it wasn't going to end at that point. He told Choate, 'You've been punching my neck and stomach with that cane, and you've been shaking your gun around pretty freely.' While he was talking, I moved toward that bar. At that instant, St. Clair said, 'I ought to take that pistol from you and shove it up your ass!' Choate then pulled his gun and spun on St. Clair. I shouted at Dave to look out. That instant St. Clair drew his pistol and shot Choate. St. Clair had not drawn his pistol before that."[13]

St. Clair kept his eyes fixed on Tilghman as the marshal inched his way toward him. "I want you to give me your gun, St. Clair," the lawman told him. St. Clair didn't respond, not even the blink of an eyelid. Tilghman continued slowly walking toward him. "I'm not going to hurt you, Dave, I just want your gun so nothing else happens."

With his chest inches from the gun barrel, Tilghman stopped and extended his hand. "Give me your gun, Dave." Slowly it was done. Tilghman stuck the gun in his waistband, then called over his shoulder at those hiding behind tables, "Anybody hurt?"

There were murmurs of denial as the nervous patrons emerged from their safe positions. Tilghman nodded to them as they cautiously moved about. He then took St. Clair's arm to lead him away. At the door, St. Clair turned toward the disconcerted saloon customers and staff and announced, "I'm not a cheat."[14]

No one responded. Tilghman motioned for St. Clair to move along, and he did so. The crowd waiting outside opened to let the pair through. A few thanked the lawman for his help as he passed by them.[15]

* * *

Armed with such stories about her husband's heroism during the desperate outlaw days of old, Zoe presented the book proposal to her publisher in March 1925. When signing the contract to write the book she never imagined the years it would take to complete the job, nor the heartbreak she would endure in the process.

Chapter 1

Kansas Life

In mid-October 1885, two men ambled down the Jones and Plummer Trail, 120 miles from the Kansas border, toward the Cimarron River. Marshal Bill Tilghman was in the lead, his eyes fixed on the spot the riders would have to ford the swollen waterway. He had a tight grip on a bald-faced mare trailing behind him. Atop the animal was a horse thief named George Synder. He was a dark-complected man in his mid-thirties with a thin moustache and a gaunt intensity that wasn't entirely healthy looking. Tilghman had journeyed to Mobeetie, Texas, to arrest Synder for stealing a horse that belonged to a politician from Great Bend named J. C. Briggs. It wasn't the first time Tilghman had made a long trip to apprehend a criminal. Unlike other lawmen who had to encroach on another jurisdiction to make an arrest, Tilghman insisted on acquiring the necessary writs from the officers overseeing the area he planned to invade. He expected the same courtesy to be shown him from law enforcement seeking to detain an offender in his domain.[1]

In the first pages penned about his life and work, Zoe made note of such professional courtesies practiced by the marshal. "My husband's career in law enforcement began in Dodge City when the country west of the Mississippi was finding its way," she wrote. "Bill traveled to Oklahoma in 1889 just before the first land rush in the nation. He served the rough Territory for thirty-five years as U. S. deputy marshal, sheriff, chief of police, and special aide to governors. His peers admired his ethics and outlaws feared his tenacity. In the end, when a new kind of frontier

William Tilghman at Dodge City, Kansas, 1882.
OKLAHOMA HISTORICAL SOCIETY

opened during the brawling oil boom of the 1920s, Bill gave his life as he had lived it—in the cause of decency and order."

Zoe could envision her husband escorting Synder to jail and contemplating his early years on the open range. His family had moved to Kansas after the military closed the fort where William Matthew Tilghman Sr. had been employed as a sutler at Fort Dodge, Iowa, selling provisions to the troops. "He grew up on the plains, and a gun was rarely far from his hand," Zoe noted about Tilghman's upbringing. "At that time, in 1862, his father and oldest brother Richard enlisted in the Union Army and fought in the Civil War. Tilghman had to do the work on the farm near Atchison, Kansas, and furnish his mother Amanda and six others with food, which mostly consisted of rabbits and prairie chickens. When he wasn't feeding the stock, milking, and gathering corn, he was practicing his shooting. In time, he was able to provide his mother, brothers, and sisters with geese and turkeys for their meals."[2]

Tilghman became proficient with a musket and a cap and ball pistol. He liked to impersonate Wild Bill Hickok with his guns. Hickok's time as a law enforcement agent in various Kansas locations was well publicized. Tilghman knew of the marshal and admired him. He met the imposing figure when he was twelve years old. Dressed in buckskins with leather fringe and a broad Plainsman's hat covering his shoulder-length hair, Marshal Hickok rode past the Tilghmans' homestead in search of a man driving a team of mules and covered wagon. The lawman stopped briefly to ask Tilghman if he'd seen such a man and vehicle. The young boy was so taken aback at coming face to face with the well-known figure that he could barely respond. Eventually, Hickok got out of the boy that indeed he had seen the man in question heading toward Atchison. The marshal thanked him for his help and rode on. That brief encounter left a lasting impression on Tilghman and, according to Zoe, helped influence his decision to become a lawman.[3]

At one time, the Oklahoma Panhandle area Tilghman and his prisoner were traveling was thick with buffalo. In 1870, the future marshal and three of his cousins embarked on a hunting trip in the vicinity he was crossing with Synder. Tilghman and his relatives filled two wagons with buffalo meat and sold it on their way back to the Kansas homestead. The following year, when he turned seventeen, Tilghman became a qualified buffalo hunter. His brother Richard joined him on the venture. They sold only the meat at first, but later took only the hides. With one shot of his Sharps rifle and using a "rest" stick for steady aim, Tilghman once killed a buffalo bull a mile away. His brother measured the distance with ropes.[4]

Hide hunting was profitable, but risky. Native Americans resented the slaughter and fought against many white hunters. Between 1871 and 1876, various members of the Senate passed laws prohibiting the extermination of the animal, but there were no agents put into place to make sure the law wasn't violated. In 1872, the Kansas legislature passed a law prohibiting the wasting of bison meat, but the governor vetoed it.[5] The absence of the massive creatures did not escape Tilghman's notice as he rode the trail with his prisoner. In his many journals about his experiences on the Plains, he admitted he was an "impetuous young man who could not imagine the consequences of the hunting expeditions in which he took part."[6]

Tilghman's years as a buffalo hunter providing game for the railroad enabled him to gain a knowledge of the terrain from the banks of the Arkansas River north of Abilene, Kansas, to the Cimarron River south of San Angelo, Texas. It was his expertise of the region and the friendly relationship he had with the Kiowa, Apache, and Cheyenne people that prompted cattleman Mart Childers to offer Tilghman a job driving his livestock that were resting southeast of Adobe Walls, Texas, on into Dodge City. Childers had more than five thousand cattle and he offered Tilghman and his former buffalo hunting crew five dollars a head for all they rounded up and drove to Kansas. The price offered was comparable to what the men received for buffalo, but neither Tilghman nor the others knew much about cattle. Childers assured them they would be taught how to "punch cows." Before Tilghman accepted the job he was informed that some of the livestock had wandered into Indian Territory and the animals needed to be retrieved.[7]

Tensions between the Native Americans and the US government were strained in 1873 when Tilghman and five of his friends signed on to be cowboys. Survey crews had been commissioned to create maps of the frontier, establish boundaries between sections of land, and determine the

Bill Tilghman traversed the plains and prairies of Oklahoma early in his life and career.
LIBRARY OF CONGRESS

best place for railroad tracks to be laid. Frustrated Indians dealt harshly with surveyors planting stakes on their sovereign land. Tilghman suspected there might be trouble venturing into tribal land to get Childers's cattle, but he believed the years he had spent on the Plains interacting with Native American leaders such as Kicking Bird and White Deer of the Kiowa and Roman Nose of the Cheyenne would help in recovering the roaming stock.[8]

After a few days training with Childers's foreman on the art of herding, Tilghman and his friends started on their way to Anderson Creek, six miles outside the rail town of Lufkin, Texas, where the bulk of the cattle were waiting. Shortly after the six men got underway, they noticed a black plume of smoke rising into the sky west of the Jones and Plummer Trail on which they were traveling. The seasoned buffalo hunters considered that Native Americans were involved. At Tilghman's urging

A young Bill Tilghman (right) posed with his cousin, Jim Elder (left), during their buffalo hunting days.
OKLAHOMA HISTORICAL SOCIETY

the men decided to ride in the direction of the smoke and the growing number of buzzards circling overhead. When the six arrived at the scene they found four slain members of a survey crew. Their bodies had been torn apart, their wagons and possessions set on fire, and their horses scattered. Graves were dug and the dead were buried. Tilghman warned the men riding with him to keep a sharp eye out for the trouble he was sure to come their way.[9]

When the novice cowboys reached the cattle camp near Anderson Creek, Tilghman met with the foreman and informed him of what they'd encountered en route. The foreman dismissed Tilghman's advice about proceeding cautiously. He believed the Indian's attitude toward ranch hands driving cattle to market were different from their feelings about settlers and surveyors. Tilghman assured him that it wasn't likely they'd be able to make the trip without disruption from members of the Cheyenne and Kiowa tribes. "What do they want from us?" the foreman asked Tilghman. "They want us off their land," he responded matter-of-factly.[10]

By the time Tilghman, his brother, their friends, and the other cowhands had been hired to drive the cattle north in the spring of 1873, Childers's herd had swollen to ten thousand head. For the first six days of the journey, churlish clouds coughed out great amounts of water soaking man and animal. Placid streams were transformed into raging torrents and the prairie sod into a quagmire. The strung-out cattle grazed as they moved. The horses carrying Tilghman and the other cowboys had a difficult time with the soggy conditions. Their hooves often sank ankle-deep and had to be pulled free from the mud suction. The riders suffered as well. Their clothes were continually soaked and heavy with moisture. The provisions they carried with them were drenched and became moldy. It was an unpleasant start in the business for Tilghman and his friends.[11]

A week after the drive had begun, a hot sun broke through and quickly dried everything. Cattle and drivers pushed on at a swifter pace. Hooves thudded, horns clicked, and the dust arose like a blanket, steadily growing thicker as the days progressed. Tilghman kept a close eye on the animals as well as the horizon. He couldn't see anyone, but knew they were being watched. Kiowa tribesmen were observing the cowhands who broke off from the main herd to look for strays and stealthily followed them. When Tilghman and another rider with extra pack horses rode away from the others in search of wandering steers, fifty Kiowa warriors stepped out of the shadows and made themselves known.[12]

Tilghman stopped his horse and the cowboy with him did the same. The two groups stared at one another without saying a word. Tilghman sensed the rider with him was concerned. In a soft voice he explained to the man that he had friendly dealings with the Kiowa in the past when he was buffalo hunting. He assured the cowhand if Kicking Bird was leading the band of braves who were eyeing the pair, he might be able to negotiate with them. While Tilghman was contemplating what to do and when, the warriors let out a loud war cry. In that instance, Tilghman knew he wouldn't be able to talk his way out of the dire situation.[13]

The Kiowas kicked their horses into a gallop toward the cowboys. Tilghman and the man with him took off in the direction they came. The pack horses they had with them as well as the stray cattle raced to keep up. The Indians divided into two parties, both hurrying after the cowhands as fast as their rides would take them. Tilghman and his coworker urged their horses to go even faster, and the animals did. The chase continued for several minutes, with the Kiowas closing the gap on the exhausted cattle and pack animals trying to keep up. Eventually the braves captured the cows and horses. Some stayed behind with the livestock while others maintained the pursuit of Tilghman and his companion.[14]

The gap between the Kiowas, Tilghman, and the other cowhand widened and narrowed throughout the chase. Tilghman considered stopping to shoot the pursuers but was convinced killing one or several of the warriors would only cause more problems in the long run. The cowboys believed their only option was to outrun the Kiowas. The Indians doggedly followed the two men into a canyon, forcing the pair up a steep hillside. When the cowhands reached the top, they realized they were trapped. Far below them on the other side was a stream that was swollen from the recent rains. Tilghman quickly surmised they would have to jump if they hoped to survive.[15]

The cowboys dismounted and coaxed their horses to make the leap first. They watched the animals plummet forty feet into the water. The dazed and slightly confused horses emerged unhurt from the death-defying jump. They swam to the bank of the stream, stumbling over rocks until they got their footing, where they stood huddled together, shaking from the experience.[16]

Tilghman and the cowhand with him leapt from the precipice minutes after making sure the horses had made it through the ordeal. The pair hit the water hard and popped to the surface moments later. Tilghman looked at the cliff towering over them to see if the warriors were at the summit. Seeing no one, the cowhands pulled themselves out of the rampaging stream and hurried to their horses. The still shaking animals could barely move beyond a walk. Tilghman and his cohort managed to lead the horses to an outcropping of rock. By then, the Kiowas were lined along the ridge. Tilghman removed his Sharps rifle from the holster on his saddle and fired a shot in the warriors' direction. The Kiowas quickly climbed off their horses and flattened themselves on the ground. They didn't return fire or attempt to follow the cowhands down the embankment.[17]

Two days after the incident, Tilghman and the other cowboy located Childers's herd and the hands driving the cattle. The foreman thought the pair had been hurt or worse. The men explained what had happened to them and confessed it took a bit to regain their strength from the ordeal. "The chase the Indians gave us was trying," Tilghman recalled later in his written account of the experience. "My horse Chief never fully recovered from the effects of that trouble."[18]

Before Tilghman had a chance to resume his duties, his friends gathered around to give him the news that his brother Richard had been killed. Like Tilghman, he had ridden off to gather stray cattle. He was overrun by Kiowas. Richard's body had been placed in a tool wagon. His friends were waiting for Tilghman to return before they buried the slain cowboy. Tilghman laid his brother to rest near a rocky meadow then rejoined the others on the drive.[19]

Childers's hired hands delivered his cattle to Dodge City and left them in the corrals near the railroad depot. He paid Tilghman and his friends the amount promised, and all hurried off to celebrate the success of the grueling run. For Tilghman the completion of the job was bittersweet. He missed his brother and was in a quandary as to what to do next. His buffalo hunting days were behind him, and although Childers offered him a permanent position with his outfit, Tilghman wasn't convinced that was what he wanted to do. He aspired to be a lawman and hoped he'd find employment in that line of work in Dodge City.[20]

In between his job as a cowhand and being hired at the Dodge City sheriff's department, one of Tilghman's friends, Bill Martin, persuaded him to ride along to a dance in Sun City, which was more than seventy miles east of town in Barber County. It was here that Tilghman met his first wife. Flora Kendall was fourteen when she and the twenty-year-old Tilghman were introduced. The couple took only one turn around the dance floor and their conversation was equally as brief, but both were smitten. He carried a mental picture of the petite, brown-eyed girl with him on his next several ventures including traveling to Colorado in search of gold, hiring on as a cowboy again and driving cattle from Granada, Kansas, to the area around Cheyenne, Wyoming, and returning briefly to buffalo hunting with Bat Masterson and Neal Brown, two men he would serve with as lawmen in Dodge City and elsewhere.[21]

In May 1877, Tilghman entered business with his friend Henry Garris. The pair were co-owners of the Crystal Palace Saloon. Sheriff Bat Masterson issued the license they needed to sell alcohol. Two months after acquiring the Crystal Palace, located across Front Street on the other side of the railroad tracks, Tilghman and Garris renovated the exterior of the building and added an awning. An article in the July 21, 1877, edition of the *Dodge City Times* reported that the improvements "will tend to create a new attraction toward the never-ceasing fountain of refreshments flowing within."[22]

"For seven years he had been a Plainsman meeting storms and deadly cold—floods, scorching summers, drought and thirst, danger of wild beasts and savage men, and the hidden terror of poison fang," Zoe wrote about Tilghman's life prior to purchasing the saloon. "He had seen sickness and wounds and death, and he had toiled heavily with his hands and all his strength. He had traveled over the whole area of the last frontier, embracing portions of five states. He knew streams and crossings and camping places; how to find the best route where no man had left a trace before him; knew high hills and landmarks and could take his course by the stars, or travel with an unerring sense of direction, to arrive at a given goal."[23]

The decision to settle in a town like Dodge City was not without complications. The wild burgh was filled with rowdy cowboys, professional gunslingers, and ruthless gamblers. In his new line of work the twenty-three-year-old Tilghman found himself associating with unsavory characters and on two occasions unintentionally found himself on the wrong side of the law.[24]

At four in the morning on January 27, 1878, five desperados attempted to rob a train outside of Kinsley, thirty-six miles northeast of Dodge. The outlaws planned to take the safe in one of the cars. The night operator at the railroad depot refused to cooperate with the would-be thieves and, because another train was soon to arrive on the scene, the robbers decided against pursuing the crime.[25]

The suspected felons rode in the direction of Dodge City and within the hour an armed posse was after them. Sheriff Masterson and his deputies managed to apprehend three of the men, Dave Reudebaugh (spelled Rudabaugh in some instances), Edgar West, and William Tilghman were arrested. Each appeared in court and Reudebaugh and West waived preliminary examinations. However, they could not pay the bail required and were remanded to the custody of the local authorities until their court date, which was set in June.[26] Bail for Tilghman, who according to the February 5, 1878, edition of the *Dodge City Globe*, was being held on suspicion of being a "wire puller" for the outlaws, was set at the same amount. He was ready to go to court immediately to proclaim his innocence, but the state wanted time to produce a witness.[27]

Tilghman was released after he posted his bail. Shortly thereafter, the charges against him were dropped. A letter to Tilghman about the matter from Edward's County attorney J. E. McArthur explained the reason why. "Dear Sir, your case was called today for examination," the correspondence began. "There being no evidence against you, I filed a motion for your discharge, entering the same on the docket. I congratulate you on your discharge, hoping that you may be so lucky in the future, as never to be suspicioned of a crime."[28]

Tilghman wouldn't be so fortunate. Two months after being accused of attempted robbery, he was accused of stealing a horse. On April 16, 1878, a rancher named M. A. Couch arrived in Dodge City with a handful of his friends and relatives in search of four horses, two of which were stolen from his neighbor. The animals were stolen in the evening hours and Couch tracked the horses to H. B. Bell's livery stable and there met Tilghman and a government scout named Jack Martin. Both Tilghman and Martin were sitting atop Couch's stolen horses. The rancher accused the pair of the theft, an accusation they strenuously denied. Couch reported the matter to the authorities and a warrant was issued for the arrest of Martin and Tilghman. "Harry E. Gryden defended Tilghman, Martin having no counsel," the April 23, 1878, edition of the *Dodge City Globe* noted. " . . . Martin has since employed Gryden to help him in the matter."[29]

The sheriff's department investigated and learned Tilghman and Martin had purchased the horses from a man named Henry Martin (no relation to Jack) who claimed to have acquired the animals legitimately from the military. The two horses he sold Tilghman and Martin were animals the army didn't need. Henry was apprehended west of Fort Dodge on April 26, 1878.[30]

Being arrested twice in a short period of time prompted Tilghman to make serious changes. He sold most of his interest in the Crystal Palace and purchased a homestead near Bluff Creek more than fifty miles north of Dodge City. At one time he had hoped to travel to Sun City and ask Flora to marry him. He considered what their lives would be like together on the 160-acre spread that was now his. The two had exchanged a few letters since their first meeting and Tilghman believed she was the one for him. Sadly, he had waited too long to propose. Earlier in the year he learned that his friend Joe Robinson and Flora had wed and were expecting their first child.[31]

Tilghman had almost put the idea of life with Flora out of his mind until he heard that Joe had been killed in a riding accident and his widow and child were left to fend for themselves. After a decent interval, Tilghman brought Flora and her son Charles to Dodge City. Before the end of 1878, the two had exchanged vows and settled on the Bluff Creek property. For a time, the couple were content. Their days and nights were consumed with working the homestead. Tilghman bought a small herd of cattle and built corrals for the horses he planned to purchase. Flora made improvements to the crude house her new husband constructed, and in the evening the pair would play with Charles, whom Tilghman eventually adopted as his own.[32]

Staying in one place for an extended period proved to be difficult for Tilghman. He enjoyed traveling the prairie and working a variety of jobs. His restless behavior didn't go unnoticed by his bride. Flora wasn't surprised when her husband accepted Sheriff Bat Masterson's invitation to serve as undersheriff. Tilghman hired a ranch hand to oversee the duties at the homestead while he helped keep peace in Dodge City.[33]

DODGE CITY'S PEACE COMMISSIONERS

Tilghman served alongside some of the most legendary lawmen in the West. He is pictured here (top, far right) with Bat Masterson (to his immediate left) and Wyatt Earp (bottom, second from left).
OKLAHOMA HISTORICAL SOCIETY

One of the first major cases Tilghman worked was the murder of dance-hall singer Dora Hand. Hand was killed by Spike Kenedy, part-time cowboy and son of a wealthy Texas cattleman. After killing the songstress by firing shots into the home where she was sleeping, Kenedy fled the scene. In early October 1878, a posse made up of the most well-known and well-respected lawmen in the territory set out to capture the offender. Members of the group known as the "Most Intrepid Posse" were Wyatt Earp, Bat Masterson, Charlie Bassett, Neal Brown, and Bill Tilghman. The posse tracked Kenedy and arrested him. He was later acquitted of the crime.[34]

Throughout Tilghman's time in Kansas, he was routinely confused with another man whose first and last names were the same as his but were spelled differently. William Tilman was frequently in trouble with the law and on occasion his misdeeds were attributed to Tilghman. Some newspaper reports of Tilman's illegal activities made a point of letting readers know "the outlaw Wm. Tilman should not be confused with the lawman Wm. Tilghman." That point was evident in articles printed in late October 1878 when Undersheriff Wm. Tilghman was on the lookout for Wm. Tilman the train robber.[35]

"It appears that Mike Rourke, Dement and Tilman were stopping at a ranch on Thompson Creek about eleven miles south of Ellsworth, Kansas, and that it was their intention to burglarize the express office at Ellsworth or to attack the train at Rock Springs, a small water station," the October 23, 1878, edition of the *Atchison Daily Champion* read. "The sheriff's posse arrived there about daylight that morning and captured Rourke in the stable. A few minutes afterward Dement came out and opened the stable door, but the officers thought at first that he was one of their numbers. He fled and was pursued, shot at, and wounded, but managed to make his escape to the woods. The gang's outfit was captured, but Tilman and Dement escaped. The officers are making a hot chase and will probably bag the rest of the gang in a few days. Rourke is now in jail at Junction City."[36]

Tilman was apprehended more than a year after the incident.[37]

In the fall of 1878, Tilghman was briefly lured away from the sheriff's office by Colonel William H. Lewis, the commander at Fort Dodge.

Colonel Lewis wanted Tilghman to act as a scout for the army. A band of Northern Cheyenne, led by Chief Dull Knife, had left their confinement in Oklahoma to return to their land in Montana. The more than 92 warriors and 262 women and children had eluded attempts by the cavalry to locate them and force them back to the reservation. They overran small settlements and ranches, taking food, supplies, and any weapons they could find. Colonel Lewis received word that Dull Knife's band had moved into southern Kansas. Tilghman, who knew the territory better than most, was tasked with determining the route and location of the Cheyenne. He informed Colonel Lewis that the band was holed up at a spot known as White Woman Creek, eighty-plus miles from Fort Dodge. The colonel assembled his troops and the soldiers, and they arrived in the area on September 27, 1878.[38]

Overnight the Cheyenne had made their way farther across the Plains and were now taking refuge in a place called Punished Woman's Fork. Lewis and his men tracked the band into a rocky canyon. The troops didn't suspect they were being lured into a situation where they had no way to retreat. Once inside the canyon, the Cheyenne warriors opened fire. Colonel Lewis was one of the many cavalrymen who were killed at the location. According to the October 17, 1878, edition of the *Southern Kansas Gazette*, "Colonel Lewis displayed rare courage and remained on his horse, the finest mark on the field. After dismounting, he moved about directing the fire of the troops until a ball in the right leg severed the main artery and brought him down."[39]

Tilghman had returned to his duties as undersheriff after his job scouting was complete. He was nowhere near Punished Woman's Fork when the battle broke out. He had accepted the colonel's assignment trusting in the intelligence the colonel had received that indicated all Dull Knife's band were in far southwest Kansas. The colonel did not know the Cheyenne had split into two groups and that one of those groups was in the southwest portion of the state traveling along Bluff Creek. Tilghman's ranch hand, wife, and son barely made it off the property before the Cheyenne band arrived. While the colonel and his men were making their way to Dodge City they could see the plumes of smoke emanating from the Tilghman homestead. The Cheyenne set fire to everything—home, corral, and barn.[40]

The Tilghmans moved into a small house in Dodge City. Flora focused on making their new place comfortable and caring for Charles, and Tilghman continued working for Sheriff Masterson until the end of the year. Masterson ran for reelection but lost to George T. Hinkle. Tilghman was out of a job when Masterson left office. He discussed his employment options with Flora and explained to her that executives with the Arizona and Pacific Railroad were hiring men to help transport materials to build rail services across New Mexico. The pay being offered was $20 a day. The couple agreed it was a good opportunity and began making plans. Flora was pregnant with their first child together and the two decided she would move in with Tilghman's parents living in Atchison, Kansas. Bill would travel to the remote railroad offices at Fort Wingate in New Mexico and return whenever he could.[41]

"The wages that had appeared so big in Kansas, proved little above the cost of feed for horse and man," Zoe wrote about Tilghman's time as a railroad freighter in the Southwest. "Bill worked for a time hauling ties made from cedar trees which were cut in the mountains. Buying supplies for the tie camp, he learned the real cost of food, wholesale, and saw a better opportunity. Soon he had set up a tent eating-house near the grader's camp. He hired people to work for him and in no time had a flourishing business.[42] He was his own cook and provided not only meat, potatoes, and beans, but pies and puddings which won great approval."[43]

Tilghman was fortunate enough to be back in Kansas when his son James was born. But his time with his family was short-lived. He had to get back to his job with the railroad and running his makeshift restaurant.[44]

In addition to hauling supplies and cooking meals, Tilghman raced horses. In a country where a horse was a primary factor in living, everybody was interested in horse racing, and the owner of a fast horse was well respected. Tilghman owned the fastest horse in the camp. There was only one instance when a gambler who had lost his money betting against Tilghman dared to accuse him of cheating and threatened his horse. Tilghman beat the man to the draw, shooting the gun out of the gambler's hand before he could get off a shot.[45]

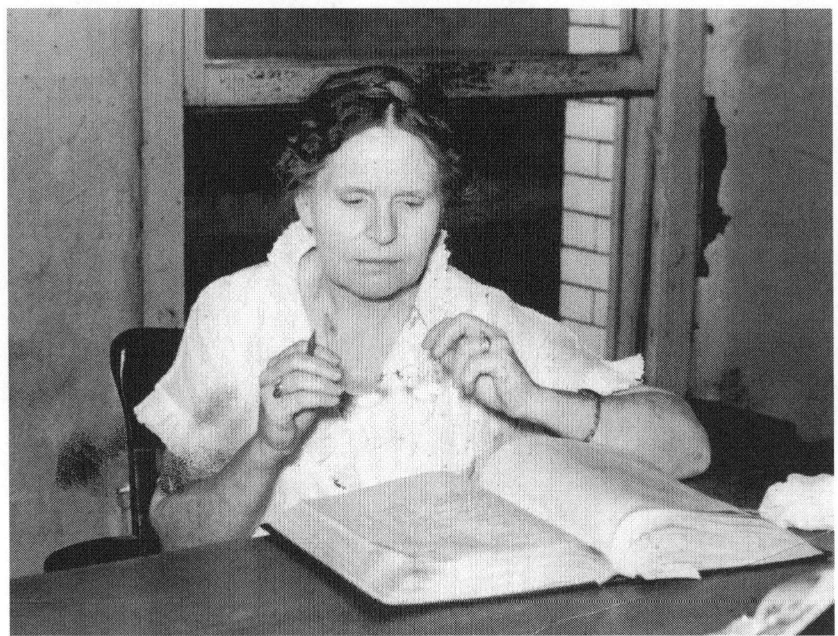

Zoe Tilghman at her desk at *Harlow's Weekly* working on her husband's biography.
OKLAHOMA HISTORICAL SOCIETY

Not long after that incident, two drunk railroad tie layers muscled their way into Tilghman's eatery and began dumping patrons' plates of food on the floor. Tilghman downed the first man with a punch to the face. The other reached for his pistol, but suddenly stopped moving when Tilghman pressed his gun into the man's stomach before the man had a chance to pull his own gun out of his holster. Both men left the establishment, but that wasn't the end. Late in the evening Tilghman spotted the offenders approaching the restaurant again. He grabbed his shotgun and stealthily made his way to a large stump just outside the canvas structure. He ducked down behind it and waited. Just as the men arrived at the entrance of the building, Tilghman stepped out, his gun leveled at the pair. The men quickly pulled their weapons, but before they could fire Tilghman shot one man in the shoulder and the other in the leg.[46]

Tilghman's business ventures in the Southwest were successful and he was able to provide well for his family. That wasn't enough for Flora, however. She wanted to be with her husband. James had become ill and died and she was devastated over the loss of the child. Tilghman traveled back to Kansas to bury his son, and when he returned to New Mexico Flora and Charles were with him. Flora dealt with her grief working long hours at the eatery. In time, the Tilghmans welcomed their daughter Dorothy to the world and the sadness over James's death subsided.[47]

When the railroad work was completed, Tilghman packed up his family and moved back to Kansas. He used the money he earned to purchase two hundred acres between Dodge City and Fort Dodge. He filled the land with cattle and invested in other types of livestock as well. In May 1883, Tilghman built a saloon in Dodge City called the Oasis and turned it over to his younger brother Frank to run.[48]

Tilghman was driven. He wanted to take care of his growing family and contribute to civilizing Dodge City. Flora wanted nothing more than for her husband to come home to her and the children every night. When Tilghman accepted the job of deputy working with Sheriff Pat Sughure in late 1883, she realized the folly of her desire.[49] She'd married a man who would always struggle to balance two competing needs—one for safety and security, and the other for excitement and the unknown. There were many evenings she sat on the wooden porch of their house on the ranch watching the trail. Everyone had gone to bed, but Flora was waiting for Tilghman. Eventually she realized he wouldn't be coming home, not then at least. She'd go back inside, make sure her children were sleeping, then crawl into bed alone. She prayed for his protection and looked forward to the possibility of seeing him the next day.[50]

As Zoe wrote about Flora's angst over Tilghman's long absences she understood how trying those times must have been. She'd echoed the same prayers and thoughts for him many times. She and Flora had that in common. What was different for Zoe as she authored the story of her husband's life was the knowledge that she would never see Tilghman again. That was something Flora never had to experience, and Zoe envied her for it.[51]

Chapter 2

Becoming a Marshal

Zoe Tilghman sat alone in her small office at *Harlow's Weekly*, studying the article that had been placed on her desk earlier in the day. The headline just above the lengthy report announced that the "Man Who Killed Veteran Peace Office William Tilghman Has Been Acquitted." The widow had circled the word *acquitted* several times with her pencil, hoping the mere act would enable her to accept the appalling verdict that came a mere six months after her husband's death. She wondered if the three sons she shared with her late husband had heard the news. The article had specifically mentioned her boys, noting that Tilghman had left behind a wife and "Tench, named for a Revolutionary ancestor; Richard, named for the first American ancestor; and Woodrow Wilson Tilghman." Tench was nineteen years old and a law student at the University of Oklahoma. Richard was seventeen and a senior in high school. Woodrow was thirteen and in his last year of junior high.[1]

Zoe was annoyed that her children's names had been listed in the newspaper story. She worried the man who killed her husband would seek revenge on the family because he had been arrested for the crime in the first place. The shooter insisted he acted in self-defense and promised to get even with anyone who doubted his integrity. Zoe's concern for her sons extended beyond threats from armed offenders. Young vulnerable men needed their fathers, and the absence of a father could lead to trouble. Zoe's focus was making sure she earned the money to take care of her family's essentials and to help fund their education; beyond that, she'd do the best she could.[2]

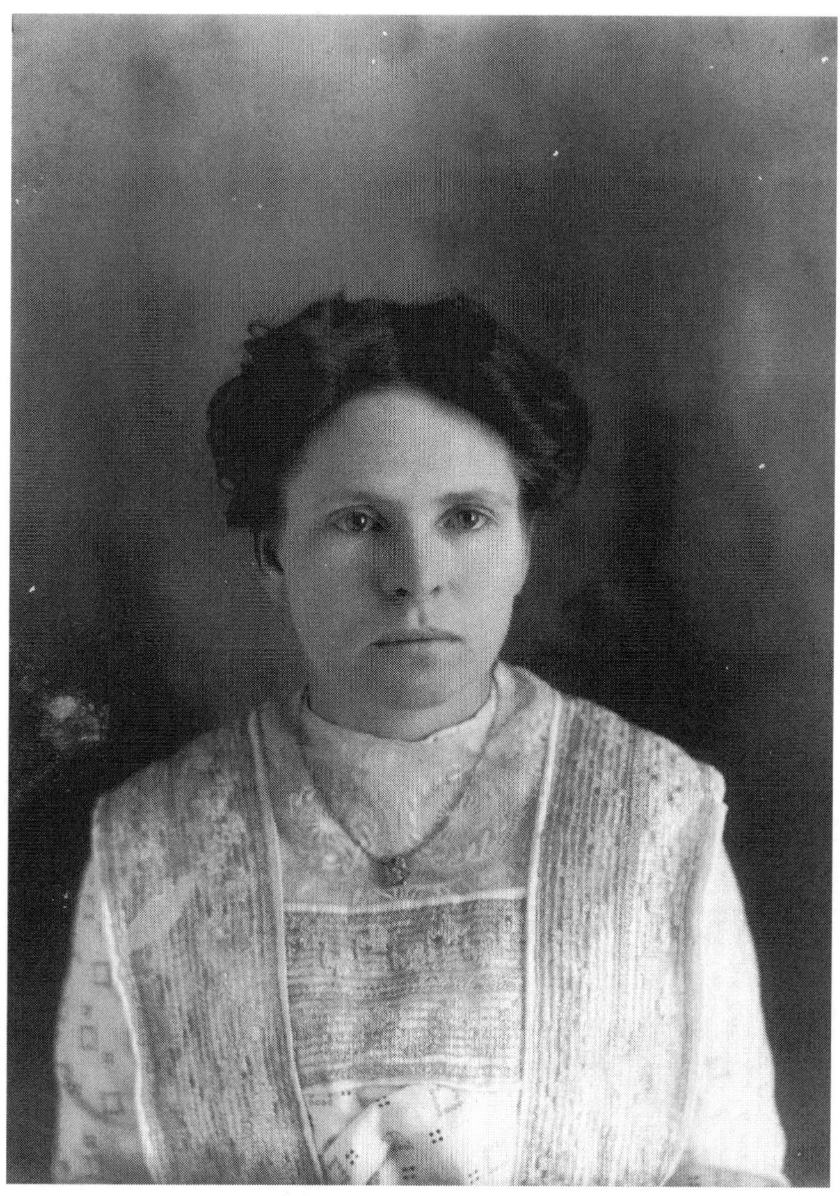

Zoe Stratton Tilghman circa 1925.
DEPARTMENT OF SPECIAL COLLECTIONS AND UNIVERSITY ARCHIVES, UNIVERSITY OF TULSA MCFARLIN LIBRARY

In addition to writing about her husband's life and times, Zoe's job with *Harlow's Weekly* included penning a regular literary column, reviews of new books about Oklahoma, biographical sketches of the state's pioneers, and contributing poems about the region. Zoe was prolific and capable of working on multiple projects at one time. Between the time Tilghman was killed in November 1924 and July 1925, she wrote her first book, *The Dugout*, and penned more than twenty poems published in *Harlow's Weekly*. Her poems not only paid homage to Oklahoma but also lamented all she'd lost to the place she called home.[3]

In her poem "Never a Song," Zoe wrote, "You have turned your heart from my prairies, the city of lights and thrills has won your love from my gracious skies and the beauty of homeland hills. I have dowered you richly and free; I have given the world a singer, but there's now never a song for me."[4]

Zoe's first poem was published in 1898 during her time at the University of Oklahoma. Born in Greenwood County, Kansas, in 1880 to Mayo and Agnes Stratton, the headstrong young woman was inspired to be a writer by her father who regaled her with tales of his days driving cattle up the Chisholm Trail. The Strattons moved to Oklahoma in the late 1890s and settled on a farm in Ingalls. Zoe's early poems, and later the books she penned, were about life in the wild territory, the brilliant landscape she desperately loved, and the people who influenced the region. William Tilghman was among those noteworthy individuals who contributed substantially to Oklahoma's history. Unlike Zoe's father, Tilghman would not be there to share with his family the stories of the struggle to grow the Oklahoma Territory into a state and how the experience shaped his character. That job fell to Zoe now and she was keenly aware of the importance of every word she wrote about her lawman husband.[5]

"Bill took up his work as a servant of the law with the same quiet determination to make good, as when he had herded cattle," Zoe wrote about Tilghman. "Being an officer meant more than a gun and a badge." Tilghman desired to learn everything he could about the law and asked Ford County, Kansas, prosecutor Mike Sullivan to teach him. Sullivan was recognized as one of the best lawyers in Kansas and happily agreed

Bill Tilghman enjoying a fishing trip with his three sons. Richard stands on his father's right, Tench is on the far left, and Woodrow stands between his father and older brother.

DEPARTMENT OF SPECIAL COLLECTIONS AND UNIVERSITY ARCHIVES, UNIVERSITY OF TULSA MCFARLIN LIBRARY

Zoe Tilghman as a young girl. The photograph was taken in 1888.
DEPARTMENT OF SPECIAL COLLECTIONS AND UNIVERSITY ARCHIVES, UNIVERSITY OF TULSA MCFARLIN LIBRARY

to take on the unique student. He admired Tilghman's drive to fully understand the legal process. He trained the officer in the proper handling and issuing of warrants and the intricacies of contracts, procedures, writs, and torts.[6]

When Tilghman was appointed city marshal in April 1884, Sullivan boasted to his colleagues that the new marshal was the "first officer he'd met out West who cared what the law really was." Citizens of Dodge City admired Tilghman's integrity as well and to show their appreciation presented him with a solid gold badge. "Wm. Tilghman, City Marshal" was engraved on one side and on the other side, "Presented by Your Many Friends. May 2nd, 1884."[7]

During Tilghman's first summer as marshal he had to deal with a number of domestic incidents. In August of 1884, a pair of prostitutes got into a brawl over a man at one of the town's saloons. Bertha Lockwood and Sadie Hudson weren't content to slap and kick one another to win the affections of their mutual lover; knives were pulled, and Sadie was stabbed three times. Marshal Tilghman arrested and jailed Bertha and she was charged with attempted murder.[8]

A week after the stabbing, husband and wife Ollie and Mollie Hart got into a physical altercation that led to the police being called to the scene. Tilghman took the two into custody but not before being hit on the head with a bottle Mollie had thrown that was intended for Ollie. Days later, Marshal Tilghman arrested a mountain of a man from Colorado who was passing through town on his way east and decided to celebrate his arrival in style. He befriended a soiled dove and showered her with gifts including a multi-colored dress. The ungrateful lady met another man at some point during the Colorado giant's visit and decided to sell the items purchased for her. When the mountain man learned of her duplicity, he began dismantling the saloon where she worked. When Marshal Tilghman reached the establishment to stop the man from doing any further damage, the interior of the business was in shambles. The jilted man was arrested, made to pay a hefty fine, and subsequently asked to leave town.[9]

If Tilghman had spent any significant time with his first wife Flora at their ranch, he would have found that his personal life was just as precarious and strained as the relationships he had to insinuate himself professionally. As marshal, Tilghman had little time for homelife. "It's day all day in the daytime and never night in Dodge," as the saying went. He knew Flora was unhappy because he wasn't around much for her and their children, but it couldn't be helped. The ranch was doing well in his absence. Tilghman had hired more hands to work the property and tend to the growing number of cattle he had acquired. Whenever Tilghman was able to be home to check on his family and ranch, he and Flora argued. He wanted to expand his cattle business to pass on to his children, but Flora insisted his regular presence in their lives would mean more. Her concern for Tilghman's safety also caused friction between the two. Flora didn't doubt his capabilities with a gun, but feared desperate characters who frequented Dodge could ambush and kill him. She didn't want to be a widow twice. Tilghman assured his wife she had no reason to worry.[10]

Dodge City had a strict policy that only lawmen could carry guns inside the city limits. Enforcement of that law was challenging at times, but taking away firearms in town lessened the chance Tilghman and other police officers could be shot. Still, there were those that didn't readily comply, and the marshal had to intercede. Those instances were harrowing, but Tilghman didn't share those experiences with Flora.[11]

Late in the summer of 1884, a pair of wild-eyed, trail-stained strangers wandered into Dodge. Both were heavily armed when they entered the Long Branch Saloon. The bartender noticed their guns and informed the men the weapons weren't allowed in town. The men announced to all in earshot that they hadn't any intentions of surrendering their guns and defied the law to take their six-shooters from them. The two grabbed a bottle of whiskey and a couple of glasses and proceeded to a nearby table where they started drinking. In between drinks the pair loudly threatened to kill anyone with a badge who came near them. Marshal Tilghman's reputation as an effective peace officer had reached beyond Dodge City, and the belligerent customers dared the well-known lawman to square off against them. "We hear tell he's fast on the draw," they shouted. "He's got a chance now to prove it. Somebody go tell him that if he's tired of living, we're ready to help him end it."[12]

Flora Tilghman, Bill's first wife. She passed away in 1900.
DEPARTMENT OF SPECIAL COLLECTIONS AND UNIVERSITY ARCHIVES, UNIVERSITY OF TULSA MCFARLIN LIBRARY

A man named Sampson let the marshal know what was going on and, in spite of the informant's warning to stay away, Tilghman picked up his pistols and headed out of his office. As he left, he told Sampson if he didn't go, gunslingers from all over the Territory would ride into Dodge ready to oppose him.[13]

When Marshal Tilghman entered the saloon, patrons and employees scattered. The resolute lawman made his way to the mouthy drifters and instructed them to give up their guns. "They're not allowed in town," he told them. The three men eyed one another for a few brief moments and then one of them quickly drew his weapon. Before he could get off a shot, Tilghman had drawn and fired his gun at the man. The second of the duo pulled his pistol but he didn't get far. He was on the floor with a bullet in his chest before the smoke from Tilghman's first shot had cleared. The marshal retrieved the dead men's weapons and ordered a handful of cowboys who were taking refuge behind the bar to help carry the bodies to the mortician's office.[14]

Such scenarios were played out time and time again in Tilghman's law enforcement career in Dodge City. When he wasn't tracking escaped prisoners or breaking up fights between rowdy cowboys, he was collecting licenses and fees for the city and keeping watch over dancehall women who were occasionally accosted. When packs of prairie wolves began attacking herds of cattle in the area, including Tilghman's livestock, the marshal decided to resign from his post in March 1886, a month before his term ended. He went home to protect his property. Flora couldn't have been happier.[15]

In late spring 1886, Tilghman traveled to Kansas City to purchase Hereford bulls and Jersey cows to replace the livestock that had been killed by the wolves. When he returned, he spent the next few months branding and rebranding the animals on his ranch. He reacquainted himself with his children and was present when his son William Jr. was born. For a brief time, all was well with the Tilghmans. Flora allowed herself to imagine that their roots had taken such a firm hold that nothing could tear them away from the land. A visit to the ranch from Dodge City Mayor Robert M. Wright brought news that put the house of Tilghman back on shaky ground. Wright let the former marshal know that the Santa Fe Railroad had plans to lay track west of Colorado and establish a new terminal that would be closer to Texas. Cattlemen from that region would be driving their herds to the new location instead of to Dodge City. Tilghman explained to Flora that Dodge only came into being because of the cattle and the railroad station. If cattlemen decided to take their livestock to Colorado, Dodge City would become a ghost town. Tilghman assured his wife that regardless of what happened to Dodge, their livelihood was their ranch, and if they had that, all would be fine.[16]

On November 16, 1886, the plains in and around Dodge City were hit with a freezing storm. Sleet and snow fell, and the wind blew violently at more than forty miles per hour. The blizzard conditions caused temperatures to plunge well below zero. Crops were wiped out as a result and livestock froze to death. The Tilghmans were unable to fully inspect the damage the weather had done to the homestead until the spring of 1887 when everything began to thaw. Replacing the livestock they lost was a possibility, but when it was discovered that the range grass the cattle grazed on was wiped out by the elements and would not be making a full return for several years, Tilghman decided against buying any more cattle. He explained to Flora they had no choice now but to move.[17]

Between April 1887 and March 1889, Tilghman worked odd jobs to support his family and earn a bit more to relocate his wife and children to wherever they decided to move. He spent time in the towns of Leoti, Coronado, and Farmer City in Wichita County, working as a peace officer. The three small cities were battling it out at the polls to see which location would be named county seat. Tilghman's job was to make sure civility was maintained in the area.[18]

On July 3, 1888, County Commissioner H. T. Trovillo and his friend Ed Prather were parading up and down the thoroughfare in Farmer City late in the evening. The men were drunk, loud, and firing their guns into the air and shooting up property. The revelry continued through the next morning. The ladies in town then asked Tilghman to step in and do something. The former marshal tracked the men down and politely asked Trovillo and Prather to stop being a disturbance. Offended, the two rode to the town of Leoti to celebrate. Later, on the night of the 4th of July, Trovillo and Prather returned to Farmer City. The county commissioner passed out on the street exhausted from the night's excursion. Prather had no intentions of slowing down and renewed his threat against the peace officer. Tilghman was enjoying a drink at the bar when Prather approached him and started an argument. He put his hand on his gun while he was cursing Tilghman. Tilghman asked Prather to take his hand away from his weapon and he refused. The consequences were tragic.[19]

"Prather seemed to lose control of himself and in his maddened frenzy, commenced drawing his gun, but with lighting speed Mr. Tilghman drew his and ordered Prather to put his gun in his pocket," the July 14, 1888, edition of the *Grant County Register* reported. "For a moment not a word was uttered, and suddenly Prather, with fearful threats, raised his pistol, when Tilghman as a last resort sent a ball crashing through the body of the would-be murderer. Prather, slightly recovering from the shock, renewed the combat by again attempting to shoot his antagonist, when Tilghman fired again with fatal precision, the ball passing through the brain and head of Prather. No one could regret the necessity imposed upon him more than Mr. Tilghman. All classes commended him for the act."[20]

When the unassigned lands in Oklahoma were opened to settlers in April 1889, Tilghman was one of more than fifty thousand people to rush into the Territory to claim a section for himself. The area where he staked his claim was called Guthrie. Overnight the town sprang into existence, plots were surveyed, businesses were built, newspapers established, and a government was formed. Tilghman was named a representative candidate on the Democratic ticket. When he wasn't campaigning for office, along with the others hoping to make it on the ballot, he was helping to clear the way for surveyors to do their work to establish the streets of Guthrie.[21]

After building a home for his family, he traveled back to Dodge City to get his wife and children. Flora was expecting their third child. In addition to relocating his family, Tilghman drove one hundred herd of cattle, fifteen hogs, and more than twenty thoroughbred horses from Ford County to his temporary home in Guthrie.[22]

Oklahoma's second land run occurred on September 18, 1891. "Bill made this 'run' from the Kickapoo country, where the Deep Fork River was the boundary," Zoe wrote about Tilghman's activity at that time. Tilghman, along with his friend Neal Brown, staked out a claim on Bell Cow Creek, two and a half miles northwest of the city of Chandler. At last, Flora and the other Tilghmans (their daughter Vonia was born in December 1890) could set down roots again. Flora, William Jr., and Dorothy unpacked and worked to get the home in order. Charles, now twenty-one, was not far away. He had completed college and was living in Guthrie where he was employed at an express company. Tilghman and Brown were partners in a horse-breeding and racehorse venture.

Both enjoyed the business, but Tilghman's primary interest was law enforcement.[23]

William Grimes, Oklahoma's first Territorial marshal, accepted the job in 1890. He established law enforcement procedures for the region that included a record-keeping system and contracted for courtrooms and jails around the Territory. He employed fifty to a hundred deputies to make sure federal laws were obeyed. Bill Tilghman was one of those deputies. The two had arrived in the area at the same time and Grimes knew of Tilghman's reputation for keeping the peace in Dodge City. Marshal Grimes hired Tilghman in 1892 along with two other men who would play an integral role in ridding the territory of crime—Heck Thomas and Chris Madsen. "It was at that time that he [Tilghman] began a service for the U. S. government that lasted twenty-one years," Zoe wrote about her husband's early police career in the area. "The Oklahoma, or Western Federal district comprised the organized Territory, and the adjacent Indian reservations, while the Eastern district covered the area of the five civilized tribes [the Cherokee, Chickasaw, Choctaw, Creek, and Seminole]. Bill held a courtesy commission in the Eastern district, which was conceded to only one or two men on each staff. It enabled them to follow criminals into the other districts. . . . Bill's work therefore ranged over the entire area of what is now the state of Oklahoma, from Arkansas to New Mexico, and from Kansas to the Red River."[24]

There was never a shortage of work for Tilghman. Between tracking rustlers who were herding stray cattle belonging to settlers who had temporarily lost track of their livestock while building their homes, and outlaws selling or transporting liquor to the Indians, the lawman was in constant demand. During the frequent time away from his ranch, capable hired hands did the necessary work. Flora oversaw the farm and stock and made occasional trips to Guthrie to visit Charles, who returned to the homestead when he could to help maintain the orchard of peach trees Tilghman had planted. The farm flourished and Flora hoped seeing the result would persuade Tilghman to turn in his badge, but that was not going to happen. An outlaw gang led by three brothers known as the Daltons was making life difficult for homesteaders who rushed into the Territory to secure land for themselves. If law and order were not imposed the promising region would be reduced to a barren wilderness. Tilghman had no intentions of letting that happen.[25]

When another major section of the Oklahoma Territory was opened to settlers in September 1892, Tilghman was there. He came as a representative of the US government in charge of a land office. Four land offices were established in four townsites—Enid, Alva, Woodward, and Perry. He made sure claims were filed correctly and interceded when individuals tried to jump lots belonging to others. He oversaw the businesses and homes being built and helped lay out the streets and organize the city government. He separated thieves from their weapons and broke up fights at newly opened saloons.[26]

Not everyone readily complied with Tilghman's directives. Such was the case in early fall 1892. A particularly disagreeable, out-of-work cowhand named Crescent Sam took offense to Tilghman asking him when he anticipated leaving town. The man had a reputation for instigating arguments and ending them with a six-shooter. Tilghman was called to the Buckhorn Saloon one evening to deal with an angry Crescent Sam who was standing in the street in front of the building firing his pistol into the night sky and challenging anyone brave enough to stop him.[27]

When Tilghman arrived on the scene Sam was howling at a full moon and shouting, "I'm a she-wolf from Bitter Creek and it's my night to howl! I'm waiting for anybody who wants to send me home." Tilghman stepped out of the shadows into the light as Sam fired two shots at the giant orb overhead. He reloaded his gun and holstered it again. Tilghman took a step toward him and stopped. Crescent Sam sneered at the lawman. A long, tense silence hung in the air. Sam was unintimidated. Any thought Tilghman had that the hostile man would voluntarily lay his weapon down faded the longer they eyed one another. "Suddenly, Sam's left hand darted toward his six-shooter and his thumb pulled the hammer back on the gun already in his right hand." Zoe recorded in the biography about the violent exchange. "Two shots and flashes came so closely that there wasn't anyone who could tell whether they came from Bill's gun or Crescent Sam's. In a moment, the answer came. The she-wolf from Bitter Creek slowly crumpled to the earth."[28]

Crescent Sam's body was moved to an area beside the entrance of the saloon. His legs were straightened out and his arms folded across his chest. Anyone else contemplating such defiance was persuaded otherwise when they saw Sam lying in state.[29]

The open Territory of Oklahoma offered many opportunities for enterprising men and women with legitimate pursuits. The same could be said for ambitious outlaws. Among the most zealous and impetuous clan of felons to invade the burgeoning region were the Dalton brothers. The very name of Dalton held people in the midsection of the country in awesome fear. Bob, Grat, and Emmett Dalton's first criminal movement came after they had been refused money owed all of them for their time serving as Osage police officers. They were especially opposed to organized law and legal injustice since their brother Frank had been killed in the line of duty. In truth, Judge Isaac Parker, operating out of the Western District of Arkansas, had appointed the Dalton brothers as deputies and posse men with the marshal's office. He ultimately fired Bob, Grat, and Emmett for rustling horses and reselling them, and then issued warrants for their arrest. The trio went on to become the first people to rob a train. The crime was committed on February 6, 1891, near Alila, California. Their efforts to ride off with the money were thwarted but not before they shot the engineer. The Dalton brothers sought refuge at a farm near Kingfisher, Oklahoma, where their mother lived with two of her other sons, their wives, and children.[30]

During the brothers' time in the Territory, they recruited six ruthless criminals to partner with them to wreak havoc on the region. Dick Broadwell, Charley Pierce, Bill McEhanie, Bill Doolin (who would later help lead the group the Dalton-Doolin Gang), Bitter Creek Newcomb, and Charley Bryant became members of the Dalton Gang. Bob Dalton was the leader of the band of men.[31]

In May 1891, the Dalton Gang robbed the Santa Fe Texas Express near Warton, Oklahoma. More than $14,000 was taken. [The amount stolen in 1891 would be equivalent to $475,000 in 2023.] On September 15, 1891, they robbed the Missouri, Kansas, and Texas Express outside of Lelietta, Oklahoma, making off with more than $3,000. The gang's next job took place on July 1, 1892, between Adair and Pryor, Oklahoma. They

Various scenes after the opening of parts of Oklahoma for homesteaders. Bill Tilghman was called on to keep order in locations such as Guthrie and Perry.
LIBRARY OF CONGRESS

robbed another Missouri, Kansas, and Texas Express train, killing one man in the process and wounding three others. The amount taken was more than $11,000. The group struck again on September 15, 1892, when they held up a train station master at the Adair, Oklahoma, depot. The bandits robbed the office safe then took cover and waited for the train to arrive. As soon as the incoming train slowed to a stop, members of the Dalton Gang jumped aboard and demanded the express guard open the safe. The man complied and the criminals took $17,000. [The amount stolen in 1892 would be the equivalent to $575,000 in 2023.] Hundreds of shots were exchanged between law enforcement and the Dalton Gang as they made their getaway. None of Bob Dalton's men were wounded, but two officers at the scene weren't as fortunate.[32]

The robbery at Adair solidified the Daltons' reputation as the most feared gang in the West. Their audacious offenses coupled with their ability to elude authorities made the group who had begun their criminal career less than two years prior notorious.

Deputy Tilghman knew of the Dalton Gang, but he hadn't yet been called on to help apprehend the outlaws. "Bill was not assigned to those cases," Zoe noted in her memoirs about her husband's job. "He was kept most of the time out of the Western District. He still lived on his claim near Chandler and was given general supervision of that part. Only a few miles east was the Creek Indian country, which was a haven for thieves, bandits, whiskey peddlers, and a starting point for raiders to pick up a horse or cow from the settler's small possessions. He was sent farther on various mail and post office cases."[33]

When US Marshal William Grimes resigned from his post in May 1893, Tilghman's jurisdiction changed. President Grover Cleveland appointed Evett Nix as US Marshal to fill the vacancy left by Grimes and tasked him with ridding the Territory of the criminal element that was riding roughshod over the law-abiding residents. Like his predecessor, Nix saw in Tilghman a strong man with knowledge of the law who, if given free rein, could make the region safe for its inhabitants. He named Tilghman Deputy US Marshal for the Oklahoma Territory and Tilghman promptly made Heck Thomas and Chris Madsen his partners in the job. Together they were known as the Three Guardsmen. "These are wonderful men, and their appointment has had a wonderful effect," Nix told a reporter with the *Kansas City Times*. "The most notorious characters in town skipped out at the first intimation that they were not wanted. Others are going."[34]

The Deputy US Marshal job paid no salary, only fees. Each man received six cents a mile while on official business, out of which he paid for transportation, board and room, and all other expenses. When he made an arrest, he received $2. He could chase a desperado for weeks, still the fee was $2 if he caught him, nothing if he didn't. If he was sent to subpoena a witness, he received six cents a mile one way.[35]

The first assignment Nix gave the men would be one of the most important of their careers. Find the Dalton Gang and arrest them.

Deputy Marshal Tilghman's dedication to taming the wild Oklahoma Territory was celebrated by grateful citizens during his time in office, and his contributions continued to be recognized years after his passing.[36]

* * *

Zoe Tilghman stood on the sidewalk in front of a row of businesses in Oklahoma City in April 1926, watching participants involved in the '89er Days Celebration Parade jockey for a position behind floats, horseback riders, and marching bands. Store windows were decorated with patriotic ribbons and bunting. Some featured photographs of the state's most notable history makers. Bill Tilghman's picture was highlighted in several displays. A short biography included in the display simply read, "Marshal Tilghman started his career in the late 1870s and served with five different local and federal agencies, sometimes simultaneously, throughout the state."[37]

City founders would like to have paid tribute to the slain lawman in 1925, but the trial of the man who took Tilghman's life hadn't concluded by the time final plans needed to be made. Tench had been invited to ride in the parade in honor of his father. A riderless, coal black horse was waiting to be led down the parade route behind the float carrying Tench. A sign across the weathered saddle, tack, and holstered Sharps rifle read "Equipment of the late U. S. Marshal, Bill Tilghman."[38]

Both Richard and Woodrow joined their mother along the parade route. They stood in rapt silence as Tench and the float traveled past them. Men on both sides of the street watching the procession removed their hats in respect and bowed their heads. Women graciously waved their handkerchiefs, dabbing a tear from their eyes when needed. Zoe was moved by the outpouring of affection. She kept her emotions close, not wanting to break. Her sorrow was private. She would express her deep longing and regret only in her writing, in short stories about love lost and dreams taken.[39]

Not long after the '89ers Days Celebration Parade, Zoe penned a poem titled "Insight." It underscored the grief and isolation she was experiencing more than a year after Tilghman's demise.

Soft, lissome body yielding in my arms,
Calm eyes with depths by white lids gently veiled.
And lips that tremble softly 'neath my own,
Responsive for an instant; then the chill,
The quick withdrawal, and reproof, whose words,
Sincere, I know, fall emptily for me;
For in that kiss I learned what you yourself
Yet scarcely know; read you with deeper truth—
Proud and calm-eyed, restrained, sweet puritan,
Fire-hearted, with rebellious pagan lips![40]

An abbreviated version of the book Zoe was working on about Marshal Tilghman was released five months prior to the parade. Titled *Outlaw Days: A True History of Early-Day Oklahoma Characters*, the publication was a record of the history of the desperados that terrorized the Territory and the lawmen who brought them to justice. The high volume of books that had sold since the initial printing reflected the affection Oklahomans still had for Tilghman. Zoe was hopeful the completed biography she was writing about him would do just as well.[41]

The much-appreciated tribute to Tilghman at the '89ers Days Celebration Parade brought back a flood of memories and helped Zoe to see that good people who passed away leave behind a part of their goodness in the faces of those paying their respects. At that moment she could see the truth of that in her sons' faces. She felt it as the horse adorned with her husband's belongings walked proudly by. There was a need to reach out and feel it once more, to have that memory to keep the soul sparks burning bright.

Chapter 3

A Shooting in Minco

A single light bulb hanging from a long wire affixed to a water-stained ceiling slowly swayed back and forth over the tops of the heads of eleven men huddled around a set of dice being tossed onto a wooden, weather-beaten floor. The modest furnishings in the small farmhouse in Minco, Oklahoma, had been crammed into a corner of the living room to make space for a craps game preoccupying the gamblers who had gathered there on October 6, 1929. James Chitwood, a bearded man in his sixties, was running the illegal game. He grabbed up the money thrown recklessly into the pot as soon as the dice stopped tumbling. In one hand he clutched a fist full of $10, $20, and $50 paper bills. He stroked his graying whiskers with the other.[1]

More than a half dozen of the men at the makeshift gaming club were regulars. All were so focused on the dice and the funds being won and lost that they failed to hear the heavy knock on the front door of the home at eleven o'clock in the evening. Finally, Chitwood answered the persistent rapping. Two men stood on the other side of the entrance and, after exchanging pleasantries, asked if they could join in the game. They explained to Chitwood that they were oil field workers who were new to the area. They admitted to listening in on a conversation some of the fellow laborers had about the action at Myers' farm and hoped they could take part. Chitwood reluctantly agreed.[2]

After the two strangers had been in the home for more than an hour, the sound of gunshots could be heard coming from the back of the house. The game was momentarily interrupted so the crapshooters could

Marshal Tilghman served with Marshal Heck Thomas and Marshal Chris Madsen for several years. The three were known as the Three Guardsmen.
OKLAHOMA HISTORICAL SOCIETY

investigate. Just as they were proceeding out of the room, an armed man crashed through the window. Chitwood quickly drew his pistol and shot the man in the neck. One of the guests Chitwood had allowed into the party, who claimed to be an oil field worker, pulled a weapon on the host of the crude gambling parlor, and fired three times. Seriously wounded, Chitwood collapsed in a heap. Both newcomers, along with the gunman who fired his weapon in the back of the house, then ran into the room with the others, leveled their guns at the eleven dice throwers and ordered them to line up along the wall. The gunmen threatened to shoot Chitwood again if anyone balked at the direction. The armed men confiscated all the money the gamblers had and took everything Chitwood had pocketed as well. Authorities estimated the thieves stole between $450 and $800. After the outlaws had scooped up their friend who had been shot, they fled the scene in a waiting car.[3]

The driver of the car was sixteen-year-old Woodrow Tilghman.[4]

Two years prior to the robbery, Woodrow had been appointed by Oklahoma Senator Elmer Thomas as a page to the US Senate. He aspired to be an attorney. Zoe was proud of her youngest son for embarking on such a worthy venture and she told him so in the numerous letters she wrote him. Woodrow moved to Washington, DC, in December 1927. His first letters home described his enthusiasm for the job as well as his need for funds to help between paychecks. "I will probably have to borrow $10.00 from Senator Thomas to get by on until payday," he informed his mother in a note written on December 6, 1927. "He told me anytime I needed any [money] to come to him."[5]

In another letter written the same day he expressed how much he missed home and reminded his mother to "send that suit." Woodrow needed a suit for his job in the capital and didn't have the money to buy a new one. "The boy that I'm borrowing this suit from needs it and I need the other one," he told Zoe. "I am flat broke. I did not eat any breakfast, dinner, or supper today, and I have already borrowed $3."[6]

When Zoe learned that Woodrow had decided to go with his brother Richard and Uncle Alfred Stratton to gamble in early October, she wasn't surprised. He was always looking for ways to acquire cash to support himself. Less than a year after living in Washington he purchased a vehicle to travel back and forth from the capital to Oklahoma. The car proved to be expensive to maintain and at times Woodrow was desperate for ways to finance his lifestyle.[7]

Zoe didn't know what had happened to Woodrow at the farm in Minco until a neighbor came to roust her out of bed after midnight on October 7, 1929, to tell her about the incident. It was then she learned that the man who was shot coming through the window had been Richard. Zoe's brother Alfred was also present as well as two of his friends, Jack Reynolds and Dude Brown. Richard was in critical condition when he was taken to the Rolator Hospital in Oklahoma City. Authorities wasted no time in tracking down Alfred Stratton and Jack Reynolds and arrested them for what they called a "raid on a gambling game." The men were charged with the murder of James Chitwood. Warrants were issued for both Richard and Woodrow for the same crime. Dude Brown, the third gunman at the scene, had escaped and could not be found.[8]

Zoe was grief-stricken and could not be persuaded to leave Richard's bedside. The bullet did not hit him in the neck as initially reported; it lodged in his liver, and the doctors predicted he wouldn't survive. As she sat with him, she pored over photographs of Tilghman and their sons on various outings and reread a few letters from Woodrow tucked inside her purse. "Dear Mother, I am sending this letter special delivery because I have not written [to] you in a long time and I want it to get to you as soon as possible," Woodrow wrote on December 19, 1927. "I got an invitation from W. P. Dawes [the son of the vice president of the United States] to a dinner at 12 o'clock, December 23. It's formal dress and I will have to rent a tuxedo for the affair. I am enclosing a copy of the *Washington Post* which gave me a pretty good write up." Zoe unfolded the clipping from the December 14, 1927, issue of the newspaper. Unlike the stories published in papers across the state about her son two years later, the report was complimentary and predicted Woodrow's "bright political future."[9]

Twenty-one-year-old Richard Tilghman died on October 28, 1929. Funeral services were held two days later in Oklahoma City and his body was taken to Chandler for burial. According to the November 1, 1929, edition of the *Verden News*, "the former Oklahoma City High School student was taken to Chickasha to face charges of first-degree murder. . . . Arrangements had been set [for his arraignment] but his condition prevented his removal from the hospital where he had been confined. The young man's physician, Dr. A. W. Nunnery, reported that the patient was irrational at times and spent a restless night before his passing. He was delirious part of the time."[10]

Given the tragic circumstances, Woodrow's attorney requested and was granted a postponement of the preliminary trial.[11]

Most newspaper accounts of the upcoming trial and the particulars leading to the killing of James Chitwood claimed Woodrow and Richard were "members of a band of robbers" and referred to the boy's father as the "legendary Bill Tilghman." An article in the January 9, 1930, edition of the *Pittsburgh Press* criticized Zoe's inability to raise her children away from gambling shacks and commented that "the trigger finger of Tilghman [had] passed to her sons."[12]

With rare exception, Zoe did not respond to the press's insults. Her focus was on Woodrow and the fate of his future. When his trial opened in the district court on January 7, 1930, she was seated beside him. Prior to Richard's passing, the police maintained that he told them he had only gone to the dice game because Woodrow was going, and he wanted to protect him. Richard denied going to the farm with the intent of robbing the gamblers. Zoe worried the judge would believe the officer's claim that Richard made such a statement and would then deal harshly with Woodrow.[13]

"Richard's father gave his lifetime to enforcement of the law," she told intrusive reporters before Woodrow's hearing. "That law turned its back on him and set his slayer free. In the face of such a lesson why shouldn't these boys and myself disrespect it? Why shouldn't my boys think they could go to a dice game? The law that set before them that disgusting lesson of injustice now comes into court with unclean hands seeking to punish them."[14]

Woodrow and the two other men in custody charged with murder pled guilty to the crime on January 9, 1930. Jack Reynolds and Alfred Stratton were each sentenced to ten years in the state penitentiary. Before the judge sentenced Woodrow, his lawyer and former mayor of Oklahoma City, Otto Arthur Cargill, issued a statement regarding his teenage client. "I do not know what the judgment of the court will be," he said. "But I want to plead to the court for this boy who has just reached his seventeenth year. He is the son of one of the most widely known and most honorable peace officers Oklahoma has ever known. His father, now deceased, died while in service for his state. He is the son of a woman who is almost nationally known through her work as a writer and poet. He has had the privilege of acting as a page in the United States Senate and also the State Senate.[15]

"He was prominent in the high school activities of the Oklahoma City high school prior to this deed. He has lost his brother through injuries received during the tragedy which is being given attention here. His mother, a widow, is bowed in grief through this terrible tragedy. I ask the court to give this boy the minimum sentence in manslaughter in the first degree, which is four years."[16]

B. F. Holding, attorney for the state, responded kindly to lawyer Cargill's request of the judge, but wanted the sentence increased by a year. "I do not want to shirk my duty as attorney for the county, but after investigating this matter and becoming more intimate with the life of this young boy and knowing his mother, I ask that he be given a sentence of five years," Holding said. "He is the son of one of the most honorable and upright peace officers the state has ever known. He has up to the time of this tragedy borne a good reputation and has never at any time been under any cloud. I myself have sons and I know the grief of this mother through this tragedy which has entered her life."[17]

The court sentenced the Tilghmans' son to five years in a reformatory. Zoe hugged and kissed Woodrow, then took him by the arm and led him to the officers who escorted him out of the courtroom. Discouraged, she sat back down in the chair she had occupied during the hearing and remained there until most everyone had gone. "Woodie must suffer from a misstep," she told the handful of reporters lingering behind. "He will return home . . . the man he ought to be."[18]

Although Zoe believed Woodrow should have to answer for his actions, she felt the punishment of five years in the Granite Reformatory was too harsh. In late February 1930, she wrote to Governor Henry S. Johnson asking for executive clemency. "The story of my husband's life and death is well known to your excellency, and I feel sure you will give it consideration," Zoe noted. "I wish, however, to call attention to the fact that the investigator who was sent to look into this killing, and who failed to get evidence enough to convict his slayer, was one W. O. Gordon who recently resigned under circumstances which also are known to you.[19]

"The state had the sacrifice of Bill's life and then protected his slayer. It allowed this dice game to exist to allow many boys besides mine into its grasp; and then when Richard was wounded the needless brutality of the law killed him. If they had waited until Richard's condition improved before moving him from the hospital to be charged with a crime, he might have lived. I feel the great injustice and failure of the law toward me and mine entitles me to ask for the parole of my boy.[20]

"Although in poor circumstances and needing help from Woody, I would be able to make a home for him and keep him from the pitfalls which come to so many friendless youths. I believe too that the tragedy of his brother's death and his knowledge of the irreparable break in my life which it has made will be a more powerful influence upon him that anything else in the world; that keeping him in confinement can serve no good purpose and that the interests of the state and society would be best served by granting him a parole."[21]

In addition to Zoe's sincere request, letters of recommendation from State Senators Uriah Rexroat, Fletcher Johnson, Gid Graham, and W. C. Fidler were filed. Senator Elmer Thomas, Congressman James McClintic, and Oklahoma City journalist Carl Held also recommended clemency. The appeal was referred to the State Reformatory Pardon and Parole board. They denied the petition on May 23, 1930. The fact that Woodrow pled guilty to manslaughter was a strong factor in the decision. Zoe insisted her son pled guilty only after the county attorney promised he would be granted executive clemency. Another element that led to the ruling was that more than five hundred citizens of Grady County signed a petition against clemency. They argued that Woodrow was given a shorter term than others convicted in the killing of James Chitwood. "He should not be released until he has served long enough to feel that he has been punished," the petition noted.[22]

"I have kept faith, but faith repudiated its pledged word," Zoe told reporters after learning of the board's decision.[23] It was difficult for the grieving mother to accept the ruling of the pardon and parole boards. The loss she experienced in a short period of time had taken its toll and she struggled to find her way again. Her work was her saving grace. Many of the poems she wrote for *Harlow's Weekly* about her beloved Oklahoma spoke not only of the wanting land but of an anguished soul in search of relief. Such was the case with her poem published in March 1930, titled "Brazos."[24]

The high, disdainful clouds sailed overhead,
Or drifted lazily in the far blue,
A sky of sapphire flame that ever drew
Away in fierce remoteness. The mirage fled,
And stern-lipped courage. On, though the wide plains grew
A burning waste, one empty, endless view
Where eyes sought vainly. "Water?" parched lips said.

To them, a miracle—a line of trees
On the horizon, as a little cloud that grows;
Won to it, with last feeble strength to plod—
A river where they drank on bended knees,
Deep, clear, sweet-flowing from the mountain snows—
And called it "Brazos de Dios"—"Arms of God"![25]

After a brief hiatus from working on her husband's biography, Zoe returned to Tilghman's story. Having dealt with attorneys and law enforcement agents in Grady County, Oklahoma, who she felt were less than honest in their handling of Woodrow's case, she was anxious to write about a trio of forthright officers—Bill Tilghman, Chris Madsen, and Heck Thomas.[26]

The three men were dissimilar in appearance but like-minded when it came to law and order. Thomas was a tall, well-groomed man from Georgia who had fought for the Union in the Civil War. Madsen was short, round, and unkempt. Born in Denmark, he served in the Danish Army and was a member of the French Foreign Legion before coming to America to hunt buffalo and work as an Indian Scout. Prior to becoming a lawman, he was a sergeant in the 5th Cavalry. In 1893, Deputy US Marshal Tilghman and his cohorts met at his ranch in Guthrie to discuss the investigation tactics they needed to employ to track the Dalton-Doolin Gang. The officers decided the best course of action would be to separate and ride the frontier from Kansas to Texas. They would stop at all the ranches and farms in between to learn what they could about the outlaws. They estimated the trek would take a month, at which point they were to meet back at Tilghman's ranch to share information.[27]

"[Bill] Doolin's raids across the country were the admiration of the West," Tilghman wrote in his journal about the fugitive. "Mounted on a superb horse, riding like the wind, halting only to breath his steed, Doolin has crossed Indian Territory again and again, like a demon emerging from the mists of night, flitting by ranch and farm, speeding and reeling mile after mile. He's slipped through the hands of many a skilled lawman."[28]

US Marshal Evett Nix depended on Tilghman, Thomas, and Madsen to track down outlaws across the Oklahoma Territory.

COURTESY WESTERN HISTORY COLLECTIONS, SPECIAL RESEARCH COLLECTIONS, UNIVERSITY OF OKLAHOMA LIBRARIES, WHCP-1165

Tilghman traveled first to Oscar Halsell's HX Bar Ranch on Cowboy Flats along the Cimarron River, thirteen miles northeast of Guthrie. At one time Bill Doolin was employed at the ranch. The marshal and Halsell had crossed paths years prior in Dodge City. The rancher had a reputation for causing disturbances in saloons in his younger days. Halsell welcomed Tilghman into his home and, after reminiscing about rowdy Kansas cowtowns, the lawman asked the cattleman about Doolin and some of the other members of the gang he helped form who used to work there.[29]

Born on August 25, 1858, in Johnson County, Arkansas, William M. "Bill" Doolin was the son of a farmer. He was seven years old when his father died, and he was left to help work the farm with his mother. In 1881, when he was twenty-three years old, Bill left home. He traveled to Caldwell, Kansas, where he found work as a freight driver hauling goods into Indian Territory. While on the prairie he met Oscar Halsell. Halsell shared with Doolin that he was looking for someone to help him build corrals at his cattle ranch and Doolin let him know he'd had experience doing just that growing up. Halsell hired him to do the job. The cattleman described Doolin as a "skinny, six-foot blonde kid who couldn't read or write." What he could do was swing an ax and split rails and no other hired hand on the HX Bar knew how to do that. In time, Doolin not only learned to rope, ride, and shoot, but how to read and print his name as well. Halsell admitted to Tilghman that Doolin became one of his most valued employees.[30]

For more than nine years, Bill Doolin plied his trade as a cowboy in Oklahoma and was considered by most in the area as trustworthy. Some of the other cowhands-turned-outlaws he rode with during that time were George Newcomb, Charley Pierce, Bill Power, and Emmet Dalton.[31]

Doolin first ran afoul of the law in 1891 in Coffeyville, Kansas, while celebrating the 4th of July at a saloon. Unaware there was a strict law against drinking in the state, authorities arrived on the scene to seize the keg of beer being shared. Doolin and his friends opened fire on the police. Two lawmen were wounded in the exchange. Doolin and the others quickly rode out of town. The former HX Bar cowhand abandoned forever the notion of a legitimate lifestyle. Shortly thereafter, he joined the Dalton Gang and participated in several train and bank robberies. But for the fact his horse became lame just prior to raiding two banks in Coffeyville on October 5, 1892, Doolin might have been shot down like Bob, Grat, and Emmett Dalton were at the holdup. Instead, he survived and went on to organize another gang with Bill Dalton, who had also missed taking part in the Coffeyville bank robberies.[32]

Besides Bill Doolin and Bill Dalton, there were eight other members of the group. They were "Little Bill" Raidler, George "Red Buck" Weightman, George "Bitter Creek" (alias the Slaughter Kid) Newcomb, Dick "Little Dick" West, Roy Daugherty alias Arkansas Tom Jones, Dan "Dynamite Dick" Clifton, Charley Pierce, and Jack "Tulsa Jack" Blake. Tilghman, Thomas, and Madsen learned a great deal about each man from the various individuals they spoke with on their fact-finding mission. Bill Raidler was an educated man from Pennsylvania who made his way into Oklahoma Territory via Texas where he had been working as a cowboy. George Weightman was a Texan who had a quick temper. Marshal Heck Thomas arrested him in 1889 for stealing a horse, a crime for which he was convicted and sentenced to three years in prison. Roy Daugherty was born in Texas, claimed to be from Arkansas, but grew up in McDonald County, Missouri. He worked as a ranch hand for a few big cattlemen in the Oklahoma Territory before riding with the Daltons. Twenty-eight-year-old Dan Clifton was one of the most mysterious members of the gang. No one seemed to know much about him before he came to Oklahoma and started rustling cattle. He was a wanted man prior to teaming up with Doolin and Dalton. After an unsuccessful career as a horse racer in Pawnee, Oklahoma, Charley Pierce joined the group. Jack Blake was a Kansas cowboy-turned-petty thief who was one of Doolin's most loyal followers.[33]

Tilghman, Madsen, and Thomas were able to acquire more information about the band of desperados, sometimes referred to as the Wild Bunch, than just their background and motivation for their criminal behavior. The lawmen learned the outlaws were frequently seen in the small town of Ingalls. Founded in 1889, the citizens and business owners there tolerated criminals because they tended to spend much of their ill-gotten gain at the saloons, hotels, and mercantile. The outlaws who chose the community as their hangout were well-behaved during their visits. They were quiet in their manner and friendly. They furnished food for socials that were held and were kind to the children who lived there. The residents loyal to the fugitives and their money, as well as the scouts working with the Doolin-Dalton Gang, made it difficult for law enforcement agents to get near Ingalls to make an arrest.[34]

Tilghman shared the information he and the other two deputies had uncovered with US Marshal Evett Nix. Nix then passed the details on to the other law enforcement agents he had working on the capture of the Doolin-Dalton Gang. Tilghman, Thomas, and Madsen attributed the gang's repeated, miraculous escapes from the law to the men and women who told them where the various posses were and how to avoid them. Together the officers learned the identity of at least three people aiding the outlaws. In addition to Cattle Annie (Anna Emmaline McDoulet) and Little Breeches (Jennie Stevenson Midkiff) there was Rose Dunn. Tilghman noted in his memoirs that the young woman who he referred to as the Rose of Cimarron was an "exquisite flower, a lovely teenager who fell in with bandits." Many historical accounts of the young woman's life note that two of her older brothers were petty criminals who knew the Doolin-Dalton Gang and occasionally spent time with them on the Dunn family homestead outside of Ingalls. It was through her brothers that she met George Newcomb. The two became romantically involved, and she was devoted to protecting him and frequently let her paramour know the location of the authorities. The blind dedication the women had to the outlaws led to incarceration and, in Rose's case, it jeopardized the lives of the very men she was trying to protect.[35]

Shortly after Tilghman, Thomas, and Madsen met in Guthrie to compare notes about the Doolin-Dalton Gang, the three received word from Nix that they were needed to help apprehend criminals in the Panhandle Territory. Believing authorities were too preoccupied with capturing the Doolin-Dalton Gang, felons had infiltrated the region and were causing chaos. Heck Thomas and Chris Madsen were sent on an expedition to Tulsa to serve several outstanding warrants. Tilghman was ordered to travel to the new town of Perry, sixty miles east of Oklahoma City, to deal with the unrest there. Hordes of landgrabbers had overtaken the town, disregarding the layout of the streets, alleyways, and parks. Illegitimate businessmen were staking out unauthorized claims on all sides of the courthouse square. Tilghman's experience with helping to establish the town of Guthrie made him a natural for the work of organizing the settlement, which by September 20, 1893, boasted more than twenty thousand people.[36]

Freight wagons hauling lumber arrived en masss and buildings sprang up like mushrooms. Whenever there was a dispute over who owned a particular lot, Tilghman was there to resolve the matter. After Thomas and Madsen concluded their job in Tulsa, Thomas was dispatched to Perry to lend a hand. According to the September 24, 1893, edition of the *Guthrie Daily Leader*, not only did Tilghman need assistance because the workload was overwhelming, but he had also taken sick and was confined to bed for several days. When the lawman was back on his feet again, he and Thomas and two other officers focused on bringing law and order to a section of the boomtown known as Hells Half Acre.[37]

There was at least one murder a day in the area dotted with saloons, brothels, and gambling houses. The population on the dark side of Perry was made up of women of ill repute, thieves, and fugitives from other states. Law-abiding citizens were terrified to go near Hells Half Acre and complained to Territorial Governor William Carly Renfrow of the numerous robberies and homicides that continuously took place there. Determined to put a stop to it, Governor Renfrow issued a directive to Sheriff Scrugg to raid all felonious businesses and shut them down. In early October 1893, Tilghman, Thomas, and a half dozen other deputies took part in the action.[38]

"In a very short time after the order was known, wheels of fortune, Faro layouts, and chuck-luck tables were piled up in innocuous desuetude on the outside of the principal resorts," the October 7, 1893, edition of the *Weekly Oklahoma State Capital* read. "The Buckhorn and Blue Bell, two of the most prominent of these places looked like deserted tabernacles soon after the clearing out of the gambling devices."[39]

Not long after closing most of the nefarious merchants and gambling halls, the governor announced that Perry was ready to hold elections. Districts were created, campaign rallies were held, and ballots were cast.

In addition to city officials being announced, councilmen met to appoint a variety of prominent citizens to various jobs. Bill Tilghman was named city marshal. He accepted the honor and named Heck Thomas as his deputy. Marshal Nix granted both men leave from their Deputy US Marshal jobs but continued their commissions so they could deal with any government work pertaining primarily to the Doolin-Dalton Gang.[40]

The dangerous thugs that populated Perry in the first three months of its existence were quickly managed by City Marshal Tilghman and Deputy Thomas. The officers forced individuals who were hanging around with no viable means of support to move on. Citizens and city officials gave Tilghman a great deal of leeway to do his job. The marshal handled such cases as locating teenage girls who had run away from home to work at local saloons and arresting drunken cowboys who had broken into gunsmith shops and stole weapons.[41]

Many times, authorities had to settle issues between themselves and lawbreakers with their six-shooters. On December 11, 1893, Marshals Tilghman and Thomas arrested two men caught in the act of stealing carpenter tools. The accused refused to give their names to the officers and threatened to kill them if they didn't let them go. The toughs' attitudes changed after Tilghman smacked one of them in the head with the butt of his rifle. Not only did they tell the lawmen who they were but confessed to a series of robberies. Firearms and muscle were used by the police in pursuit of a pair of arsonists in mid-December 1893. John Abergrass and Bert Hamilton were paid $50 each to set fire to a blacksmith shop in order that the owner of the business and building could collect the insurance. The culprits hurried out of town once the building was set ablaze, but Tilghman and Thomas pursued them and brought them back to the Perry jail handcuffed and with weapons trained on them.[42]

Another pair of troublemakers had to be strongarmed into submission by the law for indiscriminately firing their guns in public and disturbing the peace. "Missouri Lute" and a pal wearing a broad-brimmed hat were arrested last night by Marshal Tilghman," the December 14, 1893, edition of the *Evening Democrat* read. "They proved to be gigantic specimens of the 'star shooter' and were actively engaged in making 'gun plays' when they were rounded up. They showed some fight but were convinced of their inferiority when Marshal Tilghman jabbed a full-grown Colt revolver up to the abdominal organs of the ringleader, who at once ascended from his lofty perch and quietly passed the rest of the night in the city bastille. They didn't seem to object to going to jail but hated to be relieved of their artillery."[43]

In less than two months of being named marshal, Tilghman reported more than 150 arrests. Perry residents were pleased and believed offenders who dared try to break the law in the new town would not escape the vigilant eye of their police force. Residents expressed their appreciation for Tilghman's fine work on Christmas Day 1893 at the Blue Bell Saloon. One of the city founders delivered a speech acknowledging the difficulties under which the marshal had labored in preserving law and order through the first and toughest days of Perry's history. Mayor John M. Brogan presented the lawman with a new cartridge belt, scabbard, and a silverplated, pearl-handled .45 Colt revolver engraved with the words "William Tilghman, City Marshal."[44]

The cartridge belt gifted to the marshal hung on the wall of the home he shared with Zoe and his sons. Tilghman had planned to pass it on to Woodrow. Zoe made note of that in a letter to her son at the state reformatory in Granite. She hoped writing to Woodrow about his father and his legend would help him to persevere. The reformatory was lacking in programs that would help young men find purpose and make the changes necessary to arrive on the other side of their stay rehabilitated. A month after Woodrow arrived at the prison, the facility came under fire for not having sufficient employment or schooling for the inmates. Without those opportunities, Zoe worried her son wouldn't be fit for much when he was released. Ironically, prison reform was a subject Tilghman had written a great deal about later in his career.[45]

"The dream of ages, an Ideal Prison, in my opinion can never be," he noted in his journal in 1909. "But there can be, and should be, conditions within the prison which will influence and instill within one a desire to go out into the free-world and lead a normal and respectable life.[46]

"How can that be accomplished? By smaller prisons. Prisons of 250 to not more than 500 inmates. In a prison of that size each man can be treated as an individual. Classification of prisoners, and they cannot be classified according to age. I know young boys who have been raised in the slums of our cities who are so steeped in crimes, so hardened and anti-social that they are a serious problem. These poor little devils never have had a chance in life. They've had to steal for their very existence from the time they were large enough to grab something and run. They are pathetic victims of circumstances and environment. Raised among thieves and prostitutes, and often their fathers and mothers have forced them into crime.[47]

" . . . Each young prisoner should be given vocational training and have employment to go to upon his release. I believe in making all prisoners self-sustaining and paying them a small wage, and that can be done if intelligently handled. Older men and men who prefer that kind of work, I would place in farm colonies. I would place a large majority of these men on farms under supervisors. With the public's belief to the contrary, there are few prisoners who will violate their word of honor among certain classes.[48]

"Now, let us see what the prisoner is up against upon his release. Of the released prisoners about seventy-five percent make good. And that is a wonderful showing all things considered. The majority of those who make good however, are men who get help from relatives or friends or quickly find employment upon release. But it is of the other twenty-five percent of which I wish to speak. After years of imprisonment, they are released and often, into a strange world. With a five- or ten-dollar bill in a 'bull's wool' suit of clothes they are admonished to go forth and sin no more.[49]

"Now as an individual, what are his chances of going straight? Damn little, and especially so in this day and time when work is so scarce. Now he leaves prison with a vow in his heart to go straight. That is his honest and sincere desire. Possibly on many nights in his cell he has bowed down on bended knees and asked God Almighty to help him be a better man. He leaves prison and enters the free world with that exalted feeling, even the air feels different, that can be experienced only by those who have endured long years of imprisonment.[50]

"This man comes from a world of hatred, greed, fear, prejudice, ignorance, lust, and an atmosphere that is continually pregnant with perversion and degeneracy. How in God's name can a man leave an atmosphere like that without money, friends, social standing, yes, even an unequal opportunity in the free world and rehabilitate himself?"[51]

* * *

Zoe anguished over the loss of her sons. She couldn't help but blame herself for the wrong turn Richard and Woodrow took. She lost sleep wondering how Woodrow would cope in a prison environment and if he would be safe. She longed for her husband and believed if anyone knew how to manage these distressing circumstances he would. "Millions for conviction, but not one penny for rehabilitation," Tilghman wrote about the flaw in the prison system. "We owe the one day released man a debt, but for the benefit of the state if for no other reason. Parents cannot give up on their sons locked away. Without hope what is a man?"[52]

Zoe focused on Tilghman's words of hope, and by doing so it made the distressing times less difficult to bear.

Chapter 4

While Outlaws Ride

Bill Tilghman, Chris Madsen, and Heck Thomas lay on their stomachs behind a cluster of rocks, their rifles trained on a dugout three hundred yards away. The crude shelter, a rectangular hole carved into a ravine, was rumored to be the spot where the Doolin-Dalton Gang was hiding. The lawmen had sneaked into their position after midnight and were waiting until dawn to overtake the outlaws inside. The pale crescent moon above the trio shone like a silvery claw in the waning night sky. It was mid-March 1894, and it was cold. The US deputy marshals were dressed for the frigid temperature, but the occasional icy winds left them wanting more than dusters and wool chaps to rely on for warmth. Knowing the outlaws would be in custody by daybreak kept them rooted to their setting despite the elements.[1]

Six months prior to Tilghman and the others learning the criminals' location, a team of lawmen tried to apprehend the gang holed up in Ingalls. The outcome was disastrous for Evett Nix's federal authorities. Three deputy marshals were killed and most of the outlaws escaped. Law enforcement's defeat emboldened the desperados. A month after the incident in Ingalls they attended an oyster supper in Cushing hosted by the women of the church. They were overheard planning bank and train robberies. They also threatened to come after the citizens of Ingalls who had sided with the deputy marshals who raided the area in September 1893.[2]

Frustrated with the lack of progress his officers were making to catch the gang, Nix persuaded Tilghman and Heck Thomas to leave their post

US Marshals Bill Tilghman and C. F. Colcord at the opening of the Cherokee Strip in Perry, Oklahoma.

COURTESY WESTERN HISTORY COLLECTIONS, SPECIAL RESEARCH COLLECTIONS, UNIVERSITY OF OKLAHOMA LIBRARIES, WHCP-1165

in Perry and pursue a lead on the whereabouts of the Doolin-Dalton Gang. The pair would later reunite with Chris Madsen. Madsen had sent his brother-in-law, Deputy Marshal Ed Morris, and two other officers to the Ingalls area to find out if those who championed the outlaws knew where they were hiding. Morris and his coworkers arrived in town on a chuck wagon disguised as cooks traveling to Texas to work on a cattle drive. During a visit to the local saloon, Morris learned that the gang was living in a dugout on the Dunn Ranch. Rose Dunn's paramour George Newcomb survived the police raid on Ingalls and was with the rest of the gang on her family's property. Morris was informed that Rose had been seen taking provisions from the main ranch house to the dugout. Smoke emanating from the chimney of the dugout further confirmed their theory that Doolin, Dalton, and the other members of their group were indeed inside.[3]

The sun had barely begun to creep into the eastern horizon when Heck Thomas barked out an order to the outlaws inside the hillside hovel. "Doolin! We know you and your men are in there. You're surrounded by federal marshals! Come out with your hands up." The lawmen waited for a response but there was nothing. Heck gave them a sixty-second warning and promised to force the desperados out if they didn't comply willingly. The order was met again with silence. Heck pulled a stick of dynamite out of the saddlebag lying beside him, lit it, and tossed it at the dugout. It landed on the hillside above the shelter and exploded with fury. A piece of roof on the dugout flew into the air along with rocks, dirt, and vegetation. Any hope the explosion would immediately send the men inside running to escape the calamity was quickly dashed. The criminals stubbornly stayed put. The three lawmen exchanged an exasperated look and Thomas reached for another stick of dynamite. "Thirty seconds, Doolin!" Heck shouted at the inhabitants in the dugout. "The next stick will be right on your roof."[4]

Finally, the door on the dugout inched open and eight disheveled men emerged with their hands raised in the air. With guns leveled at the outlaws, Tilghman, Madsen, and Thomas approached the group. They studied the faces of the stoic criminals as they disarmed them. Although all the men who gave themselves up were wanted by the law, none of them were the gang members the officers believed to be within reach. According to one of the captured lawbreakers driven out of the shelter, the gang had been there but were warned the law was closing in. The gang had fled hours before the deputy marshals arrived on the scene. The criminals, who didn't believe they would be found, were handcuffed and left under the supervision of the guards riding with Tilghman, Madsen, and Thomas. The three well-known policemen then hurried out to pick up the trail of the fugitives.[5]

The route the outlaws took wasn't hard for the trained professionals to find. They followed the evidence (fresh horseshoe tracks, hastily made camps) of their journey to the home of a lone Native American man. It was dinner time when the three arrived and the Indian, who was expecting them, motioned for the officers to come inside. The tired lawmen enjoyed the meal prepared for them and before leaving asked how much was owed. The Indian gave them a price and added that the men who had eaten breakfast at his place earlier in the day told him the officers would pay for their meal as well. Puzzled, Madsen asked for a description of the man acting as the leader of the group. The Indian described Doolin perfectly. It was evident that the gang had anticipated their every move and had now fled into the open country with its numerous caves available to hide out. The officers paid the Indian and returned to the dugout at the Dunn Ranch. While escorting the prisoners to the jail in Guthrie the three discussed what they would do next. Tilghman's time as city marshal of Perry would end in June 1894. At that time, he would devote himself solely to the pursuit of the Doolin-Dalton Gang. Madsen and Thomas would do the same.[6]

* * *

As Zoe wrote about her husband's pursuit of Bill Doolin and Bill Dalton, she found herself thinking about the outlaws' mothers. She wondered if they knew what had become of their sons and if they ever wondered what they could have done differently. Woodrow wrote to his mother from the state reformatory in Granite and when reading his correspondence Zoe often considered how she could have kept her youngest boy from trouble. The institution was frequently in the news. Inmates attempted to escape by taking guards hostage and fought and stabbed one another in fights over cigarettes or blankets. Zoe worried that Woodrow would get out of jail worse than when he went in. She continually fought for his release, requesting prominent Oklahoma citizens to write letters to Governor William Holloway asking for clemency. Before Holloway's term ended in January 1931, he decided to grant Woodrow parole. "I knew the boy well when he was a page in the Senate," the governor told the press. "He was a victim of bad company. A large number of letters are on file on his behalf. I wouldn't give him a pardon to free him entirely, but I believe he should be paroled."[7]

In January 1931, Zoe celebrated her son's return home and the release of a book of poems she'd penned. Titled *Prairie Winds*, critics praised the work, calling it "a distinct contribution to the world's best literature." Zoe reveled in the success of her oldest son Tench's accomplishments during this time, too. Tench had graduated law school and entered the political arena as the director of an organization composed of statewide taxpayers seeking to protect public highways from being ruined by trucks carrying heavy loads. For a while it seemed Zoe's worst days were behind her and

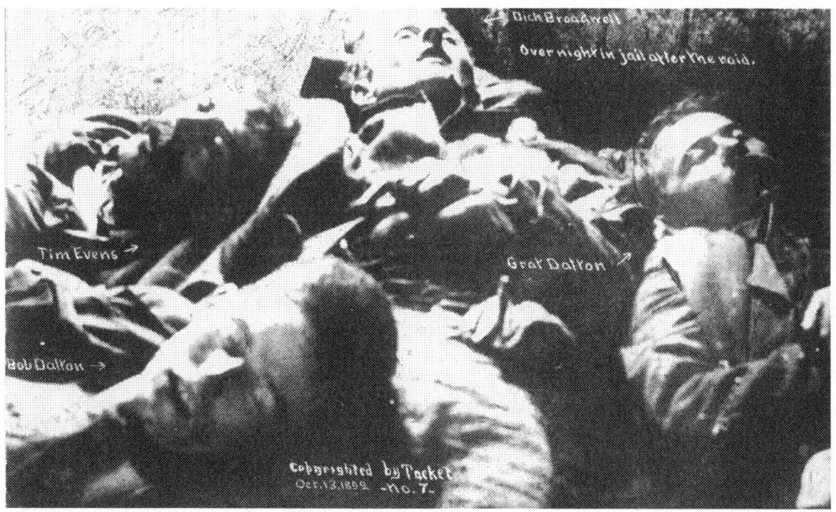

Left to right: Bill Powers (Tom Evans), Bob Dalton, Grat Dalton, and Dick Birdwell (Texas Jack) after their deaths on October 5, 1892.
OKLAHOMA HISTORICAL SOCIETY

like Tilghman focusing on the Doolin-Dalton Gang, she could now concentrate solely on her husband's biography.[8]

In May 1932, Woodrow again found himself in trouble with the law. This time he was arrested for stealing a car. Woodrow and his friend Robert Smith took C. E. Giddens's automobile from his home and were later apprehended by the police. The county attorney was opposed to trying the eighteen-year-old on the charge and requested his parole be revoked. At Zoe's suggestion Woodrow asked that he be sent back to the state reformatory to serve twenty months, the remainder of his sentence, on the condition the auto theft charge be dismissed. Zoe and Tench were at the jail when Woodrow was loaded, handcuffed and shackled, into a bus to transport him to the reformatory. He smiled reassuringly to his mother as he was taken away. Zoe waited until the vehicle was out of sight before she burst into tears.[9]

* * *

"I've met my fair share of outlaws who couldn't or wouldn't change," Tilghman wrote in his memoirs. "They were hell-bent on breaking the law no matter how many chances they were given to do the right thing." Bill Doolin was one of the men to whom the marshal was referring. Zoe wrote of an occasion in 1891, before Doolin had fallen so far into a life of crime, that he and Tilghman met face-to-face at the Turf Exchange in Guthrie. Doolin informed the lawman that he was "down on his luck" and asked Tilghman to buy him a drink. The marshal agreed and offered to help find him work if needed. Unbeknownst to Tilghman, Doolin had no intention of holding down a legitimate job. He could have chosen to turn his back on crime in the spring of 1893 when he married a minister's daughter from the area around the town of Ingalls. Instead, he decided to lead his gang in the robbery of a bank in East Texas.[10]

"Each of Doolin's gang met with a tragic fate, and their end should teach a salutary lesson to the youth of the country who might think a desperado's life an easy and comparatively safe and honored one," Marshal Tilghman noted in his memoirs. Bill Dalton was the first to be killed. He was shot at the home of Houston Wallace, where he had been living, located twenty-five miles from Ardmore. One of the posses Marshal Nix dispatched to apprehend the Doolin-Dalton Gang members surrounded the house, and when Dalton emerged Deputy Loss Hart shouted for him to halt. Dalton aimed his six-shooter in the officer's direction and Hart struck him down with his Winchester.[11]

"Tulsa Jack was first among the others to be killed in April 1895, following the holdup and robbery of a southbound Rock Island train at Dover, Oklahoma," Tilghman recalled in his journal. "Immediately after this robbery Deputy Marshal Madsen, then stationed at El Reno, [Oklahoma], was notified by telegraph and hastened to get a posse together. The posse came within sight of the bandit fugitive at a ford on the Cimarron River and a running fight ensued. Tulsa Jack was killed in the sand-hills. Charley Pierce was wounded, and three horses were slain. The officers fired to kill but the bandits aimed wildly. Bill Raidler, Red Buck, Bitter Creek, and Pierce escaped with two horses, and the next day Raidler deliberately and devilishly killed with the coldblooded carelessness of a demon of hell, a preacher sixty years of age, in order to get the minister's horse."[12]

Bill Raidler was taken into custody on September 6, 1895. Tilghman tracked the outlaw to a ranch twenty-five miles northeast of Pawhuska, Oklahoma. He was found in a log house tucked in the wooded hills. While making his way to the corral, Raidler unknowingly walked right by the armed deputy marshal. Tilghman stepped out of the trees where he had been waiting for the right time to overtake the outlaw and ordered him to throw up his hands. "But Bill's hands did not go up," the lawman noted in his memoirs. "Instead, he whipped out a six-shooter and wheeled about. Both weapons spoke simultaneously." Tilghman turned loose one barrel of the shotgun and almost instantly fired the other. Raidler fired several times also, but his shots went wild, whereas the deputy's struck the bandit's limbs in a half dozen places and Raidler dropped to the ground.[13]

Having been shot nine times, the wounded bandit was paralyzed and had to be carried into the stable for the night. The next day he was taken by wagon to Elgin, Kansas, and then transported by train to Guthrie on a stretcher. Raidler lived to stand trial, was found guilty, and was sent to a prison in Columbus, Ohio. After serving more than four years, Raidler

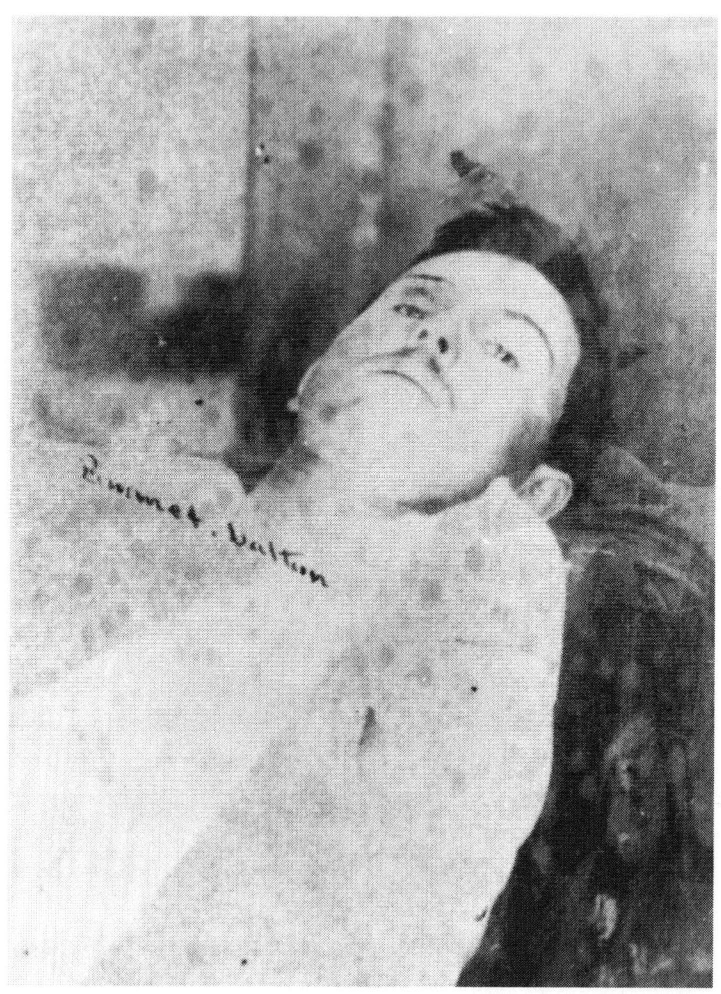

Emmet Dalton was the sole survivor of the outlaws who participated in the robbery in Coffeyville, Kansas. He was committed for life to the Kansas State Penitentiary.
COURTESY WESTERN HISTORY COLLECTIONS, SPECIAL RESEARCH COLLECTIONS, UNIVERSITY OF OKLAHOMA LIBRARIES, WHCP-1165

petitioned the court to have his sentence set aside. Ironically, he sought Tilghman's help with that matter.[14]

"I am about on the eve of making application for executive clemency, so I thought I would consult you in the matter and if possible, get your assistance," Raidler wrote Marshal Tilghman.[15]

"Now you remember I was given the full limit of the law, ten years, and I have now served over two-thirds of it counting what good time I get off, and since I have been here, I have become a total physical wreck. I am and have been for the last three years suffering from Locomator Atazia [*sic*] and its most agrivated [*sic*] form, having lost almost the entire use of my lower limbs. It might be possible if I could get out of here and get proper treatment, that I would somewhat recover before the disease gets too firm a hold on me, for they give any case of five-year standing, absolutely no hope of recovery.[16]

"So now you see the condition I am in, and if you feel that you can do anything for me or assist my friends in any way, I would appreciate it very much, and I am sure my friends would. I am sure you have no personal grievance against me, at least you ought not; you got what you was after and I got ten years.[17]

"I have been faring very well since I have been here. I am now the head clerk in the Post Office department. I have exclusive charge of all the money and stamps and stationary [*sic*] and all the mail passes through my hands; both the Warden's and prisoner's mail, but they have implicit confidence in me. I sleep in the office and have meals brought to me.[18]

"It is nearly four years since I have been locked up. I have all the privileges that any man can have in prison, but still there is nothing like liberty, and that is what I am seeking now, and if ever you did a Godly act, you will do it in assisting me in getting out of here. I know if you could see my condition, you would not hesitate a minute, and if you think I am exaggerating, write here to the Warden and get a statement from him.

"Very respectfully yours, Wm Raidler."[19]

Tilghman did intercede and Raidler was released. His sentence was eventually redacted. The outlaw who suffered partial paralysis from being shot and from locomotor ataxia (a severe progressive disease of the central nervous system, caused by syphilis) was set free in early 1903. Raidler returned to Oklahoma, married, and died in 1904.[20]

In May 1895, Charley Pierce and George "Bitter Creek" Newcomb suffered tragic deaths, being murdered by their one-time friends, the Dunn brothers. Tilghman and Thomas worked out a deal with the Dunns. They would overlook their aiding and abetting of the criminals in exchange for letting them know when the outlaws would be at their ranch next. The Dunns were to fire a shot in the air when the outlaws arrived. It was two o'clock in the morning when the deputy marshals heard the shots fired and they rushed to the scene. They found Pierce and Newcomb dead and the Dunn boys standing over the bandits.[21]

According to Tilghman, "The two outlaws had come in expecting to find shelter as they always had. They put their horses in the stable and walked toward the gate. The Dunns were standing on either side of the gate. As the visitors approached and got within range, the Dunn boys fired with shotguns, instantly killing both outlaws. After the men had fallen, the Dunns fired a shot in the air. To be sure Pierce and Bitter Creek were the outlaws in question, their bodies were sent to Hennessey, Oklahoma, to be identified by the engineer of the Rock Island Railroad. The two had robbed the rail line just prior to traveling to the Dunn Ranch. The criminals were positively identified."[22]

In the summer of 1895, Tilghman learned that a man matching Bill Doolin's description had been seen in a town in Kansas east of Dodge City known as Burden. The deputy marshal traveled to the area and discreetly discovered that Doolin had visited Burden to buy supplies. Dressed as a tenant farmer, the outlaw drove a tired team and wagon to complete the disguise. When Tilghman found out the location of the farm where Doolin was staying he made his way there. The house was next to a ravine surrounded by trees, and the lawman was able to observe the comings and goings undetected. "Necessity kept Doolin away from the secluded spot, but his wife and baby were inside," Tilghman noted in his journal. The deputy marshal kept watch over the home and its inhabitants, waiting for the gang leader to appear. Doolin never showed but his wife Edith eventually left the cabin with her bags and child in tow. Tilghman followed a safe distance behind her as she drove her wagon to the train depot in Burden. Mrs. Doolin purchased a ticket to Perry, Oklahoma, and sent a telegram to her father who lived near there letting him know she was coming to visit.[23]

Tilghman decided to check with the Burden postmaster to find out what mail, if any, Mrs. Doolin had received since she'd been in the Kansas town. Doolin hadn't written to her at all but Mrs. Pierce, the owner of the hotel in Ingalls, corresponded frequently. Tilghman then took a trip to Ingalls to have a talk with Mrs. Pierce. The innkeeper was less than forthcoming about her association with the Doolins. It wasn't until the lawman mentioned a train robbery in Texas and suggested the Doolin-Dalton Gang was responsible that Mrs. Pierce's tongue loosened. In defending the Doolin-Dalton Gang and its leader, she let it slip that Doolin was in Eureka Springs, Arkansas, getting help for his rheumatism.[24]

Armed with key information, Tilghman rode to Guthrie to report to Marshal Nix. Nix knew Tilghman was anxious to be on his way to Arkansas and suggested the officer take other deputies with him to help capture Doolin. Nix reminded him of the outlaw's threats to not be taken alive. Doolin had promised to kill any lawman who tried to arrest him as well. Tilghman assured the marshal he had a plan to get the job done alone.[25]

When Bill Tilghman stepped off the train in Eureka Springs he was dressed as an itinerant preacher complete with a long, black coat and derby hat. As he proceeded down the main thoroughfare clutching a Bible in his hand, he noticed a tall man bent at the waist walking with a cane. The man's complexion was pale, and he carried himself as though he was in pain, but there was no mistaking he was Bill Doolin. Tilghman followed the fugitive to a barbershop. There Doolin made himself comfortable in front of a warm stove and began reading a paper he had tucked under his arm. The lawman walked into the room, scanning the setting for other patrons. No one paid any attention to the lawman masquerading as a minister until he pulled a pistol from his suit pocket and pointed it at Doolin. "Put up your hands!" Tilghman ordered. The outlaw jumped to his feet and attempted to go for his six-shooter. The seasoned officer jerked Doolin's gun arm back before his hand reached the holster. Bystanders scurried out of the business, leaving Tilghman alone with the combative criminal. "Bill, you know who I am?" Tilghman asked Doolin.

"Yes, I do," he replied. "Well, you better get your hands up," the lawman told him. The desperado complied. After confiscating Doolin's gun, he handcuffed him and led him out of the barbershop.[26]

"The fact that Doolin knew him accounts for the easy manner in which Tilghman took him," the January 16, 1896, edition of the *Weekly Oklahoma State Capital* reported. "There is no other marshal that could have gotten him without a desperate fight. Tilghman is the only man on Marshal Nix's force who really made Doolin's capture a study. He was following him incessantly for many months, being very close on his trail several times. . . . The government and the railroad and express companies had outstanding rewards aggregating $3,500 for the capture of Doolin, which Tilghman will receive."[27]

A crowd of people were waiting at the Guthrie depot when the train arrived carrying Tilghman and Bill Doolin. "What were you doing in Eureka Springs?" a reporter at the scene asked the outlaw. "I was doctoring my rheumatism," Doolin responded. "I had been there about two months. I have not been a hundred miles from Oklahoma and the Indian Territory in two years. I knew the marshals were after me. . . . Did I know Tilghman? I did not know him very well. . . . I knew the man in front of me in the barbershop with his gun in my face was Bill Tilghman. I looked squarely in his eyes, and I saw in a second that he had the nerve. If it had been anyone else, I would not have hesitated to pull my gun. I saw at once that if I made a move he would kill me, so I put up my hands."[28]

Deputy Marshal Tilghman was modest about the capture. According to the January 16, 1896, edition of the *Weekly Oklahoma State Capital*, "He is known to be one of the bravest and coolest men in the United States."[29]

Bill Doolin was held in jail in Guthrie while awaiting trial. Less than two months after his capture another member of his gang was killed by a posse of Evett Nix's deputy marshals. George "Red Buck" Weightman was found near the town of Arapaho when he was shot by officers.[30]

On July 5, 1896, Bill Doolin broke out of jail along with one of his gang members, Dan "Dynamite Dick" Clifton, and immediately fled to Mexico. Before Doolin got too far, he changed his mind and rode to the home of his father-in-law in Lawton, Oklahoma, where his wife and son were living. Lawmen, including Tilghman and Heck Thomas, had suspected the outlaw might return to his family and were waiting to ambush him. Doolin was coming out of the stable when the deputies made their move.[31]

"If he had wanted to have made his escape, he could have had open roads, north, south, east, northeast or southwest or northwest, through the pasture to those high hills that you have seen many times, well, he came right down the lane, leading his horse by the tip ends of the bridle reins, walking slow in the bright moonlight, Winchester in both hands, well out in front of him, nearly in position to shoot," Tilghman wrote in his memoirs. "He was walking slow, looking first on one side and then the other. . . . He had to have known we were spying on him. . . . I hollered to him, and he shot at me. The bullet passed between me and B. Dunn. I had let one of the boys have my Winchester and I had the old No. 8 shotgun. It was too long in the neck and I couldn't handle it quick so he got off another shot with his Winchester. As he dropped his Winchester from a glancing shot, he jerked his pistol and some of the boys thought he shot once with it and the others twice and about that time Heck got the shotgun to work and the fight was over. We got him to Guthrie the next day at one o'clock. He was cared for nicely and buried close to where Charley Pierce is buried."[32]

Authorities tracked Dan Clifton to an area outside the town of Blackwell, Oklahoma, in early December 1896. The fugitive had recruited a handful of like-minded criminals to help him rob the bank in Blackwell. Deputy marshals surrounded the home of one of the thieves and opened fire on the outlaws inside. The bullet that killed Clifton passed through his body and killed a nearby cow. Clifton was pronounced dead on December 4, 1896.[33]

Newspapers erroneously reported that "Dynamite Dick" was the last of the noted Doolin Gang to be killed or captured. In truth, Arkansas Tom Jones and Richard "Little Dick" West were both still at large. Tilghman pursued West with the same tenacity he had chasing Doolin. It would take the lawman more than a year to catch the cunning desperado who had formed his own band of thieves and murderers known as the Jennings Gang.[34]

Left to right: Bob Dalton, unidentified person, and Grat Dalton after the Dalton Gang attempted robbery at Coffeyville, Kansas, on October 5, 1892.
OKLAHOMA HISTORICAL SOCIETY

According to Tilghman, the Jennings Gang's career spanned a period of only six months. Organized by Dick West, the group was named after brothers Al and Frank Jennings. Al, a former lawyer, helped lead the outlaws. Two other brothers were also a part of the group. Pat and Morris O'Malley were horse thieves and Pat was a former US marshal. "Little Dick was different from most of the outlaws," Tilghman noted in his memoirs. "While the other criminals were enjoying good warm beds indoors, Dick would lie out in the woods on a saddle blanket." Although the Jennings Gang's reputation was bad among authorities, they were looked upon merely as petty thieves until they began robbing trains. The Jennings and O'Malley brothers were hunted by US marshals and taken alive. All four stood trial and were sentenced to time in jail. Little Dick West was located by deputy marshals at a ranch southwest of Guthrie on April 7, 1898. He fought being arrested, was shot, and killed.[35]

Roy Daugherty, alias Arkansas Tom Jones, died in a gun battle against a posse in Joplin, Missouri, in August 1924.[36]

The tenacity of Deputy US Marshals Bill Tilghman, Heck Thomas, and Chris Madsen in tracking down and bringing to justice members of the Doolin-Dalton Gang, as well as other outlaws in the Oklahoma territory, earned the trio the name the Three Guardsmen.[37]

* * *

A lot had happened during Tilghman's long absence from his home chasing criminals. His ranch foreman let him know the excessive grazing of his cattle on the only fenced section of his property had caused damage to the grassland, that additional men needed to be hired to work the spread, and a bunkhouse needed to be built for them to reside. Flora (his first wife) had been unable to keep up with her usual chores around the homestead because she was ill. Prior to Tilghman's last trip, she was feeling run-down and had developed a cough. Her condition had not improved; in fact, it had gotten worse. Flora had been diagnosed with tuberculosis. She was sad about the prognosis and about ultimately leaving her children. She needed Tilghman to be with her and comfort her but, as usual, the job came first. She wept when she talked with him about how difficult it had been for her to be alone. She cried harder when Tilghman told her he was home to stay because she knew it wasn't true even if he didn't. He was driven by a vision of the wild region she couldn't see.[38]

"When I'm out there on the prairie and the wind stirs the sweet-smelling grass, I think there's nothing more beautiful in the world," Tilghman explained to Flora about why he believed the sacrifice for the job was worth it. "I think of my children and grandchildren living here in peace, loving the prairie the way I do. But there can be no peace while the outlaws ride. I suppose everyone wants to leave his mark on the land, wants to turn it over to his children better than he found it. Well, that's my way—fighting the outlaws."[39]

Flora assured her husband that she had tried to be the wife he wanted her to be but could no longer keep up the pretense. She asked him for a divorce, and he reluctantly agreed. Their property was divided and their

Zoe Tilghman with her son Woodrow at one of his parole hearings.
DEPARTMENT OF SPECIAL COLLECTIONS AND UNIVERSITY ARCHIVES, UNIVERSITY OF TULSA MCFARLIN LIBRARY

two youngest children, twelve-year-old William Jr. and eight-year-old Vonia, went with their mother.[40]

Tilghman returned to his job arresting outlaws throughout Oklahoma for offenses from mail robbery to murder and making headlines as he went along. "United States Deputy Marshal William Tilghman is one of the shrewdest man-catchers in the West," the March 31, 1899, edition of the *Weekly Oklahoma State Capital* read. "Marshal Tilghman has been upon the track of this man William Cumberledge for several months. He has watched everything that would indicate the location of Cumberledge and finally located him at Fort Madison. . . . Cumberledge is wanted for complicity in several post office robberies and is under indictment at Muskogee for horse stealing. . . . The crime for which he is at present under arrest and for which Marshal Tilghman has worked so hard to catch him, is the murdering of J. W. Fox."[41]

In between tracking criminals, Tilghman spent time with his children and even escorted his eldest daughter on a trip to St. Louis. He also took time to visit Flora. Although they were estranged, he still cared for her and was sad her health had taken such a turn. For several months Flora had traveled to stay with her parents in Ford County, Kansas. She held out hope the change in climate would make a difference in her condition.[42]

Flora Tilghman passed away at her home in Guthrie on October 12, 1900. Tilghman had been with her days before and had just returned to his home in Lincoln County when he received word that she was at the end of her life. The lawman hurried to Flora's bedside, but she died before he arrived. A large crowd of friends and acquaintances attended her funeral service.[43]

Shortly after Flora's passing, Tilghman decided he needed to sell the ranch. He told his foreman the property was riddled with too many memories and served as a reminder of how much his late wife disliked being there without him.[44]

Zoe and Flora were alike only in the way they pined for the marshal when he was away for too long. As Zoe wrote about Flora's struggles, she found herself sympathizing with the first Mrs. Tilghman. Unlike Flora, Zoe would have to suffer through Tilghman's murder and live another thirty years without him.[45]

Chapter 5

A Man Who Knows He's Right

Marshal Tilghman rode along the banks of the Red Rock River, thirteen miles southwest of Perry, Oklahoma, until he reached a small stand of cottonwoods. He surveyed the green flats beyond the trees hoping to catch sight of the man he was chasing. It was mid-May 1902. The sun was low in the sky and twilight was thickening over the plains. He was confident the criminal he was after would be passing soon. Tilghman knew the terrain so well that he hurried to the spot the outlaw had to reach to ford the river and waited.[1]

The forty-six-year-old lawman had been busy since his wife's passing in October 1900. After making sure his two youngest children were settled, he concentrated on his run for sheriff of Lincoln County. He was favored to win the election. An enthusiastic voter summed up what many Oklahoma Territory residents felt about the seasoned veteran's chances at the polls. "Well, I'm for Bill Tilghman for sheriff," the man told a newspaper reporter. "The fact that Bill Tilghman was elected sheriff of Lincoln County would be enough in itself to keep a good many horse thieves out of the county. They'd give this county the go-by." Another constituent noted, "It is the solemn duty of every voter in this county who believes in the preservation of law and order to cast his vote for Tilghman."[2]

Tilghman won the election by a large majority and began at once to do the job the public entrusted him to do. One of the first cases he oversaw involved two men named John Cofield and a Dr. Talbert. Cofield, a fifty-five-year-old farmer, lived with his wife and five stepchildren (three boys and two teenage girls) on a homestead in Parkland. The oldest of the

US Deputy Marshal William "Bill" Tilghman.
OKLAHOMA HISTORICAL SOCIETY

girls, fifteen-year-old Mary, was engaged to marry a local schoolteacher on May 12, 1901, but she died suddenly a month before the ceremony. Cofield learned his stepdaughter was pregnant in early April and asked his friend, veterinary surgeon Dr. Talbert, to help with the situation. He performed an operation to abort the baby. The procedure killed Mary. When Cofield was told she would die, he took a bottle of strychnine and fled the scene. The doctor hurried away too. The girl's mother sent for Tilghman. He arrived with a deputy who found Cofield cowering in the woods. He was arrested and taken to jail. Tilghman then set off after Dr. Talbert.[3]

As predicted, the renegade veterinarian ended up at the section of the river where the marshal was waiting. Tilghman eyed him closely as he approached, and just when Talbert was about to lead his horse into the water, the lawman stepped out from the trees with his Winchester. "Let's see your hands," Tilghman told the stunned doctor. For a long moment Talbert sat motionless, staring at the marshal's gun. As if he suddenly appreciated the desperate position he was in, he let go of his horse's reins and raised his hands in the air.[4]

John Cofield and Dr. Talbert were charged with murder. At the inquest, Mary's sister testified her stepfather had raped Mary and that the child she was carrying was his. Some of the townspeople talked about a double lynching, but Tilghman managed to reason with the infuriated Parkland citizens and convinced them to let the law take its course.[5]

Tilghman had no sooner concluded the Cofield-Talbert matter than he was summoned to the Ames Farm, several miles outside Chandler. When he reached the homestead, he found Mrs. Agnes Ames and a man named Jackson, who was the hired hand, lying dead in a cave near the house. Agnes's daughter, Adelia Smith, had suffered a gunshot wound to the arm, but managed to escape the attacker and ran to get Tilghman's help. She explained to the lawman that a strange man had come to their door the night before asking for food. He shoved a gun in her face moments after demanding a meal. He forced Adelia, her mother, and the hired hand into a nearby cave the family used to store food and take refuge during tornados. Once the trio was in place, the gunman fired three shots into the cave, hitting all of them. He returned shortly thereafter to make sure everyone was dead. The only one moving was Adelia. He ordered her out of the cave and back into the house. He demanded money and then raped her. The sound of Jackson crying out in pain prompted the gunman to hurry back to the cave. He shot Jackson two more times and Agnes once more. Satisfied they were both dead, he returned to the house. Adelia had escaped in his absence.[6]

It was pouring rain when the injured woman made it to the neighbor's home to get help. Using the detailed description of the man provided by Adelia, Tilghman rode off in search of the perpetrator. He found tracks of a horse leading from the house to where the rider had attempted to cross a small stream near where the bridge had been washed away. The horse had jumped across, and that was as far as Tilghman could track the murderer as the heavy rains had obliterated any trail to follow.[7]

Tilghman told a reporter with the *Chandler Publicist* that he "didn't believe the murder was committed to secure money, for the reason that Mrs. Ames was killed before there was anything said about money, and she would have known more of the whereabouts of the money than anyone else on the place." The county attorney believed the stranger was paid to murder the Ames family. Agnes had purchased a gun a few days prior to the killings. She told the store clerk who sold her the gun that she needed it because someone was coming for them, and she needed to protect herself and her daughter.[8]

The days before the shooting a stranger rode into town asking about the Ames family. He specifically wanted to know where Agnes Ames lived. Tilghman was confident this stranger was the man who committed the crime. He assured the outraged community that he would resume the search for the murderer as soon as he could. He was determined to catch the man and noted that "although he may be picked up at any time, the indications were that his plans for escape were well laid and that his capture would be difficult, but not impossible." Tilghman had every intention of spending as much time as needed to apprehend the fugitive.[9]

It took more than a year for Sheriff Tilghman to get his man, but he did. Jim Woods, alias Jim Alvin, was arrested in Guthrie on November 10, 1904. Not only was he a murderer, he was also a bank robber and a horse thief who was in custody at the county jail for robbing a store in

Piedmont. Woods admitted that if he'd known Tilghman was on his trail he would have put a greater distance between himself and the unshakeable lawman. Adelia Smith was summoned to the jail to identify Woods. She picked him out of more than a dozen men being detained for various crimes. Before locating Woods, the county prosecuting attorney charged Adelia's father, Angus Ames, with the double murder. Angus had been in Hot Springs, Arkansas, awaiting his own day in court for blackmail. Tilghman insisted Angus had nothing to do with the crime, arguing in court the lack of evidence leading to the prosecution's belief that he had hired Woods to kill his wife and the hired hand. Adelia was grateful to Sheriff Tilghman as was the rest of the community.[10]

"In a short time that he has been in office Sheriff Tilghman has earned four rewards, a total of $570," a report in the September 18, 1904, edition of the *Chandler News* read. "In the past few years, he has collected $7,250 rewards and spent over $4,000 in railway fares and for information in capturing desperados and criminals, and he is certainly justifying his reputation by making Lincoln County a mighty unprofitable field for criminals to operate in."[11]

With or without a reward, Tilghman was committed to his job. He believed a good lawman fought to keep the peace not only because he disliked the criminals in front of him but also because he was indebted to those law-abiding citizens who stood behind him.[12]

It was Tilghman's convictions and resoluteness that led Chief Justice of the Territory, C. H. Buford, to have the lawman make a series of arrests in the boomtown of Warwick in September 1903. Located eight miles west of Chandler, the little community was given a major boost in the summer of 1903 when the Fort Smith Western Railway Company announced they would be building a railroad through the area. Hundreds of eager land buyers gathered in the small town to purchase lots for sale. During the two-day excitement, the enthusiastic people scarcely noticed the arrival of Sheriff Tilghman and his deputy Tom Tipton. Not long after the lawmen arrived, they placed the president of the Monarch Investment Company and several of his executives under arrest.[13]

According to the September 18, 1903, edition of the *Chandler Publicist*, "The plan followed by the company in opening the townsite was this: All lots, 1,800 in number, had been sold at the uniform price of $25 cash, with the understanding that the company would make known the plan of distribution on the day of the opening. It was accordingly announced that a capital prize of the corner lot on which stands a shack dubbed by courtesy a bank building, would be awarded to the lot purchaser who came nearest guessing the number of head of livestock sold on the Kansas City exchange yesterday, every purchaser being entitled to a guess. The person making the next best guess would be allowed to select his lot from all those remaining after the capital prize was awarded; the third best guesser taking second choice and so forth to the end of the line. The guesses were being recorded at the time the sheriff appeared upon the scene."[14]

The Monarch Investment Company executives were charged with setting up and maintaining a lottery. An associate of the executives was furious and encouraged the men to resist being taken into custody. He loudly demanded to know on whose authority Tilghman was acting. Tilghman told the group who sent him and his deputy, but the boisterous associate continued to voice his objections and told the lawman, "Well, I am from Texas and will have to be shown [a warrant]." Tilghman quietly reached across the table and picked the gentleman up by the collar of his coat, and set him down among the other prisoners. The man turned out to be the secretary of the company and would have been overlooked if he'd kept quiet.[15]

* * *

The stories of the capture of Dr. Talbert, Jim Woods, and the arrest of the Monarch Investment Company executives were among the many Zoe Tilghman recounted in the biography she was writing about her husband. In the telling of the various cases, she grew to appreciate his talent and dedication more than she anticipated. She never took his abilities for granted but seeing them on the pages of the book brought all the lawman had done into sharper focus. Because she had firsthand knowledge of what he had accomplished, she was especially frustrated by an article that appeared in the April 12, 1931, edition of the *Kansas*

City Star in which the marshal and his companions were referred to as "a bunch of cowards."[16]

Written by a *Kansas City Star* reporter, the story originated in Dodge City, Kansas, and centered around the life and times of a dancehall girl named Annie Anderson. Anderson claimed to have known "all the straight-shooting characters of the early West" and lived to hear of their deaths with their boots on and otherwise. She cautioned the author against writing an article where the Western legends are made out to be heroes. "I could tell the people who write fine things about em' in the magazines a thing or two," Anderson told the reporter.[17]

She spoke disparagingly of Bat Masterson and Wyatt Earp before starting on Tilghman. "All cowards," she told the journalist. "Earp came as near being a brave man as any of them, but I noticed he never took any chances. They were men who were driven out of town. Masterson was scared out of town by an unnamed man. And I'll tell how another one left. He went at night in one of my dresses because he was scared into chills for fear Wyatt Earp was going to kill him. The man was the famous 'two-gun Bill Tilghman.' He hid under a feather bed in my house a day and a night before he ventured out in the dress. And he never came back again as long as Wyatt Earp was in town."[18]

Zoe was outraged by the story and sued the *Kansas City Star* for defamation of her husband's character. The libel suit asked for $100,000 in damages. Legal representatives for the newspaper filed a motion to quash or strike the suit. Despite the best efforts of Zoe's well-known attorney Sid White, often referred to as the "cowboy lawyer," the judge considering the libel suit ruled in favor of the newspaper and dismissed the case. Tilghman's widow was disappointed with the judge's ruling, but her spirits were lifted by a decision the US House of Representatives made around the same time regarding Bill. Congress approved a bill to compensate Zoe monetarily "for the death of her husband, caused by being shot by a federal prohibition agent." In asking the House to pass the measure, sponsored by Oklahoma Representative Fletcher Swank, Swank noted the "name of Bill Tilghman is inseparably connected with the stirring events of the Old West and he was one of the most colorful characters of the Territory of Oklahoma."[19]

The recognition Marshal Tilghman received from the US government was vindication enough for Zoe. The action taken by Congress was reported on by the Associated Press news service and the story carried in newspapers across the country, even the *Kansas City Star.*[20]

* * *

Writing the part of Tilghman's story about when he met Zoe was bittersweet for the author. Her memories of that time and the time to come were good as well as painful. Choosing what kind of information to include in the biography about their life together was emotionally trying.[21]

* * *

Tilghman had a passion for raising thoroughbred horses. It was second only to racing the stock. "There's a thrill in seeing a horse born and raised on your farm cross the finish line a nose ahead of the others in his class," he wrote in his memoirs. Breeders like Tilghman enjoyed discussing business with those who had the same preoccupation. In late 1901, he befriended a Payne County stock raiser and well-known breeder of thoroughbred hogs named Mayo Stratton. Stratton was one of Oklahoma's earliest pioneers, having moved to the Territory long before the Land Rush of 1889. Tilghman and Stratton had a great deal in common and visited one another often. It was during one of those visits that Tilghman met Stratton's daughter Zoe. The twenty-one-year-old woman was a student at the University of Oklahoma, and when she graduated, she took a teaching position at the high school where she lived with her family in Pond Creek. Tilghman showed more than a passing interest in the young woman. Zoe had gray-green eyes and dark hair and was well-spoken and self-assured. She was also an exceptional rider. She rode with her father and the cowhands cutting out calves and roping and branding them along with the hired workers.[22]

Zoe rejected the traditional idea that a woman's only ambition should be to marry and have children. She wanted to attend college and study English. She wrote poetry and stories about her family's ranch and

Zoe Stratton Tilghman shortly after her marriage to William Tilghman. Her blouse was elaborate lace bertha that Bill Tilghman had brought from Mexico.
DEPARTMENT OF SPECIAL COLLECTIONS AND UNIVERSITY ARCHIVES, UNIVERSITY OF TULSA MCFARLIN LIBRARY

aspired to make a living doing both. Zoe and Tilghman had long talks about horses, the history of Oklahoma, and the future of the Territory.[23]

The time Zoe and Tilghman spent with one another extended beyond meetings at the Stratton homestead. The lawman was occasionally required to escort individuals suffering mental issues to Norman where the state asylum was located. While in the city, Tilghman would quickly visit the college where Zoe was finishing her degree to see how she was doing. She was moved by the compassion he had for the people he brought to the facility. He had witnessed firsthand how poorly some of the inmates at the sanitarium were treated and believed the staff that ran the hospital should be fired and prosecuted. He had taken his concerns to Governor Thompson Ferguson and urged him to investigate the conditions. Tilghman's accusations and those of others who had witnessed the conditions inside the asylum led to the resignation of the superintendent.[24]

Bill Tilghman proposed to Zoe Stratton on Christmas Eve 1902, and she happily accepted. The couple was married at five in the morning on July 15, 1903, at Zoe's parents' home. The ceremony was performed by Reverend Sickels of Stillwater, Oklahoma. Mayo not only gave the bride away but also served as best man. According to the July 17, 1903, edition of the *Stroud Sun*, the reason the wedding took place so early in the morning was because the newlyweds had tickets for the train taking them to Eureka Springs, Arkansas, for their honeymoon.[25]

After spending a week in Arkansas, Tilghman and his new bride moved into the home he shared with three of his children and the housekeeper, Laura Witherman, in Chandler. The lawman's oldest son, Charles, was a cashier at the Bank of Chandler and the city treasurer. He had married Mamie King on December 25, 1900. Less than two years after they exchanged vows, Mamie died of malaria. Their eleven-month-old daughter passed away five months later. Charles was a frequent visitor at the Tilghman home. The marshal's eldest daughter, twenty-two-year-old Dorothy, his seventeen-year-old son William Jr., and the youngest child, thirteen-year-old Vonia, were polite but not overly friendly to Zoe. They kept to themselves, spending most of their time with Laura, who had become like a second mother to them. The situation was awkward for all involved. Zoe was only six months older than Dorothy and prior to her father's new wife entering the picture, Dorothy had accompanied him on business trips and helped care for her siblings. A month after Zoe arrived Dorothy decided to travel to Rogers, Arkansas, to visit friends. She felt out of place at her father's home and needed to decide what to do next. While she was away, she met David Joseph Norton, a deputy clerk of the US Court. Dorothy and Captain Norton were wed at the Tilghman home on February 3, 1904.[26]

Any idea that Tilghman would be around to help support Zoe through the awkward transition of moving into his home with his children was abandoned shortly after their honeymoon. He was well into his second term as sheriff of Lincoln County and needed to get back to work. He continued his travels throughout Oklahoma and into Kansas tracking down murderers and thieves.[27]

In September 1903, Tilghman announced to a reporter at the *Chandler Publicist* that the month had been a record-breaker in criminal business in the district court. The lawman noted that more cases were tried and a larger number of convictions secured than any other month of his experience.[28]

Local and regional politicians asked Tilghman to consider running for sheriff again. They congratulated him for "ridding the county of a good many toughs" and wanted him to stay on the job. He was flattered by the request but decided not to run for reelection. He wanted to turn his attention to his cattle ranching and horse breeding business and to spend time with his wife and family. Sheriff Tilghman spent the last week of his term of office chasing an outlaw to Amarillo, Texas. He returned to Chandler on December 28, 1904, having successfully captured the bandit and placed him in jail. "Under the administration of Bill Tilghman the office of Sheriff has been one of the best administered in Oklahoma," the editor of the *Chandler Tribune* wrote in an outgoing salute to the dedicated lawman. "Tilghman has gained Territorial notoriety, an almost national standing as an executive officer, and as he steps down and out with a reputation which cannot be but a continual source of pride."[29]

Zoe adapted to life in Chandler with Vonia and William Jr. as best she could. They preferred Laura's company over hers. She wasn't a mother or a friend, but merely their father's wife. There were times during the long trips Tilghman took pursuing outlaws that Zoe visited her parents in Payne County. While she was there, she rode her horse and wrote poetry and was always back home in Lincoln County by the time Tilghman returned.[30]

In February 1905, Zoe learned she was going to have a baby. Tilghman was thrilled and at fifty years of age, considered leaving law enforcement in favor of staying with his wife. However, a letter from the president of the United States persuaded him to remain on the job.[31]

In the course of his duties as a deputy marshal there were many occasions Tilghman had to go to Washington, DC, and it was during those times he made the acquaintance of President Theodore Roosevelt. The president was familiar with Tilghman's work and enjoyed talking with him about his time as an officer and the criminals he had encountered. Like many other politicians and law enforcement agents who knew Tilghman, Roosevelt respected and appreciated the lengths he was willing to go to apprehend fugitives. When lawyers with the St. Louis-San Francisco Railway (also known as the Frisco) sought help from the government to locate a man hiding in Mexico who had stolen a considerable sum of money from the company, the president knew Tilghman was the man to send. As special representative, Tilghman was first tasked with traveling to Mexico to meet with the country's leader Porfirio Diaz and acquire extraction papers for an embezzler named James T. Fitzpatrick. After extradition was secured, Tilghman had to find Fitzpatrick, arrest him, and escort him back to America.[32]

The fugitive was a roadmaster for the Frisco railway. He was responsible for the maintenance of the railroad and safety of the passengers for a 110-mile stretch from Oklahoma City to Sapulpa. He embezzled more than $40,000 from his employer and they were determined he be prosecuted for his actions.[33]

"Dear Zoe, I started off fine this morning," Tilghman wrote to his wife on February 12, 1905, from Fort Worth, Texas, "awaiting a fast train tonight. I leave at 8 o'clock for Mexico where I [will] receive my official papers from the American ambassador, the Hon. Powell Clayton. I think I am to go six hundred miles west to Aguacalientes. I will arrive in the city of Mexico on Wednesday. Can't tell best when I will get back but will rush through as fast as possible. So, do the best you can until I return.[34]

" . . . It is snowing here today and is very cold. It is a curiosity to see the slays [*sic*] and sleds here.

"Love to all. Hoping for the best. I am yours truly. Wm Tilghman."[35]

It took six days by train for Tilghman to reach Mexico City where he was to meet with Ambassador Powell Clayton. He presented his credentials and a letter from President Roosevelt explaining what was needed from President Diaz. While waiting to hear back from Mexico's leader, Tilghman decided to begin his search for Fitzpatrick. Armed with only a basic description of the man and a few details about his habits, the lawman made his way to the central railroad depot and began asking questions. Tilghman's Spanish wasn't perfect, but he got by and learned from a train porter that Fitzpatrick was working on a rail line that ran from Mexico City to Aguascalientes more than four hundred miles away.[36]

The following day, President Diaz agreed to see Tilghman, and the lawman explained the situation. He informed the head of the country that he had to go to Aguascalientes to find and arrest the criminal that needed to be extradited. Diaz was gracious, signed the extradition papers, and offered to have his military police accompany Tilghman. The marshal kindly declined assistance. He believed the more officers involved the more chance Fitzpatrick would have to find out and run.[37]

Although Tilghman wasn't wearing a disguise when he arrived in Aguascalientes like he had when he arrested Bill Doolin in Eureka Springs, he did try to appear more like a tourist than a policeman. He took in the sights, visited the town's hot springs, and purchased a few items at an outdoor market. He eventually wandered toward the railroad station to look around. A train was pulling into the terminal, and he watched the passengers disembark and hurry along their way. In the orderly chaos he noticed a conductor alight from one of the cars and he quickly surmised the man to be Fitzpatrick. He discreetly followed him to his home and waited for the right time to let himself into his house.[38]

The ex-roadmaster was relaxing comfortably in a chair, smoking a cigar, and reading a newspaper when he glanced up to find the barrel of a six-shooter pointed at him and Tilghman holding the gun. Fitzpatrick didn't resist arrest. Only after the pair were aboard a train bound for Mexico City did the renegade voice his opinion about the capture. "You'd never have taken me, or got away alive if I'd had half an hour's warning you were in town," Fitzpatrick told the lawman. "The boys are all sworn to get any officer that comes snooping here. They'd have knocked you in the head on the station platform or stuck a knife in your back." Tilghman almost smiled. "I knew that," he replied. "So, I didn't give you a chance."[39]

News that Tilghman had captured a high-profile fugitive was printed in papers across the Oklahoma Territory. "Tilghman Gets His Man," read one newspaper headline. The St. Louis-San Francisco Railway expressed their appreciation for Tilghman's work in a letter of thanks sent to President Roosevelt. Roosevelt shared the letter with Tilghman when the lawman was in Washington months later. The president inquired of Tilghman at that time how "a gunman on the side of law all of his life was still alive after so many experts had tried to kill him?" Marshal Tilghman replied, "A man who knows he's right has an edge on a man who knows he's wrong."[40]

On September 26, 1905, Zoe gave birth to a son. The Tilghmans named him Tench after the marshal's distant uncle who served as an aide-de-camp to General George Washington during the American Revolutionary War. "Bill was singularly devoted and indulgent to children," Zoe later wrote about her husband when Tench was born. "Even when the baby was very small, he would hold and rock him and play with him as he grew and noticed things. Wherever he went, if there was a small child, it would soon be upon his knee." Tilghman was elated with his new son. "He is a Bryan Democrat," the lawman told friends and family. The comment was in reference to three-time Democratic presidential nominee William Jennings Bryan. Tilghman was a Democrat who favored Bryan because he was a champion of popular sovereignty, political reform, social morality, and world peace.[41]

Tench grew up to be a supporter of the Democratic Party and even ran for the Oklahoma legislature. He graduated high school with honors, was an influential law student at the University of Oklahoma, practiced law at a prestigious firm, and helped bring about much-needed changes to the Oklahoma Highway Protective Association. Zoe boasted about

Tench's accomplishments during speaking engagements in which she took part at the Oklahoma College of Women and occasionally during the night classes she taught on poetry.[42]

Zoe cherished the time after Tench was born. Tilghman was home on a regular basis and busying himself with his thoroughbred stallions and his prize hogs and mules. He entered the animals in different fairs and watched his horses compete in races throughout the Territory. Zoe reflected on this moment in their history in a poem she wrote titled "Grasshoppers at West Thumb."[43]

> Still the deep-shadowed pines and crystal lake
> Chant their antiphonies of mystery
> Unto the circling mountains and the sky.
> In a dim grave, unmarked and desolate,
> My lover lies, having learned
> The last great mystery.
> Fate is not, as the ancients said,
> Old women 'neath a tree, or spinning in the sun,
> Rather, she comes so softly, where we stray,
> Even like grasshoppers in the sunlit space
> Between two mysteries, and strikes us down,
> Uncaring, ruthless, purposeful.
> Slipping behind to take us unaware.[44]

In January 1907, Zoe informed her husband they were expecting their second child. Tilghman was proud of his growing family and knew how they would benefit from his day-to-day interaction in their young lives, but he couldn't resist the needs of the Territory. Congress had been debating statehood for Oklahoma. If a bill admitting the southern part of the region and the west portion of the Indian Territory was approved, the combined territories would enter the Union as the 46th state. Tilghman was sure political leaders, including President Roosevelt, would call on him to help make statehood happen.[45]

Chapter 6

A Most Fitting Man

A mild, persistent wind caused the limbs of a naked winter tree to gently scratch the picture window outside the parlor of the enormous home of John and Mary Hale. More than two dozen men and women were seated around the couple as they watched Zoe Tilghman play the violin. Zoe's performance came at the end of the sixth annual banquet of the Round Table Club, an organization dedicated to the fine arts. After a savory meal, the hostess ushered guests into the parlor to be entertained by poetry readings, a piano duet, and a violin solo. The audience offered Zoe generous applause at the conclusion of her well-played piece and she nodded graciously to the club members. Before she left the spotlight, John Hale politely asked if her husband would again be running for sheriff of Lincoln County in the coming election. She smiled and shook her head before explaining that he hadn't said anything to her about it, but admitted jokingly that she was sometimes the last to know his plans.[1]

Zoe learned that Marshal Tilghman was a candidate for sheriff of Lincoln County while reading the March 14, 1907, edition of the *Oklahoma Weekly Leader*. Tilghman's friends and family, including his son Charles who was running for mayor of Chandler, encouraged the lawman to run. They wanted Oklahoma to become a state and believed it was incumbent on the respected pioneers of the Territory to fill positions that would help make statehood possible.[2]

"Mr. Tilghman needs no specific words of recommendation," the April 19, 1907, edition of the *Sparks Review* read. "He is too well and

William Tilghman as a young man.
OKLAHOMA HISTORICAL SOCIETY

favorably known to require an introduction to our readers. He served the people of this county [for] four years as sheriff and rendered valuable service to them that has rarely been equaled by any sheriff in the Territory. As a fearless and energetic man, he has no peers.[3]

"He has for many years been known as Bill Tilghman, the man-catcher, and that this county is in need of just such a man there can be no question.

"He is a man best fitted for this place. He's worked at similar work most of his life and when Tilghman goes after a man he is [at] his best. In fact, Tilghman has a reputation throughout the two Territories as one of the best criminal hunters we have. He is a man that pays strict attention to business. If he should be elected [he] would be found ever ready to discharge his duties."[4]

Zoe didn't ask Tilghman why he didn't discuss throwing his hat in the ring again with her. He did what he thought was best and he trusted she knew that about him. She only hoped he would be home in September when their second child was due. In the interim, Zoe helped with his campaign at Ladies' Aid Society meetings and school board functions.[5] She crafted a promotional verse to run in various newspapers across the county leading up to the primary, which read:

> A Bale to the Acre
> When you chop them to a stand, Saturday,
> leave me in the row and
> I will guarantee a full bale to the acre.
> Wm. Tilghman, Candidate for Sheriff[6]

Tilghman received the Democratic nomination for sheriff of Lincoln County in the primary. The incumbent sheriff, Lew Martin, was the Republican nominee. The race for the office between the two would be ugly. Tilghman traveled to several cities in Lincoln County with the other members of the delegation of Democratic office seekers. He gave short speeches and met one-on-one with voters. He had to work the campaign trips around his continual duties as a Deputy US Marshal. Sheriff Martin was frustrated with trying to compete with Tilghman's reputation as a marshal and his legacy in the sheriff's department. He decided to focus on the expenses claimed by Tilghman during his time in office, suggesting that they were fraudulent. Newspapers were quick to jump on the story and to seek Tilghman out for comment.[7]

"'Bill' Tilghman, candidate for sheriff, is making the race on his merit as a peace officer," the June 4, 1907, edition of the *Chandler Tribune* noted. "He can point with pride to the time when horse stealing was almost unknown in Lincoln County and when all crime was at a low ebb. The reason [for] this was that swift and sure justice overtook every attempt at criminality on account of Tilghman's splendid system.[8]

"He has spent his life running down criminals and he knows the business from a to z. People are inclined to compare the loose, unbusinesslike, incompetent administration with that of Tilghman's and to wish for the good old times.[9]

"Mr. Tilghman says that even the administration makes comparison and decided that he would be a dangerous opponent and is therefore doing all possible harm to his candidacy."[10]

Critics of Sheriff Martin made their thoughts known about his "underhanded tactics" and cited an article in the July 30, 1907, edition of the *Chandler Tribune* as an example of inefficiency during his term.[11]

"The difference between Bill Tilghman and Lew Martin can be easily seen in the developments of the Arthur Sanders' case," the newspaper article read. "A few days ago, every paper in the Territory had an account about how Sheriff Martin would start a few days for the Pacific coast armed with a requisition for Arthur Sanders, the escaped murderer. Time passed and it developed that the suspect was not the man wanted at all.[12]

"Now these mistakes are bound to happen, of course, but had Bill Tilghman been in the sheriff's office he would have kept his own counsel and no one would have ever known a thing about the matter until after Tilghman had done all the work. He goes and brings them in and then tells the reporters what he has done while Martin tells them what he is going to do and then never does."[13]

Tilghman's crusade for sheriff suffered a setback on July 28, 1907, when the marshal incurred a severe injury while driving a herd of horses to water. One of the horses turned quickly and kicked at Tilghman's ride. The hooves missed the horse and hit Tilghman just below the knee. A medical examination proved the bone was broken in two places. Tilghman's doctor confined him to bed and assured him that "it would be impossible, even under the most favorable circumstances, to do any campaign work."[14]

Sheriff Martin took full advantage of his opponent's situation and in the following months his campaign publicly accused Tilghman of being an "unscrupulous man" who overcharged taxpayers for his travel to apprehend outlaws and escort them to jails in other parts of the county. Friends and supporters were quick to come to the marshal's defense. The shameless antics continued to play out in the press until election day.[15]

On September 17, 1907, the people of the Indian and Oklahoma Territories voted favorably for statehood. The vote was certified and delivered to President Theodore Roosevelt. Three days later, Zoe and Marshal Tilghman welcomed their son, Richard Lloyd, to the world. The lawman barely had any time to enjoy the birth of his son because he needed to dispute the allegations of malfeasance leveled against him by Sheriff Martin on the front page of the *Chandler Publicist*. The headline on the September 6, 1907, edition of the newspaper read "A Whole Page of Facts Concerning Bill Tilghman and His Official Record." The article connected was incendiary and inaccurate.[16]

"Bill Tilghman advertises himself as a man-catcher. He might more fittingly refer to himself as a fee-grabber and a reward-hunter and a mileage counter. He prides himself upon his record as a deputy U. S. marshal and would have the dear people think that he learned all that there is to know about rounding up criminals while serving in that capacity. He may have learned a little along that line—his associations should have taught him something. But what made the deepest impression upon his mind was the methods he mastered of counting up mileage so as to increase his fees and of getting the rewards offered for persons whose whereabouts he knew."[17]

Tilghman responded to Sheriff Martin's charges with his own page of facts. "Compare the Record of the Two Men," Tilghman encouraged voters in the September 10, 1907, edition of the *Chandler Tribune*. "The records in the county clerk's office prove the fact that Lew Martin has been paid in sheriff's fees, jail and courthouse attendance, transportation, and expenses during two- and one-half years of his term in office as $11,074.88.[18]

"During Tilghman's term in office for two- and one-half years immediately preceding Lew Martin's term in office, the records disclose the fact that Tilghman was paid for the same class of fees $8,220.40.[19]

"During two- and one-half years Tilghman collected taxes to the amount of $15,616.83.

"During Martin's two- and one-half years he has collected $11,832.15.

"A glance at the number of persons transported to the penitentiary reveals the usefulness of the sheriffs. Here it is:[20]

Martin		
1905	Spring Term	7
1905	Fall Term	3
1906	Spring Term	12
1906	Fall Term	1
1907	Spring Term	3
		26
Tilghman		
1902	Fall Term	5
1903	Spring Term	6
1903	Fall Term	16
1904	Spring Term	11
1904	Fall Term	2
		40

"Tilghman is entitled to two of Martin's men—Jim Woods for the murder of the Ames family, and another for horse stealing.[21]

"Bill Tilghman has been pronounced by Judge Burford as being one of the best sheriffs in Oklahoma. He has been mentioned in our courthouse before juries at different times by John Embry and Roy Hoffman in the highest of terms.

"Emery Foster said just before he was nominated that Tilghman was the best sheriff Lincoln County ever had and, in his opinion, ever would have.[22]

"Will the voters take the opinion of such men as the Hon. Judge Burford, judge of the Supreme Court of Oklahoma, the opinion of the Hon. John Embry, United States attorney for Oklahoma, the opinion of Col. Roy Hoffman, the opinion of Emery A. Foster, county attorney, or the opinion of the pygmy—the editor of the Pub?"[23]

Tilghman lost the election to Sheriff Martin.[24]

Deputy US Marshal Bill Tilghman continued to be one of the most active of the deputy marshals in the new state of Oklahoma. He joined posses in search of outlaws who had murdered fellow law enforcement agents and tracked bootleggers. When Oklahoma was admitted to the Union in November 1907, Prohibition was adopted. It was the only state with Prohibition inscribed in its constitution. Marshal Tilghman was ordered to uphold the liquor restrictions using whatever means necessary.[25]

"Chief of Police William Tilghman, who made a reputation in the early days by cleaning up Dodge City, Kansas, when it was known as a bad town, has started in on a clean-up of Oklahoma City," the October 27, 1907, edition of the *Foraker Sun* read. "Seventy-five bootleggers were arrested in one day under his orders and over $1,200 of cash bonds forfeited in police court that evening. It is announced that the violators of the prohibitory law will be rearrested every time their places are found open for business."[26]

Tilghman's social calendar was as busy as his professional one. He and Zoe and their two boys attended Tilghman's oldest son's wedding in February 1908. Charles had risen from bank teller to president of the Chandler National Bank. Tilghman's daughter Dottie had married two years prior to Charles's wedding, William Jr. was attending school in Los Angeles, and Vonia was also away studying. Zoe's relationship with her husband's children from his first marriage could never have been characterized as close. Five years after she and Tilghman had wed, the best that could be said was that they were cordial to one another and endeavored to maintain friendliness at family events.[27]

Often when Tilghman was away on business, Zoe's mother would come to visit. While her mother was spending time with Tench and Richard, Zoe would write. She penned several poems about her children, stories about Tilghman's exploits, and articles about the changes experienced in her beloved Oklahoma since statehood had been achieved.[28]

* * *

In 1931, Zoe founded the Poetry Society of Oklahoma and had an opportunity to share her work with other aspiring authors. It was often said that Zoe Tilghman was as much a part of Oklahoma as the "red buds and the red earth." According to an article in the July 4, 1935, edition of the *Walters Herald*, Zoe's life in the Sooner State is a "never-to-be-forgotten pageant in Oklahoma's literary life." Her poem "Prairie Winds" serves as an example of the inspiration she derived from the land she called home and how she lamented the early days of the wild territory.[29]

> The little winds blow softly, across the prairie lands,
> Till the velvet-golden sunflowers nod, as stirred by fairy lands.
> And the little winds come whispering, whispering to me . . .
> The bitter wind goes moaning across the prairie waste,
> And ghost-gray stalks of the dead sunflowers, shiver before his haste.
> The little winds, the bold free winds, the bitter winds of storm
> Are whispering, calling, moaning, the prairies call you home.[30]

Tilghman had his own idea of how to pay homage to Oklahoma's early days. In September 1908, the deputy marshal agreed to travel to the southwest portion of the state to take part in the making of a motion picture produced by US Marshal John Abernathy and reformed train robber Al Jennings.[31] The medium was new to the country. Kinetoscope, an early motion picture device, designed to be viewed by one person at a time through a peephole viewer window, had been introduced to the United States in the mid-1890s. The technology advanced so that short pictures were being made using hand-cranked cameras called cinematographs.[32] Marshal Abernathy and Al Jennings's short picture was a realistic reproduction of a bank robbery and the attack of a wagon train by outlaws. Tilghman, Heck Thomas, and a host of other Oklahoma lawmen were asked to appear in the film as posse members tracking the bad guy. Jennings agreed to play the role of a bank robber horse thief. The film was made to show "modern Oklahomans" how lawless the region had once been and to celebrate those who helped bring about order.[33]

The finished product was shown to President Theodore Roosevelt at the capital in December 1908. "Delighted" was the president's hearty explanation at the conclusion of the Wild West moving picture.[34]

Shortly after the film was shot, Marshal Abernathy ordered Tilghman to serve papers on those people residing in the Western District who had to appear in court in the Eastern District. During the long ride, the lawman had a lot of time to think about the Abernathy and Jennings film *The Bank Robbery*. Tilghman was enamored with the process, and the experience left him mulling over the idea of producing his own moving picture. Serving legal papers wouldn't be the most exciting of all his ventures to film, but he certainly could find something exciting from his memorable past to record. Tilghman had an opportunity to relive a few of the most important and dangerous moments of his law enforcement career when he was summoned to Washington to attend the Army Navy reception at the White House. Chris Madsen, one-time Deputy US Marshal and hunter of outlaws with Tilghman in the frontier days, was also invited to attend the festivities.[35]

Tilghman and Madsen regaled President Roosevelt with stories about tracking the Doolin-Dalton Gang. The president was most interested in hearing about how Tilghman arrested Bill Doolin. Tilghman was more than happy to share.[36]

"I had been tracking Doolin for nearly a year off and on. . . . I discovered that he was living up in Southern Kansas somewhere on a farm about three miles east of Burden. I was told that a man answering the exact description of Doolin, drove in town every two weeks for provisions, driving an old lumber wagon hitched to a team managed with rope lines. I was lying in wait up there for six weeks, trying to catch him at home. When his wife left the house and bought a ticket for Perry, I thought they were going to her fathers, a preacher, and the postmaster at Lawton, in Pawnee County. I had the woman shadowed. About this time however, I got a strong scent of Doolin at Eureka Springs, Arkansas. I went there at once.[37]

William Tilghman at the Army Navy reception in Washington, DC.
COURTESY WESTERN HISTORY COLLECTIONS, SPECIAL RESEARCH COLLECTIONS, UNIVERSITY OF OKLAHOMA LIBRARIES, WHCP-1165

"Almost the first man I saw at Eureka after getting off the train was Bill Doolin. I knew Bill knew me, but he did not see me that time. I watched where he went. He went to the Davy House. I went to another place and concluded I would take a bath, and in the meantime make sure that the man I saw was Doolin. I went to a barber shop and bathroom next to the Davy Hotel. The first man I saw when I opened the door was Bill Doolin. Bill looked up, gave me a sharp glance and I brushed on past him and called for a bath. I was dressed in an unusual manner, with a derby hat, and I felt that he had not recognized me.[38]

"The bathroom was open and I went in, positioned myself so I could see when Doolin was engaged in the newspaper he had in his hands. As soon as he was, I put my gun in an inconspicuous position, quietly opened the door, and walked to where Doolin was. He did not see me until I had my gun down on him. I said, 'Bill, throw up your hands.' He got his hands about halfway up, raised to his feet, looked me square in the eye and seemed to be determining whether to put his hands up or to go for his gun. I said, 'Bill, you know who I am, don't you?' He said, 'yes, I do.' I said, 'Well, then you had better get your hands up,' and up went his hands."[39]

The president was mesmerized by the tale and shouted, "Bully!" when Tilghman was through with the account of the event.[40]

Zoe, Tench, and Richard happily welcomed Tilghman home in late March 1909. Zoe had numerous questions about her husband's trip to Washington. She wanted to know who attended the Army Navy reception, what incoming president William Howard Taft was like, and her husband's thoughts of the capital. Tilghman had little time to visit with his wife and children before receiving word from Oklahoma Governor Charles Haskell. The lawman was needed to help with a situation involving the Muscogee Creek Indians. Two deputies had been killed while attempting to arrest a tribal leader named Chitto Harjo, also known as Crazy Snake.[41]

Harjo and his people had objected to the Territory becoming a state because it meant an end to tribal governments and the further division of Native American land. Black Americans, disenfranchised because of Jim Crow laws, sought refuge among the Creeks at Old Hickory, the location where Harjo and other tribesmen ran the Creek government. During an annual meeting of the Creek traditionalists, an allegation was made that either a Creek Indian or a Black American had stolen meat from a nearby white farmer. The farmer called for the law to settle the matter, but when deputies arrived on the scene, they were driven away from Old Hickory by both the Creeks and Black Americans claiming the officers had no authority on Native land. A sheriff's posse was assembled. Deputies moved into the area to arrest Harjo and a skirmish ensued. Harjo was shot and wounded during the encounter, but he managed to get away. One man was killed and many were arrested, among them Crazy Snake's son, Legus Jones.[42]

Tilghman was named a "special officer" by the governor and tasked with leading the hunt to find Chitto Harjo. The governor reasoned that Harjo would not only come out of hiding to help his son who was in custody, but gladly surrender to the respected Deputy US Marshal, who Harjo knew personally. When Tilghman arrived at the scene of the uprising he was informed that Harjo was last seen crossing the North Canadian River ten miles from Old Hickory.[43]

During the four weeks Tilghman was searching for the Creek leader, he learned that much of the so-called uprising was exaggerated by the newspapers, while settlers who wanted the Creek Indians removed from the region had instigated the trouble that led to the exchange of gunfire. Some newspaper reports had readers believing that Chitto Harjo was going to lead his band of followers on the "war path."[44]

"It is an outrage!" Tilghman told reporters at the *Oklahoma State Capital* newspaper. "Such things have been going on in the Indian Territory for the last thirty years and this is the first time there has ever been such a newspaper row about it. . . . I saw an account of a bunch of half-grown boys in Chicago who had been drilling and had run away from home, coming down here to fight Crazy Snake." Tilghman could find no words of condemnation strong enough for those newspaper reporters who continually inflated the troubles and misrepresented the situation. As a result of the newspaper coverage, Oklahoma residents were fearful for their lives. Even Marshal Tilghman's insurance company was so frightened that the lawman was tracking such a dangerous man they cancelled his coverage. The company noted in a telegram that "the risk was too great to warrant their carrying the policy while the chief was being hunted."[45]

Tilghman combed the treacherous hills of Hickory Grove near the town of Henryetta, near to where the deputies were killed, but was unable to locate Harjo until May 1910. Harjo had retreated to Mexico and without official orders to go into the country to take him into custody, Tilghman would not continue the pursuit. The Creek leader wasn't seen again by white officers until 1911 when he made an appeal to state officials for his people to be made wards of the government.[46]

* * *

Throughout the years, as Zoe was writing the definitive biography of her husband's life and work, which included the tracking of Chitto Harjo, she was interrupted to manage serious issues. Many of these issues involved her son Woodrow. Such was the case in 1935. Woodrow had been released from jail after serving time for his part in killing James Chitwood. He'd only been home a few months when he was arrested on suspicion of stealing gasoline. It was alleged that after 1 a.m. on August 2, 1935, twenty-three-year-old Woodrow and one of his friends snuck into a filling station on South Walker Avenue in Oklahoma City and helped themselves to a tank of gas. Woodrow was charged with theft, pled guilty, and made to pay a fine. Two months later he was arrested again after a physical altercation with the owner of a local diner over the price of a chicken dinner. He and three friends he was with were asked to leave the eatery. They did so in protest. After piling into a vehicle to head out, the driver of the vehicle backed into the front of the café numerous times. Woodrow and his companions returned to the diner later in the evening and threw rocks through the front door.[47]

On November 23, 1935, Woodrow was arrested a third time for stabbing a man during an altercation at the victim's home. According to the November 27, 1935, edition of the *Oklahoma News*, Woodrow and a friend arrived at the home of the injured party, demanding to see the victim's sister. When he refused, one of the two men at his door struck him and during the subsequent fight Woodrow stabbed him. At the time of the arrest, Woodrow told police his name was Frank Jones. It wasn't until they reached the police department that Woodrow's identity was made known and he was charged with assault with a deadly weapon.[48]

Like many, Zoe struggled financially through the Depression. The money she made working for *Harlow's Weekly* paid the bulk of her expenses, but the attorney's fees for Woodrow were oppressive. At fifty-five she needed to find additional work. President Franklin Roosevelt's administration had created the New Deal program in part to aid needy individuals with finding a job. In September 1935, she appealed to the government for help but no one responded. She reached out to Oklahoma Governor Earnest Marland and his advisers, but again heard nothing in reply. In November, she went to Governor Marland's office and waited from ten in the morning to five in the evening for a chance to talk with him and explain her situation. "He wouldn't even see me," Zoe later recalled. "And as for a job, he sent out a single word 'No' as an answer. I asked for a job as a square deal. Many times, the state called on Bill Tilghman, and he always answered; the one time he called on the state, from his grave, the state refused to help in answer to his plea."[49]

Zoe wasn't the only widow in straitened circumstances. "There are others like me in similar plights," she shared with an Oklahoma newspaper reporter. "It wasn't so much that they wouldn't give me a job, but that they kept stalling me, and finally Marland flatly refused to see me."[50]

Financial relief for Zoe came in early 1936, the same month Woodrow's trial for assault with a deadly weapon was delayed by his lawyers. The Federal Writers' Project hired Zoe to help direct the writing and publishing of a guide on the history of Oklahoma. In February, it was announced that the widow of the slain pioneer peace officer would receive compensation from the government. The amount approved was $5,000.[51]

"Mrs. Zoe A. Tilghman, who recently lost a battle for a state job she said she deserved because of her dead husband's service to the state, may soon get $5,000 from the federal government," an article in the February 5, 1936, edition of the *Oklahoma News* read. "Yesterday the House of Representatives in Washington passed a bill, pushed by Rep. John Lee of the fifth Oklahoma district, which would give Miss Tilghman

$5,000. The bill now goes to the U. S. Senate where its fate will be in the hands of Senators Elmer Thomas and T. P. Gore."[52]

The funds arrived just in time to help Woodrow through another run-in with the law.

In mid-June 1936, Woodrow, along with two other men, robbed a cab driver they hired at midnight to drive them to Chickasha, fifty minutes southwest of Oklahoma City. The men forced the driver to stop and get out of the vehicle. They bound and gagged him, robbed him of the $6 he had, left him on the side of the highway, and drove away in his car. The cab driver managed to attract the attention of a motorist, and the police were subsequently contacted. Woodrow and his cohorts were arrested two hours after the robbery.[53]

The following month the trio each received seven-year sentences. Woodrow was ordered to serve his time at the Granite Reformatory. Zoe was heartbroken. She was sad and worried for her son, who didn't seem as though he'd ever be a law-abiding citizen, and despondent over her husband's memory. Each time Woodrow was taken into custody, the newspapers' account of the crimes never failed to note that he was the son of the "late Bill Tilghman, famed peace officer."[54] Zoe couldn't help but think how the scandal would have impacted his run for senate in 1910. At the urging of many longtime friends and fellow Democrats of Lincoln County, Tilghman announced his candidacy on June 14.[55]

"Having resided in Oklahoma during the past twenty-one years, and in Lincoln County for over eighteen years, I am well acquainted not only with the people of Oklahoma, but especially with the conditions and needs of the people of this district," Tilghman told the press in late June 1910. "I have strived to be a good citizen and am proud to say my family has followed that example as well."[56]

When Tilghman won the election, one of the first people to congratulate him was Bat Masterson. Masterson had always boasted that Tilghman was the "finest of all of us" and reiterated the sentiment in a telegram to the newly elected senator.[57]

The marshal's time in the office was brief. Tilghman resigned in April 1911 after being appointed chief of police of Oklahoma City by Mayor Whit M. Grant. In 1910 there was a heated battle within the state to determine which of the three cities—Guthrie, Oklahoma City, or Shawnee—would be the state capital. The honor went to Oklahoma City. Many voters were opposed to the decision, calling the location "nothing more than a vulgar Cowtown." The fight to move the capital city to Guthrie had to be settled in court. The judge ruled in favor of Oklahoma City. Mayor Grant believed if the lawlessness was under control citizens outside the city might not look so disfavorably on the court's ruling. "I have asked why I appointed Bill Tilghman as chief and here is my reason," the mayor explained in an article in the July 20, 1911, edition of the *Okmulgee Republican*.[58]

"I knew what he had done as marshal in Dodge City, Kansas, when that town was a nest of crooks and bad men. He cleaned that place up. He also eliminated the gang of degenerates and crooks at Perry when the strip was first opened. He also was a United States deputy marshal for a year. I know he is a good officer and absolutely fearless. He is the only man I know of who can be relied upon to enforce the ordinances and run the police department as it should be run."[59]

Zoe and the boys moved to Oklahoma City where Tilghman had committed to a two-year period of service. He promised at that time he'd take the family back to Chandler. Zoe assured him she would hold him to his promise.[60]

Democrats in Oklahoma City were not happy about Tilghman's appointment. They felt the job should have been given to someone who had served there as a police officer and not an "outsider." Chief Tilghman guaranteed the public that he would "enforce the law just as it is on the statute books and the city ordinances." He vowed to strictly enforce the "booze law." Many residents doubted Tilghman would be able to live up to Mayor Grant's campaign promise to shut down establishments featuring gambling and drinking. They believed Oklahoma City would continue to be a town where liquor was sold in more than thirty separate places with as much impunity as if there was no Prohibition law. "There's no more reason to allow bootleggers to openly sell liquor in the city than there is to allow thieves to deliberately steal," Tilghman told concerned citizens.[61]

Less than thirty days after being sworn in on the job, Chief Tilghman arrested fifty-five saloon keepers and the city collected $1,118 in cash fines from them. Local newspapers reported that bootleggers were so frustrated with the police department's intrusion on their business they were putting up cash appearance bonds and leaving the city. Seventeen out of thirty-eight bootleggers whose trials were set for the end of July 1911 failed to appear and their bonds were forfeited.[62]

Chief Tilghman and his officers weren't content with shuttering the juke joints; they went after bootleggers who sold liquor door-to-door as well. On August 12, 1911, a rumrunner named Frank Smith delivered a pint of whiskey to someone at a rooming house he thought was a regular customer. He didn't expect Tilghman to be on the other side of the door when he knocked. The chief of police had received a tip that Smith was selling liquor in the rear of various hardware stores. After investigating the claim, Tilghman ordered a bottle of whiskey from Smith using a secret go-between. The lawman opened the door for the man when he arrived at the delivery site and arrested Smith.[63]

Between July 1911 and February 1913, Chief Tilghman waged a quiet but effective war on bootleggers and gamblers, and because of uniformed and plainclothes officers, numerous arrests were made. In addition to substantially reducing the sale of liquor in Oklahoma City, Tilghman ordered raids on brothels and drove madams and their employees out of rooming houses and hotels in the residential districts. Political leaders were pleased with the results Tilghman had achieved and wanted him to agree to stay on with the department for another two years. He hated to leave an unfinished job and was tempted to accept the renewed appointment, but Zoe reminded him of the pledge he made to her when he took the position.[64]

The Tilghmans moved back to Chandler in the spring of 1913. Along with Tench and Richard, they were now joined by another son. Woodrow had been born on October 23, 1912. At home again the couple discussed the future and the aspirations of the fifty-seven-year-old lawman. The career law enforcement officer who had scouted for the army, tracked outlaws as a policeman, and hunted fugitives as a marshal now wanted to go after bigger game. And he needed Zoe's help to bring that about.[65]

Chapter 7

Tilghman in Pictures

By the spring of 1912, Bill Tilghman had been in law enforcement for more than thirty-five years. The job he most aspired to have within the field was that of US Marshal. He had worked with and admired former law enforcement officer turned businessman Evett Nix, who had been appointed US Marshal at the age of thirty-two. Tilghman believed his years of service made him the perfect candidate to be appointed to the position, and he hoped the two men who won the senate race in Oklahoma's first major election since becoming a state, Robert L. Owen and Thomas Pryor Gore, would agree.[1]

Both Tilghman and Zoe were thrilled when Senator Gore sent word to the lawman to let him know "if [New Jersey] Governor Woodrow Wilson is elected president, I will name Bill a United States Marshal." Gore was one of the leaders for Wilson's campaign in Oklahoma. Knowing how popular Police Chief Tilghman was in the region, the politician expected the possible appointment would prompt constituents to vote for Governor Wilson. It did ensure the Tilghman family's support for Wilson. They not only helped campaign for the governor but also were so in favor of his winning the presidency and of his platform that they named their third son after him.[2]

When Tilghman resigned as Oklahoma City police chief in February 1913, it wasn't only to fulfill a promise to his wife, but because he anticipated being appointed a US Marshal. Senator Gore was grateful for Tilghman's hard work gaining major endorsements for now President Wilson. He and Zoe had acquired letters from members of the state supreme court, state judges, union leaders, school board members, businessmen, police, and fire departments. Not only did the people the Tilghman's spoke to pledge their support to Wilson, they also wrote letters to champion Tilghman's appointment.[3]

Among the more than seven hundred endorsements Tilghman received were from men such as Democratic National Committee member Robert Galbreath. "Bill, I am for you first, last, and all the time," wrote Galbreath. "Anything I can do for you, Bill," Congressman George Neely wrote. "I'm proud and pleased to ask the appointment for this man knowing him as I do," attorney Caleb R. Brooks noted in a letter about Tilghman. Judge John H. Burford's endorsement of the lawman was also glowing. "I have personally known Mr. Tilghman for twenty years," the judge noted. "He was for many years a deputy marshal in Oklahoma, and for four years sheriff of one of the counties in which I had the honor to be presiding judge. No better, braver, truer, more discreet officer ever wore the star. He is affable, courteous, and genteel to his superiors or associates, and kind and generous to the unfortunate.[4]

"I am a Republican and speak disinterestedly. I assure you that no appointment you can make will be more fitting or appropriate, or more creditable to your administration than the appointment of Mr. Tilghman."[5]

President Woodrow Wilson's inauguration was held on March 4, 1913, in Washington, DC. Tilghman was on hand to watch the festivities. His trip to the capital was reported in several newspapers throughout the state. According to the March 27, 1913, edition of the *Bartlesville Examiner Enterprise,* a quartet of Oklahomans seeking appointments attended the swearing in of the twenty-eighth president.[6]

"William Tilghman, former chief of police of Oklahoma City, is in Washington as a candidate for the position of United States Marshal for the Western District. He has the endorsement of many state representatives and senators and counts on the backing of Senator Gore."[7]

Tilghman was treated respectfully by the incoming Cabinet during his visit but was told the appointment would not come for some months. Zoe noted in the biography of her husband that Tilghman was having health issues during this time and on doctor's orders decided not to return immediately to Oklahoma, but, instead, take some time to rest in the Colorado mountains. He hoped after a six-week stay he would be feeling better and that his appointment would have been secured. Zoe and the children accompanied the lawman on the trip that lasted until mid-September 1913. For more than three months the Tilghmans enjoyed uninterrupted time together camping, fishing, and taking long drives in and around Buena Vista.[8]

* * *

Zoe often took photos from that time to the Granite Reformatory when she visited Woodrow. Just as she had before when Woodrow was in trouble, Zoe hired a lawyer to help secure a parole for her son serving a seven-year sentence for robbing a taxi driver. Friends and fellow poets who attended the Oklahoma Writers all-day festival in early May 1937 with Zoe were aware the widow was again fighting for Woodrow's freedom. The long-suffering mother made no mention of her struggles during the event, however. Admirers of her work read aloud excerpts from her published books and poems. In between readings, Zoe fielded questions about the stories she selected to write and what inspired her. For those few hours, she was only Zoe Tilghman the writer and the focus was on her work and not her husband's legacy or her youngest son's troubles.[9]

In December 1937, Zoe was honored to learn she was one of eight women in Oklahoma to have her poems included in an anthology to be printed by New York publisher Henry Harrison. Her son Tench, now a well-respected attorney in the state, celebrated the news with his mother and during their time together the pair discussed the biography she was writing about Tilghman. The book hadn't come together as quickly as she had hoped. Work, ongoing issues with Woodrow, and her club activities created delays. Memories of her life with the lawman had consistently brought back a flood of emotions, and when she wasn't able to write about her husband's career, she focused on her poetry. The poem "More Than Forgiveness" was written in early 1938.[10]

If you come back to me,
Craving again our golden happiness,
Old love serene and unafraid,

Disloyalty confess;
Asking forgiveness now
For wandering, and, bitter lesson learned,
Seek to rekindle scattered embers where
Love altar fires once burned;
For my own sake, not yours,
Since radiance lost could never be the same
I will not know your fault. Silence your lips.
Ere they confess your shame![11]

Intertwined with the recollection of an enjoyable family vacation in central Colorado was the political wranglings surrounding Tilghman's promised US Marshal appointment. Wilson had been in office for close to a year and Tilghman had still not been offered the position. Senator Gore had continued to send notes of encouragement to the lawman telling him that "everything would be all right when the time came." Gore had troubling news when he met with Tilghman in Oklahoma City in late 1913. Governor Charles N. Haskell's staff wanted someone else to be marshal. John Q. Newell, who had been the governor's campaign manager, was appointed to the position. Gore assured Tilghman if he didn't fight Haskell's staff's recommendation for the post, he would petition the president to name him marshal of the Panama Canal Zone. Tilghman was disappointed and worried that if he expressed any frustration he'd be passed over completely. The Canal Zone appointment went to another. More promises were made to the lawman as well as requests for his patience while elected officials maneuvered to get their way.[12]

Tilghman wasn't content to simply sit and wait for something to happen. He offered his services to friend and supporter Judge Brooks Ayers Robertson's election campaign for governor and petitioned to run for sheriff of Oklahoma County. He wrote letters to supporters of the Democratic ticket for their consideration.[13]

"Dear Sir, I take the liberty to write you in regard to my candidacy for Sheriff of Oklahoma County. I take it for granted that you, as a good citizen and a good Democrat, feel interested in this important office, as protection for yourself and family.[14]

"As a citizen having the ENFORCEMENT OF THE LAW at heart, you should be interested in a sheriff THAT KNOWS HOW. Thirty-five years of my life has been spent in official work, twenty-five years in Oklahoma and Indian Territory.

"I served two terms as Sheriff of Lincoln County, and two years as Chief of Police of Oklahoma City. You, or at least all the old residents of the county, know of my official work at that time.[15]

"I have graduated through a long hard course as an officer, and will not have to be educated at the expense of the taxpayer, if elected.

"As a Democrat, you are interested in a candidate who can win at the general election in November. It is the general opinion of the leading Democrats of Oklahoma County that my official record will make me a winner.[16]

"If in your best judgement, you think otherwise, and nominate a candidate other than myself, I, as a loyal Democrat, true to my party principles, will give him my most hearty support.

"As promised before [the] election, I deem as a claptrap to catch votes. So, I have none to make other than to say to the citizens of Oklahoma County, if elected, you will get all the ability there is in me, as your sheriff in preserving law and order, and protecting life and property in Oklahoma County.

"Respectfully Yours, Wm. Tilghman, Democratic Candidate for Sheriff."[17]

Tilghman abandoned his candidacy in the spring of 1914 to help the army prepare for war with Mexico.[18]

News of the trouble in Mexico had reached Oklahoma and the rest of the nation in early 1914. For several years, the country had been run by a dictator named Porfirio Diaz who favored the rich, discarded the poor, and paid little attention to the lack of food or education for his people. The absence of concern for the average people gave way to a spirit of revolt. Francisco Madero was elected president in 1911, but he wasn't forceful enough to end the political and military strife. Rebel leaders Emiliano Zapata and Pancho Villa took up arms against the government during Madero's term in office. Madero was assassinated in February 1913. His murder caused further strife, prompting intervention from foreign governments seeking to protect the interest of their oil wells, mines, and other industries.[19] Tilghman and longtime friend and former buffalo hunter, Fred Sutton, decided to organize a company of Oklahoma sharpshooters, reminiscent of Theodore Roosevelt's Rough Riders, and travel to Mexico to help bring about order. The call to action was premature because the US War Department had not authorized enlistments. Tilghman and Sutton anticipated they would do so and wanted Oklahoma to be ready to answer the call. Sharpshooters and experienced fighters from all over the state agreed to take part in the effort when the time came.[20]

Newspapers in the region included articles about Tilghman's desire to raise a regiment of scouts to fight for the flag. Often the stories included a remark about the fact that the former police chief had yet to be appointed by the Wilson administration as US Marshal. "The much talked of appointee has failed to land the job," the April 28, 1914, edition of the *Morning Examiner* read. "Tilghman is now desperate to find his place in local law enforcement or foreign affairs."[21]

The situation in Mexico didn't rise to the level the US government felt it necessary to intervene until 1917. By that time, the former lawman had moved on to a new venture.[22]

With the need to enlist volunteers no longer necessary, Tilghman turned his attention back to Judge Robertson and his campaign. The lawman and attorney had known one another for more than a decade. Tilghman believed Robertson would make an excellent governor. He was one of the most prominent and influential representatives of the Democratic Party. Many voters recognized him as a clean, strong candidate who was familiar with the affairs of state government. Had it not been for friends like Tilghman, the judge would have abandoned his plans for the governorship when his wife passed away in June 1914. Zoe and Bill Tilghman both persuaded Robertson to continue his fight for the office and promised to help see him through.[23]

One of the judge's opponents was a former outlaw and one-time lawyer well known to Tilghman named Al Jennings. In the 1890s, Al, his brother Frank, and a handful of other men in their gang stole horses and cattle and robbed stores and trains. Tilghman's fellow officer, Deputy

US Marshal Heck Thomas, and Bud Ledbetter, along with US Marshal Evett Nix, played key roles in the capture and arrest of Al and Frank. The pair was tried, convicted, and sentenced to life in prison. Their younger brother, who was also an attorney, managed to get the sentence reduced to five years. In 1902, Al was released from prison on a technicality and in 1904, President Theodore Roosevelt granted him a pardon. After a brief venture as a traveling salesman, the former felon decided to take up law again, try his hand at politics, and become an author. His first book, *Beating Back*, was published by the *Saturday Evening Post* in 1913. In the book he detailed his time robbing trains and the inhumane conditions and barbarous treatment he and other inmates were subjected to at the Leavenworth Penitentiary. Jennings adapted his book to film, which was shown at numerous venues throughout Oklahoma during his campaign.[24]

Tilghman didn't care for Jennings and the feeling was mutual. Not only did the lawman find it outrageous that a convicted criminal could run for office, but he also resented Jennings's portrayal of the Deputy US Marshals, both in print and on screen, as cruel and ignorant. Neither spoke well of the other to the press. Jennings frequently accused Tilghman of sharing damning information with him about the other two candidates in the race, an accusation the former lawman consistently denied. An article appeared in the July 27, 1914, edition of the *Tulsa Evening Sun* announcing the appointment of Tilghman to warden of the state penitentiary if Judge Robertson won the governorship. Jennings used the report to prove how much Tilghman needed Robertson to win the election and that that was the motivation to offer confidential information to Jennings about their opponents. Tilghman dismissed the notion outright.[25]

Given his years in law enforcement, Tilghman had a definite idea as to how Oklahoma prisons should be run. He was against pardons for repeat offenders and believed in programs to rehabilitate felons who sincerely wanted to change. But Tilghman was one of many people who had been mentioned to be named warden of the state penitentiary since three inmates had escaped in January 1914, killing one man in the process and injuring three others.[26]

Al Jennings, outlaw-turned-filmmaker-turned-politician ran for governor of Oklahoma in 1914. Jennings's film inspired Marshal Tilghman to venture into filmmaking.

OKLAHOMA HISTORICAL SOCIETY

Zoe reread the papers written by her husband about reforming the penitentiaries in Oklahoma he had presented to Judge Robertson. She knew how he felt about repeat offenders. "We have to do better by lawbreakers who are sent to prison to make them less likely to return," Tilghman noted in his journal. Zoe agreed, but that objective was foreign to men running the installation where Woodrow was living. When his parole was denied in late 1937, she questioned the likelihood her son would ever recognize or turn from his wrong course.[27]

* * *

Late in the summer of 1914, the Tilghmans received sad news about Zoe's father, Mayo Stratton. The eighty-two-year-old man, a pioneer in both Kansas and Oklahoma, had passed away from natural causes. The Tilghman family traveled to Stillwater for the funeral held on August 5.[28] A poem penned by Zoe in April 1914 titled "The Pioneer" was a tribute to men like her father who first settled the territory.[29]

Forever through the fleeting centuries,
God's plan and purpose hold,
The shears of Atrope may clip the single threads,
But Lachesis still twists the cord of gold.
A hundred thousand in that April long ago,
Were gathered for the fabric of our state.
And in the tireless loom of Destiny
The flying shuttles traced the will of Fate.
Little they dreamed in those early days
Of the glory that should be:
But from dug-out and shanty, cabin, and tent,
Each to his share of the labor bent.
Some grew restless and wandered on,
And some are asleep 'neath the sod they won.
Oh, Hearts remaining, what need to speak
To you of the days when our state was young?
It is fitting we honor her natal day,
And to those she welcomed beneath her skies.

To the children who proudly can bear her name,
Commend her honor and her fame
Now and hereafter the goal we sought,
We have attained; but still before
New ways appear. We offer at the door
The benediction of the service we have wrought.[30]

Tilghman's candidate, Judge Robertson, did not win the 1914 Oklahoma gubernatorial election. Oklahoma Supreme Court Chief Justice Robert L. Williams won by 101 votes. With the possibility, although remote, of Tilghman being named warden gone, he decided to reach out to Senator Gore to ask about an appointment to a law enforcement post. The senator had just won reelection and was named chair of several high-profile committees. Once again, the politician asked Tilghman's indulgence, assuring him he was doing what he could and to give him time. The former lawman agreed.[31]

In December 1914, while Tilghman was waiting for word from the senator, former US Marshal Evett Nix contacted him. Nix was fuming. He'd been reading articles about Al Jennings's book and film and was fed up with the praise the work had received. The October 27, 1914, edition of the *Guthrie Daily Leader* referred to the picture as "the most remarkable film of its kind ever produced." Nix and his deputy marshals were featured prominently in *Beating Back* and not in a favorable way. In Nix's opinion, and in the opinion of other law enforcement agents he had hired to help capture outlaws terrorizing the Oklahoma region in the late 1880s into the 1890s, Jennings had made them the villains in his story. He portrayed himself as misunderstood, driven to a life of crime out of frustration only, and smarter than the authorities sent to track him and his gang. Nix was angry and insulted and determined that a picture showing the marshals' side of bringing about order to a lawless territory needed to be made. He had spoken with Chris Madsen about such a film and the two decided that they had to discuss the project with Tilghman. Nix wired his former deputy to let him know he and Madsen were on their way to Chandler to see him. Zoe was curious about the pair's visit. Tilghman speculated the meeting would center around the law and another job offer in the field.[32]

Shortly after the Tilghmans welcomed their old friends into their home, Nix and Madsen told Bill why they'd come. They wanted to make a film, one that accurately depicted the times. Nix informed Tilghman he had financial backing for the venture and all that was needed was for the four of them to form a partnership. On Christmas Eve the Eagle Film Company was founded with capital stock of $12,000 and the possibility of more funds being added if necessary. Nix had the title of president, Tilghman was vice president and treasurer, and Chris Madsen was designated as secretary.[33]

"Outside of Oklahoma the whole world thinks we are hero worshippers and that our heroes are the former bandits who are reputed to have terrorized the people who lived in the early days of the Territory," an article about the film company in the December 26, 1914, edition of the *Muskogee Daily Phoenix* read. "This is not the case, however, and three of the men who were instrumental in exterminating the bandits of the southwest will demonstrate it by historical moving pictures."[34]

The first movie the men planned to make was a patriotic drama titled *The Passing of the Oklahoma Outlaws*. It would focus on the ruthless careers of the Doolin-Dalton Gang and every other bandit during that time and how they met their rightful end. Magazine writer Lute Stover was hired to write the screenplay with input from the lawmen who helped apprehend the desperados, including deputy marshals Bud Ledbetter, Bill Tilghman, Chris Madsen, Evett Nix, and John Hale. Tilghman's good friend and neighbor J. B. Kent was hired to film the action and co-direct. Kent was recognized by most in the region as an expert photographer. Cowboys and cowgirls from the Miller Brothers 101 Ranch Wild West Show were hired to play a variety of roles alongside the former marshal and deputy marshals. Specifically, some of the Wild West Show performers who would be in the picture were Ed Lindsay, a remarkable rider, and his wife, who was just as exceptional a rider as her husband; Lem Rogers, Montana Williams, and Bill McNamee; and Miss Lulu Lomland, a superior horsewoman. Roy Daugherty, also known as Arkansas Tom Jones, the sole survivor of the Doolin-Dalton Gang, would also appear in the film and provide insight from the outlaw's perspective, sharing what was happening when. Four years prior, Arkansas Tom had gained early release from prison. News that the convicted criminal had been hired by the same lawmen who tracked him down and arrested him was reported in newspapers across the state. Some questioned the wisdom of employing the bank robber and murderer, but Nix insisted the outlaw had reformed and brought an added credibility to the film, as opposed to Jennings's biased picture where actors portrayed many of the major roles.[35]

The bulk of the filming of *The Passing of the Oklahoma Outlaws* would be done at the location where the desperados were shot or captured or where the battles with the marshals took place. The producers assured the newspaper reporters following the Eagle Film Company's progress that the picture would show, in addition to the historical facts, all the romance that went into outlawry in the early days of the Territory and the fatal ending of every bandit's life.[36]

Production on the Eagle Film Company's first picture began in Chandler, Oklahoma, on January 18, 1915. Tilghman and the other key players estimated it would take thirty days to complete the filming. The cameras and actors drew a lot of attention in the communities where *The Passing of the Oklahoma Outlaws* was shot. According to the January 29, 1915, edition of the *Chandler News Publicist*, the people of Sparks, Oklahoma, were thrilled to have their "little city in the movies." Tilghman, Madsen, and Nix, and the others involved with filming were happy with the warm reception they received everywhere they traveled in Lincoln County.[37]

Whenever the principal players were together on location, they made time to discuss the production. Tilghman and Bud Ledbetter had a great deal to do with breaking up the noted gangs of bank and train robbers that infested Oklahoma, and the two often compared notes and choreographed certain scenes. In early February 1915, a reporter with the *Chandler News* was on hand while the lawmen were talking about the different six-shooters and rifles they used on the job and how and where to shoot a man to ensure sudden death. To an outsider the conversation might have sounded bloodthirsty, but they were striving for authenticity in the film. Both admitted to having been up against many ticklish propositions in their work, and only their quickness on the draw and their ability to shoot where they looked served to save them.[38]

There were some setbacks in filming *The Passing of the Oklahoma Outlaws*. Evett Nix became ill and was forced to return to his home in St. Louis to see his physician. In his absence, Tilghman assumed the former marshal's duties but had to delay production entirely at one point due to his mother's death.[39]

"Dear Zoe, mother was buried at 2 P.M. today," Tilghman wrote to his wife at their home in Oklahoma City. "The funeral arrangements were good and the display of flowers was beautiful and tonight, Dear Little Mother is again sleeping beside Father on the hill west of Chandler.[40]

" . . . We are getting along fine with the work; have been getting some great scenes filmed. Nix is still in St. Louis where he is suffering with a bad cold and his doctor has ordered him to stay in bed. He wrote today that he could not get here before Monday so I have got my hands full here. I will try and get down home just as soon as he comes. Love to the boys. . . . Your Truly, Wm Tilghman."[41]

The Eagle Film Company finished filming their first picture on March 12, 1915. Except for a few extras, everyone was sent home. Tilghman, Madsen, and Kent the cameraman stayed on to film a couple of extra scenes. The abbreviated crew was in Chandler working around Tilghman's ranch on March 27, 1915, when one of the former lawman's ranch hands galloped up to him and announced that both banks in the town of Stroud had been robbed by Henry Starr and his gang. Starr was the alleged nephew of notorious robber and livestock rustler Belle Starr. He started robbing banks with his own gang in the late 1890s, and in 1903, he killed one of Judge Isaac Parker's deputies.[42]

Stroud was fourteen miles away from Tilghman's homestead. After clarifying with his employee that indeed Starr had robbed two banks at the same time, he removed the blank cartridges from his gun and replaced them with real bullets. Just before Chris Madsen and Bill Tilghman began their trek to Stroud, Tilghman asked his hired hand how he'd heard about the crime. The ranch hand told him that Henry Starr had phoned for him. Starr had been captured by the townspeople after being shot. The townspeople took the outlaw to the local doctor's office but had no intention of handing him over to the authorities after he was treated.

Starr was afraid he was going to be lynched and he wanted Tilghman to protect him.[43]

When Tilghman arrived in Stroud, there were several armed men waiting outside the jail. Four of the five men who helped rob the banks with Starr had tried to escape, but more than two hundred residents of the town stopped the thieves from getting away. They surrounded the outlaws in a grove close to the scene of the crime and refused to leave the criminals alone even after they had been locked in their cells. Tilghman weaved his way through the crowd of angry citizens lining the street outside the doctor's office. Starr was lying on an examination table when Tilghman entered the physician's workplace. The wounded desperado was happy to see him. He told Tilghman the doctor had removed the bullet from his leg where he was shot but that the leg was broken in several places. Starr wanted to know if Tilghman could get him out of

Peoples National Bank of Stroud, Oklahoma, was one of two banks robbed by outlaw Henry Starr on the same day.

COURTESY WESTERN HISTORY COLLECTIONS, SPECIAL RESEARCH COLLECTIONS, UNIVERSITY OF OKLAHOMA LIBRARIES, WHCP-1165

Stroud and moved to a jail in Chandler. Tilghman promised, with the help of Lincoln County Deputy Sheriff George Wilson, that he would.[44]

Starr was transported to Chandler via a westbound Santa Fe train Tilghman flagged down at the Stroud depot. Tilghman and Wilson kept their guns in plain sight to warn furious residents against taking the law into their own hands. When the express car bearing the injured bandit arrived in Chandler, hundreds of people were at the station to meet it. News of the robberies and of Tilghman's intervention had circulated quickly. Starr was offloaded from the train on a cot, placed in a hay wagon, and escorted to the jail, which was in the basement of the courthouse. The entire crowd followed along.[45]

J. B. Kent filmed the outlaw's move from Stroud to Chandler and the footage was later incorporated in the picture.[46]

The Passing of the Oklahoma Outlaws premiered in Chandler on May 26, 1915, at the Ogden Theatre, and patrons fully appreciated the production.[47]

"Bill Tilghman and Bud Ledbetter were as natural as life, and were recognized by the audience as soon as they appeared in the scene," the May 27, 1915, edition of the *Chandler Tribune* reported. "Apart from the main characters who appeared in this picture many of the prominent men and women of this city were shown in small parts.[48]

"J. B. Kent has always been conceded as a good motion picture photographer and last night's picture showed that he is a real artist at his profession; these pictures were among the clearest and most lifelike that have been shown here."[49]

The Passing of the Oklahoma Outlaws was presented in six reels and was ninety-six minutes in length, and the film spanned a twenty-five-year time period. Tilghman and the other producers traveled throughout the state during the months of June and July showing the picture at venues from Adair to Yukon. In addition to seeing the film, patrons could purchase a booklet written by Lute Stover, Tilghman, Nix, and Madsen about their days as officers in the Territory. It was the first complete written account of the men and the events depicted in the picture. The movie and the booklet included two stories not covered in the newspapers at the time they happened. One of those stories was of the time Deputy US

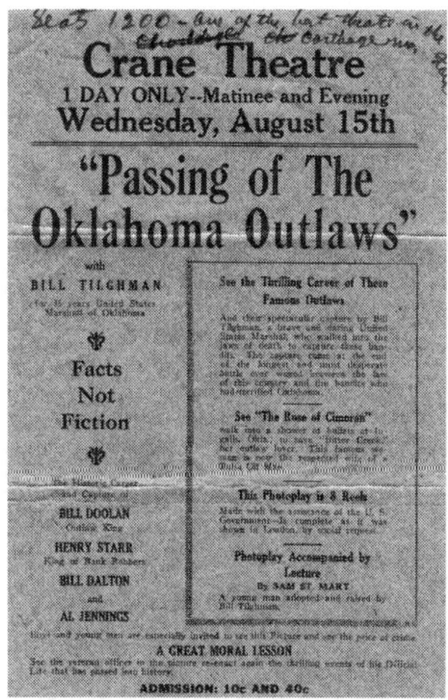

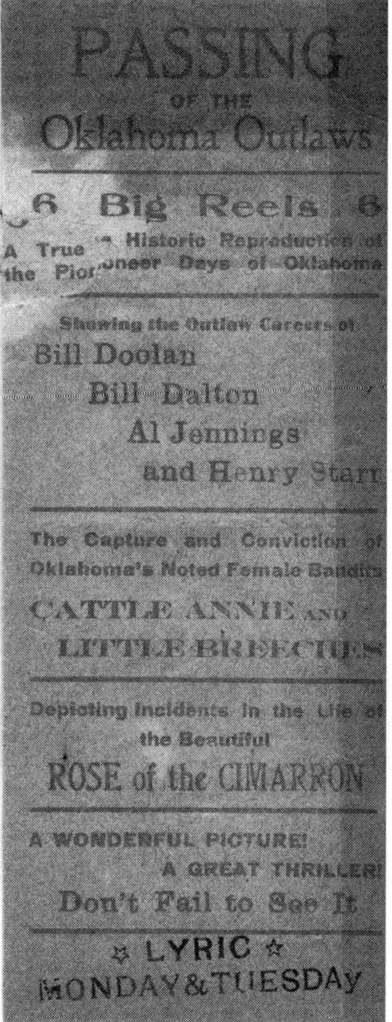

Audiences across the country flocked to the theaters to see *The Passing of the Oklahoma Outlaws*. Posters such as these were circulated in many cities and towns.

DEPARTMENT OF SPECIAL COLLECTIONS AND UNIVERSITY ARCHIVES, UNIVERSITY OF TULSA MCFARLIN LIBRARY

Banners and signage outside theaters across Oklahoma let theatergoers know the film *The Passing of the Oklahoma Outlaws* was based on fact, not fiction.
DEPARTMENT OF SPECIAL COLLECTIONS AND UNIVERSITY ARCHIVES, UNIVERSITY OF TULSA MCFARLIN LIBRARY

Marshal Bill Tilghman entered a dugout where the Doolin Gang was hiding and the other focused on a young woman, referred to as the Rose of Cimarron, who was romantically involved with one of the outlaws.[50]

Before each showing, one of the former deputy marshals would give a short lecture to the audience about their work, the history of the Oklahoma Territory, and the making of the film. The response from most ticket buyers, who paid from fifteen cents to a quarter to see the picture, was positive.[51]

"*The Passing of the Oklahoma Outlaws* is a motion photo drama with a splendid moral, and pathos and sweetness, and thrilling scenes and incidents depicting actual events of consuming interest to Oklahoma citizens, does not intend in the least to glorify crime or criminals, rather they have the opposite effect," the July 1, 1915, edition of the *Daily Ardmoreite* reported. "They impress vividly and permanently the unfailing, sure, and tragic end of a criminal career."[52]

Praise for the picture came from several influential members of the state supreme court too. " . . . I want to congratulate you upon your success in so thrillingly and truthfully portraying the gradual emergence of Oklahoma from turbulence and outlawry into peace and respect for law and order," Chief Justice Matthew J. Kane wrote Tilghman in a letter dated August 13, 1915.[53]

"I have been a resident of Oklahoma during all the period covered by your picture and knew in a general way of many of the incidents thrown upon the screen and the great changes for the better which have taken place as a result of the dominance of the forces of law and order over the element that preys.

"But to have the drama which it took years to enact in real life, vividly and faithfully flashed before my eyes within the course of an hour or two, proved to be an experience altogether novel, exciting, instructive, and pleasurable. I cannot conceive how anything but good can result from [the] public exhibition of your film. Very Truly, Matthew J. Kane."[54]

Presentations of the Eagle Film Company's picture continued through the summer and into the fall at theaters from Paducah, Kentucky, to Vancouver, Washington. Evett Nix, Chris Madsen, and Bud Ledbetter had jobs they needed to return to and couldn't be at every showing.

Tilghman attended every presentation. He realized early on that every seat in the movie house filled when at least one of the lawmen made a personal appearance. Tilghman anticipated the film would earn back the funds the producers invested in the project by the end of the year.[55]

His long absence from home took a toll on Zoe and their boys. She was pleased the film was a success, but she and the children longed for Tilghman to return to Oklahoma. "Dear Will, your letter received, and was so glad to hear from you; also glad of the money," Zoe wrote to her husband on September 1, 1915.[56]

"It is awfully dull and lonesome without you. Woodrow misses you worse all the time, I think. I supposed he would get used to it. The other day he begged me to telephone for you; and when I would not, he got off my lap and ran to the phone before I knew what he was doing; and he said, 'I want my Daddy to come home.' He spoke very plain and the operator told him you would come. He also called again today and would have called twice, but I headed him off. He talks of you so much; says you will get him new shoes, and take him to the fair and to the sand pit. When I was dressing him in the morning he said, 'I want Dad to come home right now.'[57]

"Tench has had a bad cold for a week and I have been giving him quinine and cough syrup, and wet cloths on his throat, and calolactose[*sic*]. He is getting better now and will be in good shape by the time school starts. I think Richard came in yesterday with a fever and at first, I thought it was because he swallowed a marble; and I gave him medicine. But this afternoon the fever came up again and I called up Dr. Wallace. He said that there is a great deal of such fever since this cold spell. He told me to give quinine strong, and break it up at once. So, I got the medicine and started on him.[58]

"I hope you can make the Denver show pay. I suppose you are glad to have Mr. Nix gone. Is it next week you are booked at Cheyenne? Take care of yourself all you can. I am afraid the lecture and all will make it hard for you. I wish I could hear you. With love from all. Zoe A. Tilghman."[59]

In subsequent letters to her husband, Zoe stopped short of insisting he come home. She wasn't the kind of woman who would make demands and Tilghman wasn't the kind of man who would tolerate them. Until he was able to hire a staff that could market and show the film for him from time to time, Tilghman would remain on the road. The picture provided a modest income to support his family, and he wouldn't give it up until the appointment Senator Gore promised came through. Zoe wrote a letter to the politician to remind him that her husband was counting on him. She included endorsements she was sure the senator would recall from men such as Dennis Flynn, a one-time delegate to Congress for Oklahoma. "I've known Mr. Tilghman for twenty-five years," Flynn noted. "In my judgement there is no more competent man to be found in this state or elsewhere. He is honorable and trustworthy and has had years of experience. . . . "[60]

More important to Zoe than having her husband home was seeing him get what he deserved. Senator Gore was the only one who could make that happen.

Chapter 8

A Promised Appointment

Zoe and William Tilghman's oldest son's wedding was held on a day of blue skies and sweetly rising heat in mid-July 1939. The local newspapers that covered the ceremony wrote of thirty-four-year-old Tench's many accomplishments. "He attended the universities of Colorado and Oklahoma and is a member of Delta Tau Delta Fraternity, and the Army and Navy Club," an article in the July 16, 1939, edition of the *Daily Oklahoman* read. "He is a captain in the field artillery reserves and is a member of the law firm of Blakemore, Ludington, and Tilghman. Zoe beamed with pride as she watched Tench exchange vows with Doris Tucker. The service took place at the post chapel at Fort Sill, which was decorated with palms, ferns, gladioli, and garden flowers, and lit by candles.[1]

Zoe described the special day in her weekly letters to Woodrow, who continued to serve time in jail. Had he been free, the chance he would have been invited to the nuptials would have been questionable. Tench was frustrated with his brother's inability to stay out of trouble. He was frustrated with his mother at times too. Money Tench gave Zoe to help her make ends meet was often filtered to lawyers to aid Woodrow in his legal troubles. The brothers' relationship was strained. Tench resented the grief Woodrow brought their mother. Zoe had always suspected there would be trouble with her youngest child. In a letter to Tilghman written in October 1917, Zoe shared her thoughts about their sons with her husband, noting how dependable twelve-year-old Tench was compared to ten-year-old Richard and five-year-old Woodrow. "He [Tench] is remarkably well able to take care of himself; also, he is trustworthy, and not likely to be led into mischief, which would be the danger with Richard and Woodie."[2]

Woodrow was aware of the sacrifices Zoe had always made for him and periodically expressed his gratitude in cards he sent her. In late summer 1939, he sent her a card that read: "Underneath the current of the busy every day, I can feel your presence, Mother. In a hundred little ways, and am grateful remembering the days that used to be. There is happiness in knowing you are still the same to me." Before signing the card, he wrote, "The verse is perfect—and the stairs [on the front of the card] remind me of the many steps you've taken for me. I love you. Woodie."[3]

While poring over the journals Tilghman kept during his time on the road showing *The Passing of the Oklahoma Outlaws*, Zoe found notes he'd written expressing the same sentiment Woodrow had. The lawman turned filmmaker was grateful for his wife's devotion and all he was able to pursue because she kept things going at home while he was away. "You're doing a fine job with the boys," Tilghman remarked in a letter to his wife in early 1916. "I'm anxious to see what kind of men they will become."[4]

Throughout most of 1916, Tilghman appeared at theaters in locations from Salt Lake City, Utah, to Houston, Texas. Newspaper advertisements for the film reminded potential customers that "Powerful William 'Bill' Tilghman will personally lecture and explain the wonderful picture. Don't fail to see this wonderful man in his fight to free his own state and other states adjoining of rebellious characters." Zoe was doing her part to promote her husband's picture. She authored a detailed article about the making of the film that was published in various newspapers across Oklahoma. She read those articles aloud to audience members at authors' clubs in Oklahoma City.[5]

The Tilghman's were reunited in July 1916. The former lawman felt he'd been away from his wife and children for too long. He decided to take the family on another trip through Colorado. After a couple of weeks vacationing in the Garden of the Gods, Zoe, Bill, and their three children traveled east to St. Louis to spend their winter. Tilghman planned to show his film at various venues in the city. He rented an

William Tilghman at the opening of his motion picture *The Passing of the Oklahoma Outlaws*.
OKLAHOMA HISTORICAL SOCIETY

apartment and Zoe enrolled eleven-year-old Tench and nine-year-old Richard in school. Woodrow was only four and had to stay home with his mother. In January 1917, the Tilghmans headed back to Oklahoma. *The Passing of the Oklahoma Outlaws* was scheduled to premiere in Lansing and Detroit, Michigan, the following month. Zoe decided against following Tilghman and placing the boys in another school. She returned to Oklahoma with the children and they resumed their former routine. Tilghman struggled after Zoe left, not only because he missed her and his sons but because his health was failing. Letters written to Zoe in early February 1917 explained the extent of his illness.[6]

"I took an ex-ray examination this morning at 9 o'clock and another at 3 o'clock and am ordered back again in the morning at 10 o'clock," Tilghman wrote to his wife about his visit to the hospital in Ann Arbor on February 2. "They have worked me pretty faithful since I have been here but I can't learn if they have discovered anything yet. I am confined in the medical ward with twenty other patients. . . . I just heard from

Bill Tilghman (right) and Chris Madsen in 1916.
OKLAHOMA HISTORICAL SOCIETY

Chris Madsen today. He will be showing the film at a little town 35 miles north of here tonight."[7]

Tilghman was first diagnosed with ulcerative colitis, an inflammatory bowel disease that causes swelling and sores in the digestive tract. Physicians at the hospital where Tilghman was staying believed the ailment was brought on by stress and recommended surgery. Zoe had suspected something might be wrong with his stomach long before he was hospitalized. "He was living largely on malted milk," she wrote in her memoirs. "When he was at home, I used to make him a custard every day." On February 6, Tilghman wrote Zoe from the surgical department and asked her to travel to be with him and to bring Woodrow with her.[8]

"I wrote [to] you yesterday in regard to the operation," Tilghman informed Zoe. "I think the thing to do is to go on with it. So, I will probably not wait until I hear from you. . . . I went down in town yesterday and sent Tench a book he asked for. Please let him know.[9]

"There is an excursion up on the Wabash Saturday. I hope you will come up here. I will be disappointed if you can't do it. But please bring Woodrow. Think the matter over seriously and do just as you think best. If you should come, you are due in Detroit at about 8:30 A. M. You arrive at the Union Depot. I am about two hours from the Union Depot in Ann Arbor.

"Do as you think best in the matter. Love to all. Yours Truly, Wm. Tilghman."[10]

Prior to Zoe reaching Ann Arbor, Tilghman wrote her several letters to keep her abreast of what was happening with him. In a letter dated February 8, 1917, he shared his concerns over their finances and how he needed to get back to work showing the film.[11]

"When a person leaves the hospital and then comes back, he loses his place and then has to await his turn so he is liable to be turned back for two or three weeks by going away. That is the reason I don't want to go away. And the doctor tells me I should be operated on soon. So, I have first got to wait. I wrote [to] Mr. Nix to come up if he possibly could. I am afraid of losing my films if I let anyone here handle them for me and there is a good chance to make some money if I can get them to work."[12]

The date for the surgery Tilghman needed was postponed for more than a week. The hospital was crowded and there were men and women in front of the former sheriff who needed treatment more desperately. The cost to stay in the facility was $2 a day.[13]

Zoe was with Tilghman during his recovery after surgery. She couldn't stay long because Tench and Richard were alone and she worried. She hated to leave her husband and tried to convince him to hire someone to manage the bookings for the film and the showings. She believed managing the presentations and the constant travel was adversely affecting his health. Tilghman was still holding out for a marshal appointment from Senator Gore and until the offer came, ticket sales from the film were his primary source of income.[14]

By early May 1917, Tilghman was making plans to return to St. Louis to show *The Passing of the Oklahoma Outlaws* to more patrons. He was told that the theaters there were taking in from $25 to $40 a day.[15]

"Dear Zoe . . . I have a booking here for Thursday the 3rd and Saturday I have bookings in two different theaters. They are both small theaters. I am hustling awfully hard to fill in some of the dates next week. Am not trying to do anything after the 10th of the month. Will hustle as hard as I can until then. Williams [another filmmaker] and I showed together last Wednesday at the Metropolitan. We had expected a good house and we were expecting to do some good business. It rained all afternoon and night but we took in $45. After paying advertising and settling up, I got $9 for my part.[16]

" . . . Don't get discouraged. Lots of hope for better times. Am sorry to hear you've been suffering with headaches. Love to you all. Tell the boys not to forget their dad. Yours, W. T."[17]

Tilghman couldn't hustle as much as he had hoped because when he arrived in St. Louis he was struck with another serious medical issue. This time it was his appendix that was giving him trouble. Tilghman didn't share his ailment with Zoe or let her know when he was scheduled for surgery. She found out after the fact.[18]

When the school year ended for the Tilghman boys, Zoe brought the children to Chicago where their father was going to show his film next. During the six weeks the Tilghmans were together Bill shared with

Zoe how much he was still hoping Senator Gore would honor his promise. Being away from home for so long and the health problems he had experienced left him exhausted and longing to return to law enforcement. Show bookings had slowly declined since April when the United States entered World War I, but there continued to be an audience for moving pictures. *The Passing of the Oklahoma Outlaws* was shown in fewer theaters but they were always sold out. As a result, Tilghman was working less and making better money, but he would have traded it all for a job as a United States Marshal.[19]

Back in Oklahoma, with all three of the Tilghman boys enrolled in school, Zoe decided to write a letter to Joseph Tumulty, secretary to President Woodrow Wilson, about her husband and remind him of what the politician had assured him would transpire.[20]

"Dear Sir, four years ago a certain appointment was made, and this promise was given with it," Zoe's letter dated October 24, 1917, began. 'The President has recognized your services and endorsements. He has promised POSITIVELY to give you an appointment in lieu of the one you asked. Keep quiet, let this other man be confirmed: and you have the President's word that you will be taken care of later.'[21]

"Wm. Tilghman accepted that promise. By it he was tied hand and foot. He could make no fight for himself. He trusted in the word of the President and waited as he was told. He has waited four years. Now he asks the keeping of that promise.

"But you may say, the President did not make such a promise. Then, Mr. Tumulty, is the name and authority of the President of so little moment, that it may be assumed and used by any man to suit his own purpose? The President, I am sure, would not of his own accord, defraud the meanest citizen in even the most trivial matter. Has he so little regard for the honor of his name and the dignity of his office that he will permit it to be used thus falsely? And act in ignorance of it?[22]

"The President will soon be called upon to reappoint the man whose confirmation was secured by the use of his name. If he signs that appointment, he says one of two things: I refuse to keep the promise I made. Or I hereby approve the false use of my name and make myself a party to the fraud so perpetrated.

"You who know him well, I do not know him, but I stake all my faith that he would not knowingly do this thing. Am I wrong?[23]

"Mr. Tumulty, then please tell him that: A positive and definite promise was made in your name, Mr. Wilson. This man has waited four years. He now asks you to keep that promise if you really made it. If not, he asks you to repudiate the whole transaction. And it is put squarely up to you either to approve or repudiate it.

"We ask for justice, who have been cheated through the use of his name. It surely is Mr. Wilson's affair, both as a man and as a President. I beg and pray you to tell him of the matter in the name of honor and justice, both for himself and us. If he cares so little for the honor of his personal work or the dignity of his high office that he approves what has been done, let us hear it plainly. This is a personal matter though it arose through departmental business and is not to be 'referred.'[24]

"I have made strong statements, but I beg you to believe that this letter is written in all respect. As a suppliant for justice, I ask for a hearing and a verdict. Very Respectfully, Mrs. Wm. Tilghman."[25]

Tilghman wrote his own letter on the matter and addressed it to Oklahoma Senator Robert Latham Owen.[26]

"Dear Senator: In a conversation I had with you in your office in Washington, D. C. Tuesday afternoon October 23rd, you said you did not know what influence caused Senator Gore to endorse Mr. John Q. Newell for United States Marshal for the Western District of Oklahoma four years ago.

"I did not at that time fully inform you of what I knew to be Senator Gore's reasons for endorsing Mr. Newell for the Marshalship and I now take the liberty to do so. It was purely a matter of personal politics with Senator Gore. This information was given [to] me by Senator Gore in his room in the Skirvin Hotel in Oklahoma City ten days before Mr. Newell was appointed marshal.[27]

"He said, 'Bill, I now have the fight of my life on my hands and if you will lay down in your race for the United States Marshalship as a personal favor to me at this time, I can name a man other than yourself that will strengthen my political fences.'

"Senator Gore was involved in a scandal with Mrs. Minnie Bond of Oklahoma City at that time. He further told me that he had the right and authority to name the United States Marshal of the Panama Canal Zone and if I would lay down my fight for the Marshalship in Oklahoma, he would name me for the United States Marshalship in Panama.[28]

"Through a feeling of sympathy for the Senator and believing he was sincere in his promise made to me, I consented to quit the race for Marshal of the Western District.

"Mr. Newell at that time had never performed an official act and had no qualification as an officer. He had no endorsement by the Democrats of Oklahoma. He had never distinguished himself as a party worker in Oklahoma other than assist ex-Governor Haskell as his campaign manager in the Western District when he, Governor Haskell, made his campaign against you for the United States Senator in 1912. As you well know, in one of the most villainous, vile, slanderous campaigns ever waged against any candidate for any office in Oklahoma.[29]

"In consideration of his services rendered, Mr. Haskell in his campaign, demanded of Senator Gore Mr. Newell's appointment which was given with the promise of Mr. Haskell that he would line up his political forces in the state for Senator Gore.

"Judge Robert L. Williams gave me a very strong letter of endorsement for the appointment of marshal now on file in your office with the copy of my endorsement filed there in 1913. Later the judge became a candidate for governor and on being informed that I was supporting another candidate for the governorship, called Senator Gore and told him that if he would endorse Mr. Newell for Marshal and Mr. Newell would appoint Duke Stallings of Durant Chief Deputy for the marshal's office, he would in a quiet way, line up his political forces throughout the state for Senator Gore. Duke Stallings is now Chief Deputy United States Marshal.[30]

"You can readily see that by uniting the combined politics of Mr. Haskell and Judge Williams throughout the state, Senator Gore could very materially strengthen his political fences in his campaign for Senator. Being a much-interested person at that time, I gathered this information from reliable sources and it is true.

"In regard to my ambition at this time I feel and believe that by virtue of my official work for the government in Oklahoma covering a period of almost a quarter of a century as a Deputy United States Marshal, exerting my best official ability to maintain law and order and protect life and property, I am now entitled to recognition.

"And in consideration of my loyal party work for President Wilson during the primary campaign of 1912, I am entitled to recognition.

"Sincerely Yours, Wm. Tilghman."[31]

After more than a year and a half away from home, Tilghman returned to Oklahoma in mid-November 1917. The *Oklahoma News* celebrated the former Deputy United States Marshal and Oklahoma City police chief's homecoming with a front-page article. "I've been in fifteen different states since I left here," he told the newspaper. Tilghman's friends and fellow officers were pleased to see him. They too were frustrated that his appointment had not come through and asked those in support of him to make their thoughts known to the president. On December 5, 1917, Oscar D. Halsell, an owner of one of the grocery stores in Oklahoma City, sent a letter to the White House on behalf of the townspeople.[32]

"Woodrow Wilson, President. His Excellency: Please find enclosed and attached hereto a petition asking for the appointment of Wm. Tilghman for the Western District of Oklahoma.[33]

"This petition is signed by the business and professional interests of Oklahoma City and others. There is a condition existing in this state that demands a man in the marshal's office of good judgement, long experience, fearlessness, and a past record that cannot be questioned.

"A great deal of our trouble is over with as soon as Mr. Tilghman receives a commission. If he does, for the reason that the violators of the law knew him, and they are not going to take many chances, he being a US Marshal.[34]

"We are entitled to better protection than we have had in the past and there isn't any question but that Mr. Tilghman can give it to us. Very Truly Yours, The Williamson Halsell Frazier Co., O. D. Halsell, President."[35]

The issue over Tilghman's promised appointment to US Marshal for the Western District became a heated and much publicized matter in January 1918. Dr. John Q. Newell, who had initially been named to the post, had served four years and his term was set to expire. Newell, who wanted to remain marshal, needed to be reappointed. President Wilson was now aware that Tilghman was also a candidate for the position. Hundreds of recommendations and endorsements for both were submitted to state leaders. After more than a month deliberating on the subject, the president decided to keep Marshal Newell on the job.[36]

Disappointed over the decision, Tilghman turned his attention back to the film. Now that he knew he would not be a government-appointed marshal, he resigned himself to supporting his family solely from the ticket sales from *The Passing of the Oklahoma Outlaws.* The money it had cost to make the picture had been recovered. The only out-of-pocket expenses were renting the theater space and promoting the showings. The only drawback was the time Tilghman would again be away from his family.[37]

From May 1918 to April 1920, the former lawman traveled across the country with the film. In many places the theaters were sold out and records were set for the number of patrons who had seen the picture.[38]

On the home front, Zoe continued to manage the household and the raising of her sons as well as contribute to the family's income. The November 30, 1919, edition of the *Daily Oklahoman* featured an article about the publication of a story she had written titled "The Wives of the Walking Sun." The tale was that of a Native American who was forced to make a choice between his two wives by order of the government, which required Native Americans to conform to the white man's custom of having one wife only.[39]

"Mrs. Tilghman is well qualified to write such a story, having made her home in the Indian Territory and Oklahoma since 1887 with her father, M. E. Stratton, located at what is now Osage County and engaged in the raising of cattle," the article read. "Mrs. Tilghman is a graduate of the University of Oklahoma and while a student there served as editor of the *Umpire* which was then the official university publication. She has contributed verse to *Ridgeway Magazine*, adventure articles and stories to the *Woman's Home Companion* and other publications."[40]

Zoe wrote to Tilghman to let him know when she sold stories to the various magazines in the region. He praised her talent for the written word and periodically mentioned how he'd like her to pen the story of his life in Oklahoma. "When you're home for good, you can work on that yourself," she encouraged him.[41]

In late spring 1920, Tilghman decided *The Passing of the Oklahoma Outlaws* could continue playing in theaters without the presentation he always made before the film was shown. Fellow Oklahomans had once again suggested Tilghman as a candidate for marshal. His reputation in law enforcement and position on the average citizen carrying guns to protect themselves from the increased threat of crime were the key reasons residents wanted him in office.[42]

"Reputable citizens of a community should be issued official permits to carry guns for self-protection at night during the present crime wave sweeping the country," Tilghman told reporters in an interview with the *Morning Tulsa Daily World*. "I heartily disapprove of the suggested law making gun-carrying a felony. All the hijackers carry guns. Why prevent respectable citizens carrying them when a gun is the only protection citizens have in times like these? Such a law would play into the hands of the holdups. The man who carries a gun for protection is not a coward, as has been suggested, but the man who does not carry one is a fool."[43]

Tilghman's interest in the job had waned a bit since 1918. He wanted to be home with his sons and thoroughbred horses at this point in his life. Tench and Richard were both involved with school projects and their accomplishments were noted in the weekly paper. Tilghman wanted to see them participate on the debate team and play sports.[44]

Throughout the summer and into the winter of 1920, Tilghman busied himself with his campaign for sheriff. The disappointment over not being appointed a US Marshal had eased, and he felt a renewed spark for the work. He hadn't lost his appetite for producing films, however, and when cameraman J. B. Kent asked to meet with him in November 1920, Tilghman leapt at the chance. Kent was passing through Oklahoma City on his way to the Miller Brothers 101 Ranch to film the cowboys and cowgirls who worked there. Tilghman had an idea for a new film he wanted to present to him titled *The Making of a State—Oklahoma*. The picture was to be the true history reproduction of the events that occurred in the territory from the years 1870 to 1920. According to the synopsis Tilghman wrote, the film would "show Oklahoma from a wilderness inhabited by Native Americans and buffalo, through the different transformations it passed up to 1920 when the state became one of the greatest commonwealths of the United States."[45]

Tilghman and Kent agreed to meet again when their schedules permitted to discuss when to begin shooting the film.[46]

A call for help from Oklahoma Governor James B. Robertson prompted Tilghman to temporarily set aside his drive to return to law enforcement and make another film. Governor Robertson's life and career was being threatened by members of the Ku Klux Klan. The organization had invaded Oklahoma in early 1920 and in a brief time gained a foothold in communities throughout the state. Politicians who opposed the existence of the Klan risked floggings or other violent acts. Robertson's problems with the group began when he made it a rule that no officer of the state militia could be a member of the Klan. The order adversely interfered with the Klan's plans to control the police. Leaders of the terrorist faction vowed to make the politician regret his actions.[47]

The Klan's initial battle against the governor involved the demise of the Citizens National Bank of Okmulgee. The bank's failing during post–World War I depression wasn't unusual. Many banks throughout the nation failed. Numerous depositors, such as those who did business with the Citizens National Bank of Okmulgee, were left with nothing when the business collapsed. A year prior to the failure of the bank, it had taken over the Guaranty State Bank of Okmulgee. That action proved to be a positive one at the time. The bank was in a solvent condition and sold for more than its liabilities. Stockholders received a profit from the sale. When the Citizens National Bank of Okmulgee failed, patrons blamed the handling of the takeover of the Guaranty. Klansmen seeking to capitalize on the incident began a smear campaign against Governor Robertson and Fred Dennis, the man he appointed as state bank commissioner. The implication was that the governor had stolen funds from

Marshal Tilghman visited officials in Oklahoma City several times to discuss the trouble with the Ku Klux Klan.
LIBRARY OF CONGRESS

the bank, leaving depositors destitute. Governor Robertson vehemently denied the accusation and quickly ordered the state attorney general to investigate. The Klan anticipated such an action and while the matter was being reviewed by the state lawyers, they forced local officials to impanel a grand jury to hear the charges.[48]

Amid the scandal, the governor had the presence of mind to send for Tilghman. Tilghman was also an enemy of the Klan, and during a meeting with Robertson he assured the politician that there were many citizens in the state who were against the organization. Governor Robertson asked Tilghman to be the head of his security detail. Robertson believed the Klan would stop at nothing to get him out of the way now and wanted the former Deputy US Marshal at his side. Tilghman was more than willing to offer his services and recruited two other veteran lawmen to help, Chris Madsen and Bud Ledbetter.[49]

The grand jury proceedings began in the superior court at Okmulgee in early March 1922. Roman Catholic Judge H. R. Christopher presided over the hearing. When he was made aware of the Klan's influence over the jury, he ordered a dismissal of the case. Outraged by the action and the fact that a Catholic was presiding, the Klan summoned the county attorney to review the judge's decision. The county attorney determined that Judge Christopher "had been impelled by sinister influences to dismiss the jury," and declared that "within two hours, indictments would be returned against state officials and others in connection with the bank's failure." The Klan threatened Judge Christopher and his family with bodily harm and he left the state, returning to his old home in Chicago.[50]

Another grand jury was called, but the new judge assigned to the hearing was dismissed because he was a Klansman and had discussed pending cases with Klan members. Before another judge could be named, Governor Robertson ordered the bank commissioner, Fred Dennis, to retrieve the books of the failed bank from the state banking department in Okmulgee to be turned over to the grand jury. Dennis was petrified of the Klan and refused to obey the governor's orders. He resigned and left the area.[51]

Governor Robertson decided to retrieve the books and take them to the grand jury himself. Accompanied by Tilghman, Chris Madsen, Bud Ledbetter, and a host of other officials such as former railroad police officer Fred Cooke and former undersheriff William H. Crume, the politician arrived at the courthouse with the documents unharmed. It came as no surprise to the governor that the members of the Klan-selected grand jury indicted him. A subsequent, impartial investigation resulted in Governor Robertson's eventual acquittal. However, the damage the bank scandal had on his political career was irreversible. Although Robertson was unable to maintain the governorship, he was eternally grateful to Tilghman for recruiting a team of men who protected him through a particularly harrowing time in office.[52]

Leaders of the Oklahoma chapter of the Ku Klux Klan weren't willing to overlook Tilghman's association with Governor Robertson or Tilghman's staunch objection to the organization. Midway through his campaign for sheriff, Tilghman received an invitation from Klan headquarters letting him know if he joined the group, they would get behind him and elect him to office. "I'd rather cut off my right arm," he told them in his written reply. "If I go into the sheriff's office, I'll be there to uphold the law. I will go in free, not bound to anyone."[53]

An article in the March 2, 1922, edition of the *Oklahoma News* noted that although Tilghman had been out of law enforcement for a time he should not be considered out of the game. "Bill Tilghman hasn't figured in enforcement circles since he quit the chief of police office here, believing he would become US Marshal for the Western District. J. Q. Newell got the plum from President Woodrow Wilson and held it for eight years," the article read. "Tilghman is as picturesque as ever. He doesn't betray his almost seventy years. His step is still strong and he has the virility of most men two decades less aged.[54]

"His history has been recited over and over, each time a thrill to youth and grownup alike. This is the man who is attempting to come back as a law enforcer into a new age when crime methods have changed much."[55]

Democrat and prominent member of the KKK, Tom Cavnar, beat Tilghman in the primaries and with the full support of the Klan behind him, Cavnar went on to be elected sheriff of Oklahoma County.[56]

Tilghman wasn't in Oklahoma when Cavnar took office. Shortly after the primary he went back on the road with *The Passing of the Oklahoma Outlaws* in what would be one of the last times he would show the film. Audiences were still interested in the picture, but three years had passed since the film's debut and Tilghman's enthusiasm for the product had dwindled greatly. His ulcers were troubling him again and while at a film event in Battle Creek, Michigan, the pain became so overwhelming he was admitted to a hospital for treatment. Zoe sent Tench to be with his father and to help him make it home before Christmas.[57]

Zoe's job at *Harlow's Weekly*, writing regular columns and contributing poetry for the publication, filled the financial gaps between Tilghman's periodic work for government officials, as in the case with Governor Robertson, and the ticket sales from showing his film. Victor Harlow, owner and managing editor of the paper where Zoe was employed, thought it was tragic the state didn't have a pension fund for public servants like Tilghman, or paid them enough so they had something to put aside in times of need.[58]

Harlow believed, as many others did in Oklahoma, that no other man in the region had as much to do with the thinning out of the outlaws as Bill Tilghman. "Tilghman devoted his entire life in law enforcement and he should be compensated beyond the modest pay received," the newspaper editor insisted. "Men in private business are paid two, three, four times as much for operating a business of comparable magnitude. A physician of equal standing and competence earns several times as much.[59]

" . . . The State of Oklahoma fails to pay its public servants. The salaries ought to be at least something like an approximation of the value of the long years of service, and the exceptional ability necessary for the type of service which the state needs and demands."[60]

Residents in Oklahoma City hadn't forgotten the former Deputy US Marshal's contributions to settling the once wild Territory. They expressed their appreciation for the lawman at a celebration for newly elected Governor J. C. Walton in early 1923. After Walton took the oath of office, he and other influential individuals rode in a parade through town. Tilghman was one of those distinguished history makers recognized on January 10. More than thirty thousand people lined the streets to cheer for the Oklahoma pioneers. Some of the other dignitaries with Tilghman were Wild West showman Zack Mulhall and General Roy Hoffman, organizer of the Oklahoma National Guard.[61]

Shortly after the parade, Tilghman went back on the road to show his film to yet another audience. At the conclusion of special showings of *The Passing of the Oklahoma Outlaws*, he would explain the outlaw's life and the methods used by the deputy marshals in their capture. After his talk, he was often asked about his time in law enforcement in Dodge City, Kansas, and his days as a Deputy US Marshal. Tilghman answered such queries candidly and, given the chance, he elaborated on how the criminals he battled differed from those in the 1920s.[62]

"There is another gang of bad men growing up," the legendary peace officer told an audience in Albuquerque in October 1923, "but they are what I call yellow hearts. The Ku Klux Klansmen are yellow streaked.

They hide their faces under a mask, and go in gangs to take a coward's revenge on people who they think have earned their hatred.[63]

"It is just a question of whether Governor Walton enforces the law or whether we live under the Ku Klux Klan. Oklahoma City and Tulsa both brought in big majorities against Governor Walton because they are the strongholds of the Klan, but there is the rest of the state to reckon with.

"Texas, Louisiana, and Oklahoma are in control of the Ku Klux Klan. In some places it is practically impossible to get a conviction against a man if he is Klansman. Two district attorneys, police officers, and even the judges are members of the order. They join it for ulterior purposes, political advancement, and self-protection from the consequences of their own unlawful acts."[64]

In 1923, the seasoned law enforcement officer continued to be called upon for help from high-ranking politicians. In November of that year, Governor Martin Trapp (who succeeded Governor Walton after his impeachment) summoned Tilghman to his office to handle a problem involving convicts at a prison camp at the state capitol. The men had been brought in to work on the interior and exterior of the capitol building. The governor had heard rumors that the inmates were planning to break out of the minimal security camp and wanted Tilghman's advice on how to handle rebellious felons. Governor Trapp valued Tilghman's direction. He'd met the former sheriff when he was a boy and respected his years of experience dealing with lawbreakers.[65]

Tilghman agreed to do what he could, but needed to know why the prisoners were upset enough to consider escaping. According to the governor, his predecessor, who had arranged for the convicts to make the improvements to the grounds, had promised them pardons when they concluded the work. Governor Trapp refused to honor the alleged pledge. The guards watching over the inmates were also upset with the government. The legislature under then-Governor Walton's watch had refused to appropriate money for their pay. The integrity of the guards was now called into question. For the safety of the public, Governor Trapp wanted the prisoners returned to the penitentiary and he wanted Tilghman to make it happen. The former lawman promised the politician he would handle it.[66]

Tilghman's first order of business was to have the governor send for the state militia to assist. Military orders were prepared and a unit was dispatched to Tilghman for instruction. He stationed the soldiers around the camp, then arranged with the railroad to make a special car available to transport the convicts back to prison. Within forty-eight hours the men had been safely returned to their cells.[67]

Encouraged by Tilghman's ability to quickly resolve a potentially explosive situation, Governor Trapp dared to ask the former lawman for help with another issue. Former Governor Walton had ordered the parole of numerous prisoners and several of those men had since broken their parole. Governor Trapp wanted those violators apprehended and returned to jail.[68]

At the age of sixty-nine, tracking outlaws was like old times to Tilghman. In less than three months he'd taken into custody all those who had defied the terms of their parole. "I was trailing bad guys when hell was frosty and the jack rabbits still wore horns," he joked with the governor. "It's just what I do."[69]

Tilghman proved himself to be more than capable to continue being a lawman. Shortly after his seventieth birthday, he received an offer to return to the job full-time. There were problems in an oil boomtown east of Oklahoma City, and Governor Trapp believed Tilghman was the man to send to set things right.[70]

Chapter 9

Death of a Marshal

Zoe Tilghman stood in the front room of the Oklahoma City home she shared with her husband and three sons, staring out the window. In the distance she could see the faint trace of Tilghman driving away in his well-used Ford. He bounced up and down over the unpaved road, dust trailing behind him. It was late summer 1924 and Tilghman was off to Cromwell, Oklahoma. At the request of Oklahoma Governor Martin Trapp, he had accepted the job as chief of police for the town that had been referred to as the "wickedest in the United States." Although she never said it aloud, Zoe didn't want him to go. The sciatica that had plagued him for many years had been acting up and he was in constant pain. He refused to give in to the torment, however, insisting that it would pass if he kept busy.[1]

Just prior to accepting the Cromwell job, Tilghman had been employed by the state to help defuse a situation in McAlester between the striking miners at the Kali-Inla Coal Company and the guards for the coal mine. The Oklahoma National Guard had been dispatched to the area to keep tensions from escalating, but the bitter feelings between nonunion miners who had replaced striking miners had intensified. Gunfire had been exchanged on both sides and the presence of the state troopers had insignificant impact. Acting as a state operative, Tilghman went in to investigate the shootings and bring about a peaceful resolution to the dispute. The former Deputy US Marshal managed the matter so well, Governor Trapp didn't hesitate to ask Tilghman to take care of things in a lawless section of Seminole County.[2]

In the fall of 1924, Marshal Bill Tilghman was sent to the rowdy oil town of Cromwell, Oklahoma, to bring about law and order.
OKLAHOMA HISTORICAL SOCIETY

"In August, a group of citizens from the boom oil town of Cromwell asked the governor for aid in establishing order there," Zoe later wrote. "The sheriff's office of the county was giving little aid, or was unable to, in the face of rampant crime, bootlegging and dope peddling. The US Prohibition forces were supposed to curb the latter, but this too was inefficient.[3]

"They had plans to incorporate the town and they wanted Bill Tilghman to become city marshal. They would provide one assistant and the salary was good. . . . Bill went. The place was tough. A large criminal element of thieves, gamblers with alcohol and narcotics lived to prey on the oil field rough necks who had money to spend in their brief periods in town. The two men hired as assistants, successively quit. Bill worked on."[4]

Zoe's description of the town was based in part on her letters from Tilghman, letters from the governor, and newspaper reports. The condition of the wild burgh was thoroughly explained to Tilghman before he took the job by W. E. Sirmans, secretary of the Chamber of Commerce.

"It's only fair that you know," Sirmans warned. "We have a boom town of about 5,000 people. . . . As soon as we started out, the graft collectors realized that would stop their money, so they set up a fight, and we found that the sheriff refused to commission any man we wanted. The county attorney refused to help, and in fact, they tied our hands so we cannot do a thing."[5]

Tilghman found Cromwell to be exactly as advertised. The landscape was thick with oil derricks. Massive sections of pipe were stacked near mining shacks and mining equipment, stray tool pieces and wood shards from derricks that had been rocketed into the air by oil gushers were strewn about, and puddles of mud and oil were all around. Among the businesses on the main thoroughfares were numerous taverns, dance halls, and houses of prostitution. "This is a bad place," Tilghman wrote to his wife shortly after he arrived, "and these modern criminals are not like your old outlaws that had a sense of honor and gratitude, and decency in certain ways. These dope runners and the like would sooner shoot you in the back than meet you face to face."[6]

Tilghman was sworn in as chief of police on Saturday, September 14, 1924. He wasted no time in helping to make Cromwell a safer and more desirable place to live. He functioned as sanitary officer and general welfare custodian as well as policeman. One of the first directives was the installation of water barrels for fire emergencies. He also ordered the trash and debris that littered the streets and alleyways around businesses to be cleaned up. By the end of the month his focus had shifted from the exterior of the storefronts to the businesses themselves. He shut down and padlocked the doors of twenty-five pool halls and arrested owners who had violated the Prohibition Act. Dancehalls too had been closed temporarily but were allowed to reopen on October 2, with a warning to the proprietors that the first sign of violating the law would result in the closing of the businesses. Many merchants and individuals referred to as "undesirables" decided to leave the area rather than adhere to the rules.[7]

"The party of officers in Cromwell has struck terror into the large list of law violators and an exodus has been in progress all week," the October 4, 1924, edition of the *Shawnee Morning News* reported. "Captain Tilghman, who is in command of the local situation, is one of the best known of the early day Oklahoma officers. He was chief of police of Oklahoma City for many years and it was through his leadership that several lawless bands of the early days in Oklahoma were exterminated.[8]

"In most oil field villages 'cleanups' are almost weekly occurrences, but the 'joints' always open again sooner or later. But those who have been deprived of their daily 'nip' are viewing the situation with pessimism in Cromwell.

"If Captain Tilghman gets orders from 'higher up' to keep the joints closed, you can just bet your bottom dollar Cromwell will be 'tight' is the way one Cromwell citizen put it.[9]

"Captain Tilghman has a number of capable assistants, among them being Deputy Sheriffs Bud Gardner, Hugh Reynolds, Bob Chandler, Jim Roberts, Constable Z. R. Lane and G. A. Holloway, a special officer and newspaper man."[10]

Zoe followed the progress Tilghman was making cleaning up Cromwell through the regular reports in *Harlow's Weekly*. The couple discussed his work on Sundays when he returned home to visit. "It's not a bad town entirely," Tilghman shared with Zoe in mid-October. "It's a little wild maybe but not mean. There are some shady business dealings that need to be handled." One of the "dealings" had to do with the way the dance hall girls were being brought in to work at the various establishments. Tilghman suspected the Mann Act was being violated. The Mann Act made it a felony to transport women or girls across state lines for immoral purposes.[11] A prerequisite to Cromwell's incorporation was the elimination of such practices. "The town has been painted as a modern Sodom and Gomorrah," Tilghman told Zoe. "Even if the town incorporates, vice is going to exist there as long as the town remains the nightly gathering place for men in the oil fields. The trick is controlling the illegal acts."[12]

Tilghman confessed to his wife that he hadn't seen one gunman and that there hadn't been any gunfights. There had been plenty of fistfights he had to break up, but no gun battles. "There are more black eyes here per city lot than in any other city, town, or village I have ever visited," he told Zoe. "It seems to be a sort of distinction to have a black eye. It indicates that the owner has been around town long enough to get acquainted with the folks there, and be accounted as an old inhabitant."[13]

Transforming Cromwell from a rowdy, lawless community to a location where families and polite society could live peacefully might have come about more quickly had Tilghman had a jail to house the criminals he arrested. The men and women he apprehended had to be transported thirteen miles away to a jail in Wewoka. The chief promised city officials there would be more law enforcement after a jail was built.[14]

One of the individuals Governor Trapp sent to Cromwell to help Tilghman bring about order was Mabel Bassett. Bassett was the state commissioner of charities and corrections. She informed the governor that Tilghman had a long, hard road to go to reform the town. In her opinion, "The conditions were worse than that of Tia Juana, Mexico." She added that more than two hundred drug addicts were on the prowl nightly. "We are making headway," Tilghman assured Trapp in a letter. "The number of dope fiends has been reduced in the weeks I've been here."[15]

Zoe worried about Tilghman and the types of criminals he was encountering. "For the first time in his life he was face-to-face with the narcotics business in full stride," she later recalled in her memoirs. "It was no good to arrest the wretched addicts, little help to arrest a peddler, for another quickly took his place." Bill was determined to find the source.[16]

Tilghman and his three deputies often made their rounds late at night because that was when cars came and went from Cromwell to Tulsa and Juarez, Mexico, and back again, carrying whiskey, women, and drugs. Stops were made and outlaws were placed under arrest, but Tilghman discovered that drug dealers were delivering and trafficking their merchandise in broad daylight too. They deposited shipments of dope in a can or box, set it with other cans or boxes of like labels on the shelves of a grocery store, and peddled it out in small doses. The drugs, which were in small capsules, were sold for $1 each. The peddler would drop the drugs on the ground when and if he saw Chief Tilghman or his men approaching. When the officers searched the culprit, he had nothing on him to warrant an arrest. Tilghman continued to believe the only way to stop the illegal business was to get the manufacturers and wholesalers of both the dope and whiskey. According to Zoe, Tilghman had learned the identity of those manufacturers, which only two or three top men knew. "I'm going to get them, and then I'm coming home, he promised me."[17]

Governor Trapp, state representatives, and law-abiding Cromwell citizens were pleased with the work Chief Tilghman and his officers had done. From October 1, 1924, to October 20 of the same year, traffic in narcotic drugs had decreased seventy-five percent and of the more than 120 reported "hop-heads" in the town when Tilghman first arrived, only 25 remained.[18]

Not everyone applauded the lawman's efforts. Deputy Sheriff of Seminole County turned Federal Prohibition Officer Wiley Lynn did not care for Tilghman and resented his presence in Cromwell. Born in Madill, Oklahoma, in May 1888, Wiley Ulysses Lynn was a mechanic early in his life. He opened his own garage in his hometown and offered car owners the "very best repair work." He married Ollye Maude Banks in 1905 and the couple had two boys. In addition to running his own business he was involved with local government, serving in the assessor's office as a collection agent.[19]

After working as a special enforcement officer for the county under Oklahoma Governor Lee Cruce, he ran for Madill chief of police in mid-1912. Lynn lost to Jim Blalock and then decided to run for constable. He won the election but resigned his position five months later. He took a job as an oil field mechanic with the Rosana Petroleum Company in Wirt, Oklahoma, in 1917 and was drafted into the army the following year. He was later rejected because of a physical disability.[20]

In 1920, Lynn was one of six candidates for sheriff of Marshal County. His campaign ads boasted that he was "a man with a conscience," but he was a plaintiff in more than one lawsuit involving defaulting on loans and nonpayment of bills to local merchants. Lynn lost the election for sheriff and returned to his job in the oil field.[21]

Sheriff Tom Christian made him a jailer in 1923. His rate of pay was $50 a month plus expenses, but his financial struggles continued to mount. Bill collectors sought him out on a regular basis. In an attempt to help Lynn through his difficulties, Sheriff Christian promoted him to deputy and raised his pay. Lynn was tasked with tracking those in the county making and selling alcohol. By mid-year he'd helped with the

Artist's drawing of the altercation between Bill Tilghman and Wiley Lynn.
AUTHOR'S COLLECTION

arrest of a handful of men in possession of corn whiskey. The amount reported to have been seized in each event differed from the amount the suspects told authorities they had, leading some to believe the arresting officers had helped themselves to the product either to keep or sell.[22]

After more than a year with the sheriff's department, Lynn was appointed a federal marshal by Franklin E. Kennamer, the incoming US district judge of the Eastern District of Oklahoma. Critics of the appointment claimed Lynn was given the job in part because of his family's longtime association with the judge. Kennamer and Wiley Lynn's father were close friends. He was assigned to the Holdenville territory where he was charged with enforcing the National Prohibition Act. His work would take him to many cities including Cromwell.[23]

Lynn wasted no time earning a reputation as the federal agent dedicated to ridding the area of illicit liquor trafficking. His first major arrest occurred in mid-June 1924 when he made the largest still capture of any officer ever recorded in the region. A combined total of seventy barrels of liquor was confiscated from seven stills and seven men were taken into custody. Lynn made similar raids on farms where whiskey was being stored in bottles buried underground and hidden in the trunks of cars on the property.[24]

On Wednesday, August 13, 1924, a week before Tilghman arrived in Seminole County, Lynn, along with four other law enforcement agents, destroyed a large quantity of liquor and demolished several gambling joints in Cromwell. Several people were expected to be arrested for gambling and possession of intoxicating liquor, but it didn't come about as expected. Rumors abounded that Lynn pressed charges on some of the violators but let others go for a price. When he wasn't on the job, Lynn kept company with dance hall girls, bootleggers, and other felons. Some believed Lynn must have had the same character to surround himself with the likes of them and they questioned his integrity.[25]

The insinuations were just that. There were never any charges made against Lynn or proof brought forward to show he was corrupt. In fact, state officials praised Lynn for the work he had done during the month of August, particularly in Cromwell, which resulted in eight injunctions. Officials in Washington applauded Lynn's efforts as well and noted in the records at the Prohibition headquarters in Oklahoma City that he "bore the distinction of having made the biggest monthly average of still captures in his jurisdiction."[26]

Lynn's success primarily in Holdenville notwithstanding, Governor Trapp, his staff, and leaders from the town of Cromwell wanted the lawlessness brought further under control there and that's why Tilghman was made chief of police. His primary objective was taming the town the press deemed a "defiant pest hole of debauchery." Lynn had no intention of making the job easy for Tilghman. He was appointed Federal Prohibition Officer assigned to the area and had proved he could do the job without the help of the aged, albeit legendary lawman. "He [Tilghman] arrested a bootlegger and sent him to jail at the county seat," Zoe recalled in her daily journal. "Next day, he was back in business. The sheriff's office when Bill telephoned, said, 'Mr. Lynn phoned us to let him go.' Tilghman knew then there would be trouble. Professional jealousy had reared its ugly head."[27]

According to Zoe, Tilghman and his officers were always investigating leads in an attempt to track the main dealers of both the drugs coming into town and the liquor. In late September 1924, the chief learned of a shipment of narcotics coming from Mexico. The shipment was to be flown into a barren section of the oil fields near Cromwell sometime on or before Halloween. He also discovered that five thousand dollars had been paid to an unknown law enforcement agent for protection. Tilghman suspected Lynn was the agent but lacked the necessary evidence to prove it.[28]

Regardless of how difficult Lynn made his job, Tilghman was a stubborn warhorse for law and order who had pledged to make Cromwell respectable. Acting on a tip about alcohol coming in from a neighboring county, on October 17, 1924, Tilghman and his officers seized a one hundred gallon still filled with whiskey found in an abandoned shack three hundred yards across the Okfuskee County line. Both the liquor and the still were subsequently destroyed.[29]

Two days later, Tilghman led a raid on a gambling room in town and arrested fourteen men. Games were in full operation in the back part of a general store on Main Street when the chief of police arrived on the scene. After confiscating $71 on the tables, Tilghman marched the lawbreakers to jail.[30]

Wiley Lynn would later claim that Tilghman had a habit of keeping some of the money he impounded during an arrest for himself. He also accused Tilghman of taking the alcohol he confiscated during the raids he led and either selling the liquor or turning it over to bootleggers. Associates of Lynn's would later confess that Lynn was the officer who operated in such a way and not Tilghman. Those same associates and acquaintances of Lynn's who saw him after ten o'clock on the evening of November 1, 1924, noted he had been driving around Cromwell drinking. They also witnessed Lynn in the company of two known prostitutes at that time. Lynn was chauffeuring the women and an army sergeant around Cromwell. They were drinking and all of them were being loud and obnoxious. It was around that time that the trouble between Lynn and Tilghman became heated and a physical altercation ensued.[31]

Since Chief Tilghman had come to town, he'd put a stop to drunken miners and oil field workers firing their weapons indiscriminately. Few had dared to violate the directive. So, when the lawman heard a gunshot outside Murphy's Café where he was having coffee with one of his deputies, he hurried out of the building to investigate. As he exited the eatery, he saw Lynn at the end of the boardwalk holding a gun. "What the hell are you doing out here?" Tilghman asked gruffly. Lynn approached Tilghman with his gun in his hand, and the lawman walked toward him holding his own gun.[32]

School commissioner Hugh Sawyer saw Lynn quickly walking toward Tilghman with his gun drawn and tried to intercede to disarm him. In the meantime, Tilghman moved in to meet Lynn's attack. When the two met a scuffle ensued. Tilghman was using both arms to keep Lynn from pointing his gun at him. Lynn, seeing an opening and using his free hand, reached for another gun he had in his suit jacket pocket. He leveled the gun at Tilghman and fired three bullets into his chest.[33]

The veteran lawman sank to the street, unconscious, and his colleagues and townspeople rushed to him. Wiley Lynn ran back to his car and sped away from the scene with his passengers by his side.[34]

Chief Tilghman was carried to a secondhand furniture store and placed on a sofa. He died shortly thereafter.[35]

"At home, I had the house in order and a chicken dressed for Sunday," Zoe later recalled about the day she learned what had happened. "The telephone jingled. 'Cromwell calling,' the operator said. 'Is that you, Bill?' I queried. A strong voice answered. 'Mr. Tilghman has been shot. . . . We want you to call Governor Trapp. Tell him to call the Caldwell Drugstore.' Slowly I took in the words, 'Mr. Tilghman has been shot.' I answered dazed. 'Yes . . . yes . . . I will.'[36]

"Tench, who had enrolled in the University in September, was home for the weekend. I told him, 'We must go. . . . You get out the car. . . . ' I called the governor's residence and Mrs. Trapp answered. I gave her the message. She would call the governor who was at a meeting.

"Tench and my brother and I made hasty preparations to go. The two younger boys were with some of their friends. The telephone rang again. It was the Oklahoma City Chief of Police who had worked under Bill. I told him I was leaving. His voice was husky. 'Mrs. Tilghman . . . don't go. . . . He's . . . dead.'[37]

"The terrible word registered, but tears did not come. In a state of shock, I still moved and spoke. I hung up the phone and told the others. Richard came in, tears on his cheek. 'Is it true?' he cried. Woodie, the youngest came and I told him. He burst into pitiful crying. I too wept."[38]

On Monday, November 3, 1924, Governor Trapp ordered federal and state authorities to investigate Tilghman's killing. Lynn, who told police when they caught up with him that he acted in self-defense, also noted how sorry he was for what had happened. He expressed regret over the incident to M. S. Meadows, the Federal Prohibition Director for Oklahoma, but insisted the confrontation was brought on when Tilghman threatened his life. According to the November 3, 1924, edition of the *Daily Ardmoreite*, "The first shot that brought Tilghman to the scene to investigate, was fired accidentally when Lynn's thumb slipped from the hammer of his revolver. Mrs. Rose Lutke, one of the occupants of the car in which Lynn was riding, declared that Tilghman fired first at Lynn. 'He had his gun in my side and threatened to kill me,' Lynn said. 'It was a matter of kill or get killed. I don't believe Tilghman fired.'"[39]

Tilghman was well-respected by many Cromwell citizens and revered by the officers with whom he served. They scoffed at Lynn's self-defense plea and remarked to the press that Lynn had brought the trouble on himself by consorting with members of the underworld. Lynn was charged with "shooting and killing one Bill Tilghman while acting within the scope of his authority." Fearing Tilghman's supporters would overtake the guards at the Seminole County jail where Lynn was being held, he was moved to an undisclosed location.[40]

Zoe was shattered by the death of her husband, and learning the details of the incident only made matters worse. "About one o'clock in the morning the day after Bill was killed, I was in bed, but sleepless," Zoe recalled in her memoirs. "Much later I slipped downstairs to find Tench alone in an armchair. I urged him to get some rest, but he was there all night.[41]

"Daylight came slowly. I rose and dressed. It was too early for the paper but I went outdoors, walked up the street and came to the big bundle of Sunday papers left by a truck. Feverishly I paced up and down until the carrier boy came.

"Black headlines stared at me. The murder had been early enough that a pretty full story had been available. The identity of the killer was not known but came out that day. Wiley Lynn, the Deputy Prohibition Agent had surrendered himself to the US commissioner at Holdenville.[42]

"Visitors came in a stream. Our next-door neighbor carried us all over there for meals. Members of the family came. Bill's sister Josie arrived that night. There were plans to be made. Bill's body was brought from Cromwell. They took me to see him, lying on a couch, so still, so strange. I touched his brow and spoke a few words over him."[43]

Several stories came out during the government's investigation into the case. Lynn told authorities he was going to Murphy's Café to ferret out bootleggers operating there. Rose Lutke and Eva Caton, both prostitutes from a bordello called The Cozy Room, were going to assist Lynn in finding the main dealer. W. P. Thompson, an officer from Fort Sill, came along for the ride. Lynn did indeed have a warrant to search the business for whiskey. According to Lynn, he was walking toward Murphy's Café when Tilghman and another man whom he didn't know rushed out and told him he was under arrest. Lynn declared he tried to tell Tilghman who he was, but Tilghman retorted that it didn't make any difference, he was under arrest. Lynn said he put his hands up in the air and Tilghman took a gun from his hip and shot at him. Tilghman also grabbed him by the throat and began to choke him.[44]

Eyewitnesses to the incident, starting with the moment Lynn fired his weapon, stated that the gun was shot on purpose because he wanted to get Tilghman in the street. They also noted that Lynn was the one issuing threats, not Tilghman.[45]

The announcement that Tilghman's funeral would be held on November 5, 1924, ran in newspapers across the state. Governor Trapp ordered his body to lie in state in the capitol where people could pay their respects. Zoe was among those in attendance.[46]

"The funeral took place in the First Presbyterian Church of which Bill and I were members," Zoe recalled in her memoirs. The pastor, Reverend W. Clyde Howard, gave a brief and moving service. 'We honor today a prince of a man . . . ,' he said. The pallbearers were Governor M. E. Trapp, J. B. A. Robertson, Brigadier General Roy V. Hoffman, Alve McDonald, US Marshal, and two of Bill's former deputies, W. Crume, and G. W. Swanson. Both were now prominent businessmen in Eastern Oklahoma.[47]

"We were on the train for Chandler. Many old friends waited there, autos were ready for us and a long procession formed. On the main street, before every place of business, flags hung at half-mast from staffs set at the edge of the sidewalk. At the cemetery were several automobiles of people from Cromwell, men and women who had honored and loved him. Some spoke to me of how they admired him. They brought flowers. They had intended to go to Oklahoma City the day before to see him lying in state, but learning that the burial would be at Chandler, which was nearer, they came there.[48]

"The next week two men came to me who had been closest to Bill at Cromwell. One of them had picked up his gun where he fell, and brought it to me. It had not been fired. They gave me the intimate story of those last two days and of the murder. Oh, how I grieved and could best express my sorrow in verse."[49]

I shall remember how your eyes locked deep into my heart,
And knew that aye, in life or death, my soul of yours is part.
I shall remember how your hands held mine with tenderness,
That made my pulse unbidden leap beneath their swift caress.
I shall remember how your voice held nameless melody,
That drew my very soul to hear its deep-toned threnody.
I shall remember how you loved
When other days shall be
In days and nights when all my life
Is work and memory.[50]

Less than a week after Tilghman's funeral the state charge against Lynn was changed to murder. The federal court claimed authority over the matter but state officials won out. Fearful Lynn would somehow manage to escape justice, Zoe retained an attorney to help prosecute him. Lynn's murder trial was held in the District Court of Seminole County at Wewoka on May 22, 1925. The accused caused a stir in the courtroom before the proceedings were underway. When guards searched Lynn for weapons, they found he'd brought a loaded, pearl handle, silver-plated, automatic pistol to the hearing. The gun was confiscated.[51]

In the opening statement, Lynn's lawyer, W. W. Pryor, told the judge and jury that their client was acting reasonably given that Tilghman was interfering with an officer's duty. Lynn claimed he was going to Murphy's Café to serve a warrant and to arrest those peddling whiskey on the premises. Prosecutors told the jury in their opening remarks that Tilghman was acting as he should have as chief of police in trying to disarm an individual disturbing the peace.[52]

The defense counsel told the court that Tilghman had been sent to Cromwell by Governor Trapp contrary to the wishes of Seminole County authorities. Pryor said that when Lynn alighted from a motor car in front of the dance hall and walked up to Tilghman he had put away his pistol, which was discharged accidentally, but that Tilghman drew his gun and leveled it at the federal officer. Pryor added that Lynn called out, "Don't, Uncle Bill, this is Lynn." Tilghman allegedly responded, "I don't care who it is. I have you where I want you and am going to kill you." Pryor then asserted that Tilghman fired the first shot and that Lynn did not use his gun until Tilghman backed him against the wall and started to throttle him. He said Lynn drew the second gun then and fired in self-defense.[53]

According to the May 22, 1925, edition of the *Tulsa Times*, "Pryor charged that Tilghman took three gallons of liquor from a federal officer at one time and sold it, offering later to divide the proceeds of the sale when the federal representative asked what had been done with the liquor." He went on to accuse Tilghman of attempting to give Cromwell a bad name so he could use the city as a background for a motion picture sponsored by him showing the development of Oklahoma.[54]

The defense spokesman explained to the court that the women in the car with Lynn were there because he needed them to search the females he planned to place under arrest who were working out of the café.[55]

The state's attorney, S. P. Freeling, however, drew a different picture of Mrs. Lutke. Freeling told the judge and jury that Lynn, Mrs. Lutke and Eva Caton, who were owners of a brothel in another town, and Sergeant Thompson were all in the car drinking liquor given to them by Lynn himself. According to Freeling, Eva Caton was drunk and out of control. Sergeant Thompson was in a drunken state too, and Rose Lutke and Lynn had also been drinking to excess. Lynn shouted profanities at the occupants of a passing vehicle before falling out of his own car. After Lynn killed Tilghman, Lutke asked him why he did it. Freeling said that Lynn told her to "shut up" and then he drove them to the home of Park Crutcher, the United States commissioner at Holdenville, and surrendered.[56]

Sergeant Thompson was one of the first witnesses to take the stand and related the details of the evening. He admitted he had been drinking but said he was not intoxicated.[57]

John R. Striff, a former oil well driller, testified he heard Lynn yell at people to get out of his way and scream profanities at them as he drove into Cromwell. He testified he saw Lynn shoot into the street and heard the shots later that killed Tilghman.[58]

Zoe was present in the courtroom listening to the events leading up to the death of her husband. She cried softly into her handkerchief as they described the gunfight and the shooting that ended Tilghman's life.

She occasionally glanced at Lynn, who wore an impassive expression as the attorneys were making their statements.[59]

The defense introduced witnesses that said Tilghman had made threats against Lynn. Rose Lutke, on cross-examination, admitted she knew Lynn had a search warrant and that she was with him to help find whiskey at Murphy's Café. The prosecution struggled in the hearing. They planned to put Eva Caton on the stand to testify that Lynn had been drinking and doing drugs, but she mysteriously disappeared. Two other chief witnesses for the state also went missing.[60]

On May 26, 1925, the jury returned a verdict of not guilty.[61]

After the court had discharged the jury, Lynn rose and walked from the room. In the hall he was surrounded by a group of friends who patted him on the back. He offered a few words to his supporters and members of the press. "I have tried to fight a clean fight and have endeavored not to introduce evidence tending to blacken the character of Uncle Bill or anyone else," he said. "I have respected the family and have tried to spare them."[62]

Zoe Tilghman was escorted out of the courtroom by friends and family. A newspaper reporter stopped her as she was leaving and asked her for a statement. "The outcome of this trial has added a supreme dishonor to the law of Oklahoma," she replied. "Today, the measure of shame is full."[63]

Not long after the trial, Judge Mathews, who presided over the hearing, shared his thoughts about the case with Tilghman's longtime friend, General Roy Hoffman. "To all persons of average intelligence and experience, it was clearly apparent that the evidence presented by the defense was unnatural and could not be accepted as true by any thinking person," he said. "I was convinced by evidence that it was a cold-blooded assassination. . . . It is to be regretted that a man's reputation should be subjected to the perjured testimony of such wreckage of humanity as appeared for the defense in that case."[64]

Although Lynn was freed from the murder charge, he still had to answer for coming to court armed. "The court cannot conceive of a man so bold, so insolent," the judge announced. He sentenced Lynn to ninety days in jail for contempt of court.[65]

In July 1925, Lynn was arrested on an intoxication charge while at a rooming house with Rose Lutke. He was ordered to pay a fine and released.[66]

Over the next eight years, Lynn would be in and out of trouble both with the law and at home. His wife left him and he lost touch with his children.[67]

In mid-July 1932, Lynn was in a gunfight with Oklahoma State Bureau of Investigation Agent Crockett Long. Long had arrested Lynn several times prior to the shooting incident that took place in Madill, Oklahoma. Lynn approached Long at the local drugstore with his gun drawn. Long pulled his gun to defend himself. The two men fired their weapons simultaneously. Both were killed.[68]

"Bill Tilghman has been avenged," Zoe told reporters who tracked her down with the news. "I'm glad Wiley Lynn is dead. I'm sorry another good man had to be sacrificed before Lynn met his due. I'm glad he died the way he died for he was a hardened criminal whose life fittingly was ended by bullets. No jury can acquit him for killing Crockett Long. A higher jury has passed sentence upon him." In that moment Zoe clearly recalled the words she'd said to her husband as she stood over his lifeless body. "Wiley Lynn will die someday before a smoking pistol." She'd been right, but as she admitted later in her life, it was little consolation.[69]

Chapter 10

Marshal of the Last Frontier

Zoe Tilghman sat behind her desk in her small office at *Harlow's Weekly* watching a sign painter stencil her name across the front of the closed door. Two months had passed since her husband had been killed in the line of duty. She was tired and a bit lost. In early 1925, Zoe became the primary breadwinner in the family. Making ends meet and caring for her three sons while grieving was at times overwhelming. The full weight of the circumstances fell heavy on her in mid-January 1925 when she was informed that Tilghman's last month's salary of two hundred dollars would not be paid. Zoe would have to fight for the funds but was too weary to think about mounting a campaign to persuade the powers that be to give her Tilghman's earnings. All she could manage at the time was to catalog such challenges to include in her book about her husband's time as marshal of the last frontier.[1]

"I knew from the time we laid him away that it would be my task to write the story of Bill's life," she wrote years later as she reflected on her life, "but earning a living and keeping a home left little time for writing. Eventually, I set myself to do a thousand words a night. I missed some nights of course, but in time I would have a book. For the early parts, I had his own notebooks, without which any story of this period would have been impossible. I had official records and I contacted a number of his old friends and associates to help with some details."[2]

Prior to approaching the editor of *Harlow's Weekly* for work, Governor Martin Trapp offered to find Zoe a job, one that might have allowed her more time to write Tilghman's story, but she declined the politician's

Marshal Tilghman lying in state in the rotunda of the Oklahoma State Capitol.
COURTESY WESTERN HISTORY COLLECTIONS, SPECIAL RESEARCH COLLECTIONS, UNIVERSITY OF OKLAHOMA LIBRARIES, WHCP-1165

assistance. "I felt a state job might be uncertain, lasting only as long as the new administration was in office," she recalled in her memoirs. "The field of teaching was overcrowded. I applied at various places for other work, but no luck.[3]

"I had a few things published in magazines and a number of poems in *Harlow's Weekly*. I had some personal acquaintance with the president, Victor Harlow. I thought I could qualify as a proofreader. And I told him, 'I think I'd like to work for you.'[4]

"Victor Harlow was a scholar turned businessman. He had the keenest analytical mind I have ever known. He was a man of vision, broad sympathies, and understanding. He had been president of a small college. He had served as the first clerk of the State Board of Affairs and he knew both the theories and the practical workings of government. He had personal acquaintance with most of the political figures of state.

"Mr. Harlow was active in his church and for many years an important worker in the chamber of commerce. He was chairman of their committee which worked to make Oklahoma City the center for public meetings and conventions. Though his publishing company was a fairly large concern, it was not too large for his personal supervision.[5]

"*Harlow's Weekly* was only one item of the business. It was modeled on the then important *Literary Digest*, but restricted to Oklahoma only. It dealt with public affairs, carried articles about public men and news in various fields. Also, it used poems by Oklahoma writers.

"Mr. Harlow knew my training and background. He had the skill and insight to utilize that and to help me develop it. I was to be the literary editor of the *Weekly* and surely it was an ideal job for me. I grew up in Oklahoma. I had the background of the pioneers and through Bill I had had a closeup of public affairs. I had shared his interest in politics. From him I learned practical knowledge and some ability to read between the lines of a political situation.[6]

"One handicap of the beginner was spared me. I was not a new worker. I was Mrs. Bill Tilghman and though I never made any attempt to capitalize on that everyone from the president down treated me with respect. My desk was near the front of the line of offices and the outer door. If there has been any one thing of significant service in my life, I think it was the work I did in this position in promoting and encouraging writers.

"In time I was entrusted with any work of the *Weekly* except the lead political articles. I learned to prepare copy on the linotype, saving costly corrections. I had to know the spelling of names, of every legislator or public man, as well as geographical or other special words. I shared with Mr. Maxey, final proofreading. I made up the dummy for the print shop and when time pressed, I could make up from the start the paper as a whole, standing beside the makeup man and directing him as he made up the pages from the galleys.[7]

"I give this here as a summary of the work through the years. Not all of it of course was on me at any one time. My salary increased gradually from $15 a week to $25 and we managed to live, somehow. I had sold my car, of course, and for a year or two walked to and from work."[8]

Zoe's oldest son, Tench, took a job to help support the family. He was a sophomore at the University of Oklahoma pursuing a degree in law when he took time off to concentrate on earning money. Richard and Woodrow remained in junior high and high school and during various breaks, traveled to nearby towns to show Tilghman's film, *The Passing of the Oklahoma Outlaws*. They were only able to exhibit the motion picture for a short time since the films eventually wore out. Zoe could not afford to replace them. She often wished she could have purchased new prints, believing if that had been possible her sons would have been too preoccupied to get into trouble. "The pair would have been busy with their father's films with no time to visit gambling houses," she lamented.[9]

Richard's body was laid to rest next to his father in 1929 at age twenty-two. Woodrow was in and out of jail the rest of his life. After gaining his freedom in the 1940s, Woodrow was arrested for armed robbery in 1950. He was sentenced to twenty-five years in prison. Zoe hired lawyers to represent her son at his hearings and to file subsequent clemency pleas. She sacrificed her own comfort and discretionary income to pay for Woodrow's defense. He died on March 1, 1981, in Fort Worth, Texas.[10]

Tench not only received a law degree from Cumberland University in Lebanon, Tennessee, but went on to join the military and was attached to the headquarters of General George Patton's Third Army. He landed in southern France with Patton's forces in July 1944 and took part in the historic sweep across France. In March 1945, he was awarded the country's highest military honor, the Croix de Guerre of France. After the war he returned to the United States where he made a career in the army, rising to the rank of lieutenant colonel. He and his wife had one child. Tench passed away on August 13, 1970, at the age of sixty-four.[11]

"Throughout the course of my life, particularly after Bill's death, my work, my writing was my only refuge and I think saved me from utter breakdown," Zoe wrote in her memoirs. "My first book, *The Dugout*, was published on a royalty basis by *Harlow's* in 1926. I had written it before Bill's death. While it had no wide circulation, it won praise. The editor of *The Author and Journalist* said, 'It is real literature.' More than one person declared that he could not lay it down, but read it at one sitting.

A good beginning but I could not follow it up. Writing for the *Weekly* with my other work, and home-keeping seemed to take all my energy. *Outlaw Days in Oklahoma* with my name was the next book. Then a revised edition of *The Little Red Book*, which Bill had prepared for sale at theaters where the picture was showing, was published under my name also in 1928.[12]

"It was not until 1936 that I penned another big book. Mr. Harlow suggested that I do a life of Quanah Parker, the Comanche chief. He felt that Oklahoma should have something about our Indians and was thinking of a series of three or four. Quanah's mother had been Cynthia Ann Parker, a white child carried off by the Indians when she was about six years old. She grew up as one of them and married the chief of the band. She was recaptured by the Texas Rangers in 1860 and returned to her Texas relatives."[13]

The manuscript was approved by Reverend White Parker, Quanah Parker's son, as an authentic biography. It was published by *Harlow's* in 1938, with the title *Quanah, the Eagle of the Comanche*. The name Quanah means eagle.[14]

"Between these [books], however, came a book of my poems entitled *Prairie Winds*, published by *Harlow's* in 1931," Zoe noted in her memoirs. "But it did not include all I had published. I wrote a good many after that until, after a shattering tragedy, my muse flew away. I had technical skill, but no more poetic ideas. In time, I occasionally authored a poem, but sometimes not one in a whole year. And though I had some publications, my best work was in the past.[15]

"The University Extension Division held evening classes in Oklahoma City. I became a teacher of poetry writing. My first class went well and I developed my lectures and notes. In every session part of the time was devoted to criticism of students' poems. I applied the system of Professor Parrington's, poems written on the board with no author's names. With chalk in hand, I changed and criticized, calling on the class, gradually training them to criticize and improve."[16]

In 1934, Zoe founded the Poetry Society of Oklahoma, which had the largest membership of any literary organization in the state. She helped publish three anthologies for the society featuring poems specifically relating to the state.[17]

Zoe turned sixty in 1940. She had been a professional writer for more than twenty years and had achieved some minor success, but was still struggling financially. She had spent a great deal on legal assistance for Woodrow and had little or nothing left. "Tench, who was then stationed in Turkey, sent me a check monthly which he could ill afford," she later recalled. "I worked some at writing and sold a few things, little more than enough to buy paper and stamps. Then, with a one-year scholarship, I went to Norman weekly for a conference on fiction writing with Professor Foster Harris of the School of Professional Writing. I had by this time decided that I was no good at fiction, but with some ability as a historian and fact writer. Foster approved [of] the work I did, but the editors did not. However, the work with him undoubtedly did me good and from then on, I sold occasional articles.[18]

"One day Victor Harlow again sent for me. His publishing company had weathered the Depression, but it was now engaged almost entirely in publishing schoolbooks. Leaning back in his swivel chair he looked at me across the desk and wasted no words. 'I want you,' he said, 'to write some books on the real Indian, suitable for auxiliary reading in schools.' Again, I was on familiar ground for in addition to growing up in Oklahoma, I had read everything available in her history.[19]

"I followed somewhat the plan of the Indian books. Each event or period was told as seen through the eyes of a young person. It was history dramatized and again like the Indian books, it was a correct picture of the people and life of that time whether white or Native American. There were fifty stories taking the history from the first Spanish explorers to statehood. We stopped at this point because from that point on the history became political and beyond the interest of children. The book was accepted as a textbook by the state board. I wrote in all seven books. Two with women heroines. Each book pictured a different tribe and area.[20]

"In the 1950s a change came in the magazine field. Most of the large output known as pulps faded out and the number of slicks diminished. There was also an increased interest in factual writing.[21]

Zoe Tilghman appeared on the Art Linkletter Show in the late 1950s to talk about her career in writing and Bill Tilghman's legacy as a lawman.
DEPARTMENT OF SPECIAL COLLECTIONS AND UNIVERSITY ARCHIVES, UNIVERSITY OF TULSA MCFARLIN LIBRARY

"I wrote a number of articles for the magazine *True West.* I wrote more than a few stories that the editor of the magazine did not pay me for. Indeed, *True West* owes me $27.63 for work I did fact checking. I corrected errors in many of the magazine's articles. For a while, their policy was to print only true material and there would be garbled versions of some events. Some were honest mistakes of the writers and others due to mere neglect in getting data. One instance was a story of Quanah Parker with several errors which a simple reference to the government records would have prevented.[22]

"I began to get letters with comments and inquiries and soon came to be recognized as an authority on things Western. Once or twice the magazine sent me an article to look over before they would use it. For the area of Oklahoma and western Kansas in the Indian and cattle days, I do consider myself an authority, but not by any means for all the West.[23]

"I answered all the letters as well as I could and thus formed a wide circle of friends. Many had made reference to Mr. Tilghman or asked about him. Some gave me valuable information. Letters came from England and Germany and I now have a group of greatly prized friends. Two of them visited the old home of the Tilghmans in Snodland parish in Kent and sent me photos of the church and the earliest Tilghman tomb about six hundred years old. It was considerably sunken in the earth.[24]

"Now and then I was invited to speak before a club or a conference. I had recognition from writers' associations. The New York Public Library research department listed me as an authority and referred one or two writers to me. This resulted in some delightful contacts and friendships. The author of the *Golden Anniversary of the History of Oklahoma* asked me to serve as a consultant on the book."[25]

In addition to fact checking for *True West*, Zoe also served in that capacity for articles written about the history of Oklahoma for *Oklahoma News*. The job offer came after the newspaper ran a story about Bill Doolin in December 1938. Zoe took exception to some of the details in the story and wrote the editor to share her concerns.[26]

"*The True Story of Bill Doolin* published in last Sunday's *News* is so full of errors that I feel impelled to write to you. Perhaps you will wish to print this in the Letters to the Editor section—perhaps not.[27]

"The girl Doolin married was not named Mathews, but Edith Ellsworth. Her home was at a little country store post office place called Lawson about where the town of Quay is now located. It moved to Quay when the railroad was built. It is seventy-five or eighty miles from the Old Halsell ranch which was near the town of Pleasant Valley on the Guthrie-Ripley branch of the Santa Fe. The ranch was abolished when the country opened in 1889. Up to that time Doolin had been a law-abiding cowhand and sort of foreman under O. D. Halsell.[28]

"The reference to 'rustlers' is approved western fiction style. But did not fit in the Territory. There was no big business of rustling because every ranch in the country belonged to the tight organization of the cattlemen and there was no one who could take care of a lot of cattle, change brands, and market them."[29]

The editor of the *Oklahoma News* did print Zoe's letter, which was five pages long. She commented on numerous so-called facts the author, Ned P. De Witt, got wrong. The letter led to a regular column. Whenever anyone submitted a question about the history of the area, Zoe would answer them in her biweekly feature.[30]

By August 1948, Zoe had completed the biography she had started on her husband in 1925. "I rewrote the book four times," she recalled years later. "Once I threw away a hundred thousand words and began anew. But by 1948, it was done. I had, in the process, learned a good deal about writing. I had hoped that some time Bill's life would be the object for a moving picture. . . . *The Marshal of the Last Frontier* was published in 1949 by the Arthur H. Clark company, leading historical publishers, as Number III of their Western Frontiersmen series.[31]

"Before this, however, I received a letter from Mr. Mitchell Gertz, a leading agent in Hollywood. He was interested in the Tilghman story. I sent him a copy of the manuscript. But evidently, the name of Tilghman was not known to the Hollywood producers and it took Mr. Gertz years to impress upon these people the importance of Bill Tilghman in the American scene.[32]

"Hollywood was blinded by the phony publicity given to other lawmen and overlooked the genius contributions that Tilghman made in creating law and order in the Territory. Years passed by and no offer of any consequence was made.

"Late in 1959, I was invited to Los Angeles by a film company. All expenses were to be paid and I had a Cinderella adventure for some ten days. My first plane journey, inside view of the studios, personal meetings with Mr. Gertz and with producers and actors, a brief appearance on television, press interviews, and luncheons.[33]

"I stayed with an Oklahoma City friend, who on weekends, took me about to other places of interest and to meet friends.

"On my return, my son and his wife and daughter met me. Tench had retired from the army as Lieutenant Colonel. After trying Florida for some months, they found the Oklahoma call stronger. Suzie [Tench's

Marshal Tilghman's saddled horse was led in the '89ers Day Parade on April 22, 1925.
COURTESY WESTERN HISTORY COLLECTIONS, SPECIAL RESEARCH COLLECTIONS, UNIVERSITY OF OKLAHOMA LIBRARIES, WHCP-1165

daughter, Zoe's granddaughter] had to go back to her college, but Tench and Doris stayed with me for some weeks until they could buy a home. After the years of absence, I was happy to have them near me once more."[34]

Among those readers who did recognize Marshal Tilghman's contribution to law and order and who wrote Zoe letting her know their thoughts on the biography was President Dwight D. Eisenhower. On July 1, 1958, the president penned a letter to Zoe expressing his gratitude for the book.[35]

"Dear Mrs. Tilghman, As Bryce Harlow reported to you, I had hoped to be able to receive from you personally your book on the life of your husband, the famed Bill Tilghman, but official engagements made it impossible.[36]

Lieutenant Colonel Tench Tilghman.

DEPARTMENT OF SPECIAL COLLECTIONS AND UNIVERSITY ARCHIVES, UNIVERSITY OF TULSA MCFARLIN LIBRARY

"Now, however, I have your book at hand and have read with great pride and appreciation your fine inscription to me. For your message (including the Latin passage which I shall have deciphered) and for your thoughtfulness in making this book available—one that will surely provide fascinating reading about a period always of great interest to me. I am grateful indeed. Bill Tilghman is a great man in the Old West, and I shall prize the story of his life, told as only one could who lived it with him.

"With best wishes, Sincerely Dwight D. Eisenhower."[37]

Marshal of the Last Frontier was well received not only by politicians like President Eisenhower, but by critics from coast to coast. Joseph Henry Jackson, the highly respected *San Francisco Chronicle* and *Los Angeles Times* book reviewer, noted that "Mrs. Tilghman's book is well organized and clearly told. It reflects not only one man's life but the story of an enormously significant period in the growth of the U. S. I dare say people will argue forever about which man of all the well-known ones was the West's greatest peace officer, but one thing is certain, Bill Tilghman's name belongs well up near the top."[38]

The Hollywood agent who was initially attracted to Zoe's book about Tilghman managed to get the manuscript into the hands of several executives who produced television westerns. Although they weren't interested in dedicating a series around the legendary lawman's life and work, they were impressed with Zoe's writing. She was offered a job contributing stories for the television show *Death Valley Days*.[39]

In 1960, the eighty-year-old author, poet, and screenwriter shared her thoughts about westerns in an interview with a reporter from the United Press. "There's too much gun play in television westerns," Zoe noted in the article. "TV's westerns over-emphasize the shoot-em-up business and there was much more to the job. It lacks a long way of being history," she said. She conceded that there was "a certain amount of accuracy in the setting" portrayed, but it wasn't everything.[40]

Zoe recalled that Tilghman was genuinely tough when necessary but was a far cry from some of the lawmen on film. Adept with either hand, he packed just one six-shooter—two were too heavy. "Bill was a high-class detective, using methods like those of the FBI nowadays. None of the others were."[41]

One of the last photographs taken of Marshal Bill Tilghman in 1924.
OKLAHOMA HISTORICAL SOCIETY

Zoe shared a similar perspective on her husband's character and work in a feature article *Life Magazine* did on Tilghman and the biography she penned. "My husband was one of the West's great peace officers," she shared with the publication. "He hunted down famous outlaws and killed men when he had to. But Bill was more than an expert gunman who fought on the side of the law. He and other men who also held dangerous jobs as sheriffs and deputy marshals did the work of civilization along the whole frontier.[42]

" . . . T-V westerns give a false picture of pioneer lawmen like Bill. He hated to kill and never boasted about it. But he knew some men had to be killed before the West could be a safe place for homes and families to exist in."[43]

The success of *Marshal of the Last Frontier* and the notoriety Zoe received writing for *Death Valley Days* prompted many supporters of Tilghman, his legacy, and Zoe's ability to capture the lawman's life in word to send letters expressing their appreciation for what she and the legendary officer had done. One such letter came from Jesse James III dated November 14, 1954.[44]

"Dear Mrs. Tilghman: If I had had your address while down at Guthrie and Oklahoma City very recently, I would have dropped around to see you. My grandpa, Old Jesse Woodson James, often spoke of your husband and had great admiration for him. I had met Bill several times in the years past at Ponca City on one occasion and several times down around Muskogee if my memory serves me right.[45]

"I wonder if Orrington 'Red' Lucas is still alive? When grandpa Jesse came out of hiding in May 1948 at Lawton, he had a broken hip and was pretty miserable. In July, for the most part we were in Guthrie, Oklahoma. We then went to a bone specialist on or about July 29, 1948, in Chicago so the aged man could be treated.

"I also met Bat Masterson once or twice and met and knew Red Lucas. That is why I am writing to you thinking perhaps you might know where he is now. I last saw him at the Cooper Hotel in April 1953. If alive now he must be around 98. Red Lucas, an old time U. S. Deputy Marshal in the early days, worked mostly in Oklahoma.[46]

"Red knew the James boys very well since 1878 or 1879, and was one of the dozens of grand old pioneers and ex-gunmen that gave us very valuable help and cooperation. Grandpa Jesse was not the only old timer that had been declared 'officially dead.' You can perhaps name, and I can name quite a few others that had faked up funerals so they could wiggle out of a bad bit of trouble that way.[47]

"Grandpa Jesse was actually born April 17, 1844. He was to pull the biggest hoax ever pulled upon the American people via just a lot of politics, back on April 3, 1882, in St. Joseph, Missouri, when two factions got together and had him declared 'officially dead.'

"After a man or woman is once declared 'legally' dead, or if he or she stays out of sight for over seven years, in the eyes of the law of our land, he or she will be as dead as ever will be even if he or she comes back later on in life.[48]

"Grandpa died in Granbury, Hood County, Texas, on August 15, 1951, during one very hot and sultry late afternoon about 6:45 P. M. There I buried him myself four days later. Kinfolks, old friends, old pals, ex-outlaws, and peace officers of the early days had come by the hundred to see him while alive and at his death. Historians, identification men of our great and modern crime bureaus, came off and on to study this strange case. Great judges, and historians also came by.[49]

"Old lodge brothers of the K and P Lodges, Odd Fellows, and the Masonic Lodges from Texas to Illinois, from Georgia to California and Florida, came around to see him personally as we traveled back and forth across the nations. Sitting back and watching a great old cantankerous warrior handle himself as he faced the world with a broken hip, over a hundred years old, and with a lot of pain and misery every moment he took a breath. Yes, there are a few, and just a very few, who because they had set themselves up as self-appointed experts, would dare call all our grand old pioneers, liars.[50]

"To my notion and many others, Bill Tilghman, Wyatt Earp, Bat Masterson, John R. Hughes, and several more were just about tops and the most respected and honest peace officers the west ever saw.

"Grandpa always said that Bill Tilghman was a man most capable and honest in his judgement and as a peace officer kept many a wild man

Zoe Tilghman in front of a portrait of her late husband.
OKLAHOMA HISTORICAL SOCIETY

from getting into trouble or going to prison. Grandpa said that there was many and many an old cow-waddie that some officers would have shot and killed because it would have been easy, but not Bill Tilghman. He said that Bill saved his life once in Caldwell, Kansas, by simply disarming him and another fellow in a saloon. Otherwise, some lead would have been flying all over the place as both fighters were drunk anyway.

"Yours Very Truly, Jesse James III."[51]

Zoe was grateful for the correspondence but doubted most of what James wrote.[52]

Of all the types of writing Zoe tackled, she was most prolific in poetry. She preferred to express her sentiments about Oklahoma, her children, and her husband in verse. Her poem titled "Eternal," one of the last she crafted, is an homage to the life she shared with Tilghman:[53]

White moths above the clover,
And the tall grass bent with dew,
A thrush in the hawthorn thicket,
And the dawn up flashing new.
Yet whiter than clover blossoms,
Sweeter than call of bird,
Fairer than May-time sunrise,
And rose by the dawn-wind stirred.
Your love in that hour given,
Whatever life's loss or gain,
However its myriad voices,
Of passion or joy or pain.
May rise, I keep that unchanging,
And more than their clamor strong,
Deep in my heart—the echo
Of an eternal song![54]

Zoe Tilghman died on June 13, 1964, at an Oklahoma City nursing home. She was buried at the Oak Park Cemetery in Chandler next to Marshal Tilghman. She was eighty-three years old.[55]

Notes

Prologue

1. Zoe A. Tilghman Historical Document Collection, *Chicago Chronicle*, August 22, 1895, *Belleville Telescope*, August 29, 1895, *Bill Tilghman: Marshal of the Last Frontier*, pg. 135-136, *Marshal of the Last Frontier*, pg. 210-211.
2. Zoe A. Tilghman Historical Document Collection, *Chicago Chronicle*, August 22, 1895, *Belleville Telescope*, August 29, 1895.
3. Zoe A. Tilghman Historical Document Collection, *Marshal of the Last Frontier*, pg. 210-211, *Butte Miner*, August 24, 1895, *Taloga Advocate*, September 7, 1895.
4. Zoe A. Tilghman Historical Document Collection, *Bill Tilghman: Marshal of the Last Frontier*, pg. 133-135.
5. Zoe A. Tilghman Historical Document Collection, *Bill Tilghman: Marshal of the Last Frontier*, pg. 133-135.
6. Zoe A. Tilghman Historical Document Collection.
7. Ibid.
8. Ibid., *Salt Lake Telegram*, October 13, 1923, *Sioux City Journal*, November 4, 1923, *Florence Bulletin*, February 7, 1924, *Life Magazine*, May 18, 1959.
9. *Dodge City Globe*, July 15, 1884, *Ford County Globe*, July 8, 1884, *Dodge City Times*, July 10, 1884.
10. *Dodge City Globe*, July 15, 1884, *Ford County Globe*, July 8, 1884, *Dodge City Times*, July 10, 1884.
11. *Dodge City Globe*, July 15, 1884, *Ford County Globe*, July 8, 1884, *Dodge City Times*, July 10, 1884.
12. *Dodge City Globe*, July 15, 1884, *Ford County Globe*, July 8, 1884, *Dodge City Times*, July 10, 1884.
13. *Dodge City Globe*, July 15, 1884, *Ford County Globe*, July 8, 1884, *Dodge City Times*, July 10, 1884.
14. *Dodge City Globe*, July 15, 1884, *Ford County Globe*, July 8, 1884, *Dodge City Times*, July 10, 1884.
15. *Dodge City Globe*, July 15, 1884, *Ford County Globe*, July 8, 1884, *Dodge City Times*, July 10, 1884.

Chapter 1

1. *Dodge City Globe*, October 20, 1885, *Journal Democrat*, October 17, 1885, *Thunder Over the Prairie*, pg. 26–30.
2. *Life Magazine*, May 18, 1959, *Memoirs of William Tilghman*, Handwritten by William Tilghman.
3. *Life Magazine*, May 18, 1959, *Memoirs of William Tilghman*, Handwritten by William Tilghman.
4. *Life Magazine*, May 18, 1959, *Memoirs of William Tilghman*, Handwritten by William Tilghman.
5. *Weekly Commonwealth*, June 26, 1872.
6. *Life Magazine*, May 18, 1959, *Memoirs of William Tilghman*, Handwritten by William Tilghman.
7. *Bill Tilghman: Marshal of the Last Frontier*, pg. 47–48, *Marshal of the Last Frontier*, pg. 101–102.
8. *Marshal of the Last Frontier*, pg. 101–102, *Memoirs of William Tilghman*, Handwritten by William Tilghman.
9. *Marshal of the Last Frontier*, pg. 101–102, *Memoirs of William Tilghman*, Handwritten by William Tilghman.
10. *Marshal of the Last Frontier*, pg. 102–105, *Memoirs of William Tilghman*, Handwritten by William Tilghman.
11. *Memoirs of William Tilghman*, Handwritten by William Tilghman, *Bill Tilghman: Marshal of the Last Frontier*, pg. 49–52.
12. *Memoirs of William Tilghman*, Handwritten by William Tilghman, *Bill Tilghman: Marshal of the Last Frontier*, pg. 60–62, *Marshal of the Last Frontier*, pg. 103–105.
13. *Memoirs of William Tilghman*, Handwritten by William Tilghman, *Bill Tilghman: Marshal of the Last Frontier*, pg. 60–62, *Marshal of the Last Frontier*, pg. 103–105.
14. *Memoirs of William Tilghman*, Handwritten by William Tilghman, *Bill Tilghman: Marshal of the Last Frontier*, pg. 60–62, *Marshal of the Last Frontier*, pg. 103–105.
15. *Memoirs of William Tilghman*, Handwritten by William Tilghman.
16. Ibid.
17. Ibid.
18. Ibid.
19. *Memoirs of William Tilghman*, Handwritten by William Tilghman, *Marshal of the Last Frontier*, pg. 118–119.
20. *Memoirs of William Tilghman*, Handwritten by William Tilghman, *Marshal of the Last Frontier*, pg. 118–119, Zoe Tilghman Handwritten and Typed Research Notes, *Marshal of the Last Frontier*, pg. 103–105.
21. *Memoirs of William Tilghman*, Handwritten by William Tilghman, *Marshal of the Last Frontier*, pg. 68–70, Zoe Tilghman Handwritten and Typed Research Notes, *Marshal of the Last Frontier*, pg. 107–108.
22. *Dodge City Times*, July 21, 1877.
23. Zoe Tilghman Handwritten and Typed Research Notes.
24. Zoe Tilghman Handwritten and Typed Research Notes, *Memoirs of William Tilghman*, Handwritten by William Tilghman, *Great Bend Register*, January 31, 1878.

25. Zoe Tilghman Handwritten and Typed Research Notes, *Memoirs of William Tilghman*, Handwritten by William Tilghman, *Bill Tilghman: Marshal of the Last Frontier*, pg. 67–68, *Dodge City Globe*, February 1, 1878.

26. *Winfield Courier*, February 7, 1878, *Dodge City Globe*, February 5, 1878.

27. *Dodge City Times*, February 16, 1878.

28. *Atchison Weekly Patriot*, February 23, 1878, *Great Gunfighters of the Kansas Cowtowns, 1867–1886.*

29. *Memoirs of William Tilghman*, Handwritten by William Tilghman, Zoe Tilghman Handwritten and Typed Research Notes, *Dodge City Globe*, April 23, 1878.

30. *Hays City Sentinel*, April 27, 1878, *Memoirs of William Tilghman*, Handwritten by William Tilghman, Zoe Tilghman Handwritten and Typed Research Notes.

31. *Memoirs of William Tilghman*, Handwritten by William Tilghman, *Bill Tilghman: Marshal of the Last Frontier*, pg. 68–69, Zoe Tilghman Handwritten and Typed Research Notes, *Marshal of the Last Frontier*, pg. 153.

32. *Memoirs of William Tilghman*, Handwritten by William Tilghman, *Bill Tilghman: Marshal of the Last Frontier*, pg. 68–69, Zoe Tilghman Handwritten and Typed Research Notes, *Marshal of the Last Frontier*, pg. 153.

33. *Marshal of the Last Frontier*, pg. 154–156, *Memoirs of William Tilghman*, Handwritten by William Tilghman, *Bill Tilghman: Marshal of the Last Frontier*, pg. 71–74, Zoe Tilghman Handwritten and Typed Research Notes.

34. *Dodge City Times*, October 12, 1878, *Sumner County Press*, October 14, 1878, *Oswego Independent*, October 26, 1828, *Marshal of the Last Frontier*, pg. 141, *Thunder Over the Prairie*, pg. 26–27, *Memoirs of William Tilghman*, Handwritten by William Tilghman.

35. *Ford County Globe*, October 29, 1878, *Memoirs of William Tilghman*, Handwritten by William Tilghman.

36. *Atchison Daily Champion*, October 23, 1878.

37. *Emporia Ledger*, December 5, 1879.

38. *Dodge City Globe*, January 7, 1879, *Marshal of the Last Frontier*, pg. 154–155, *Memoirs of William Tilghman*, Handwritten by William Tilghman.

39. *Southern Kansas Gazette*, October 17, 1878.

40. *Marshal of the Last Frontier*, pg. 154–155, *Memoirs of William Tilghman*, Handwritten by William Tilghman, *Atchinson Weekly Patriot*, January 4, 1879.

41. *Marshal of the Last Frontier*, pg. 155–157, *Memoirs of William Tilghman*, Handwritten by William Tilghman, Zoe Tilghman Handwritten and Typed Research Notes.

42. *Marshal of the Last Frontier*, pg. 155–157, *Memoirs of William Tilghman*, Handwritten by William Tilghman, Zoe Tilghman Handwritten and Typed Research Notes.

43. *Marshal of the Last Frontier*, pg. 155–157, *Memoirs of William Tilghman*, Handwritten by William Tilghman, Zoe Tilghman Handwritten and Typed Research Notes.

44. *Marshal of the Last Frontier*, pg. 155–157, *Memoirs of William Tilghman*, Handwritten by William Tilghman, Zoe Tilghman Handwritten and Typed Research Notes.

45. *Marshal of the Last Frontier*, pg. 156–158, *Memoirs of William Tilghman*, Handwritten by William Tilghman, Zoe Tilghman Handwritten and Typed Research Notes.

46. *Marshal of the Last Frontier*, pg. 155–157, *Memoirs of William Tilghman*, Handwritten by William Tilghman, Zoe Tilghman Handwritten and Typed Research Notes.

47. *Marshal of the Last Frontier*, pg. 158–159, *Memoirs of William Tilghman*, Handwritten by William Tilghman, Zoe Tilghman Handwritten and Typed Research Notes.

48. *Memoirs of William Tilghman*, Handwritten by William Tilghman, Zoe Tilghman Handwritten and Typed Research Notes, *Dodge City Globe*, April 3, 1883, *Garden City Herald*, May 5, 1883, *Journal Democrat*, April 5, 1884, *Marshal of the Last Frontier*, pg. 160–161.

49. *Marshal of the Last Frontier*, pg. 160–161, *Dodge City Globe*, March 25, 1884, *Journal Democrat*, March 29, 1884.

50. *Marshal of the Last Frontier*, pg. 160–161, *Memoirs of William Tilghman*, Handwritten by William Tilghman, Zoe Tilghman Handwritten and Typed Research Notes.

51. Zoe Tilghman Handwritten and Typed Research Notes.

CHAPTER 2

1. *Duncan Banner*, May 29, 1925, *Wewoka Capital Democrat*, May 28, 1925.

2. Zoe A. Tilghman Handwritten and Typed Research Notes.

3. Zoe A. Tilghman Handwritten and Typed Research Notes, *Okmulgee Daily Times*, October 13, 1925, https://gateway.okhistory.org/ark:/67531/metadc2017330/.

4. *Atoka County Jeffersonian*, June 11, 1925.

5. Zoe A. Tilghman Handwritten and Typed Research Notes, https://gateway.okhistory.org/ark:/67531/metadc2017330/, *The Oklahoman*, August 9, 1936.

6. *Bill Tilghman: Marshal of the Last Frontier*, pg. 138–139.

7. *The Globe*, May 6, 1884, *Bill Tilghman: Marshal of the Last Frontier*, pg. 83–84.

8. *Dodge City Kansas Cowboy*, August 9, 1884.

9. *Dodge City Democrat*, August 16, 1884, *Memoirs of William Tilghman*, Handwritten by William Tilghman.

10. *Dodge City Kansas Cowboy*, August 29, 1885, *Dodge City Globe*, March 31, 1885, *Bill Tilghman: Marshal of the Last Frontier*, pg. 84–85, *Memoirs of William Tilghman*, Handwritten by William Tilghman, Zoe A. Tilghman Handwritten and Typed Research Notes.

11. *Memoirs of William Tilghman*, Handwritten by William Tilghman, Zoe A. Tilghman Handwritten and Typed Research Notes, *Bill Tilghman: Marshal of the Last Frontier*, pg. 84–85, https://www.gunpolicy.org/firearms/citation/quotes/11281.

12. *Memoirs of William Tilghman*, Handwritten by William Tilghman, Zoe A. Tilghman Handwritten and Typed Research Notes, *Bill Tilghman: Marshal of the Last Frontier*, pg. 85–87.

13. *Kansas Cowboy*, August 23, 1884, *Bill Tilghman: Marshal of the Last Frontier*, pg. 85–87, *Memoirs of William Tilghman*, Handwritten by William Tilghman, Zoe A. Tilghman Handwritten and Typed Research Notes.

14. *Kansas Cowboy*, August 23, 1884, *Bill Tilghman: Marshal of the Last Frontier*, pg. 85–87, *Memoirs of William Tilghman*, Handwritten by William Tilghman, Zoe A. Tilghman Handwritten and Typed Research Notes.

15. *Marshal of the Last Frontier*, pg. 162–163, *Dodge City Globe*, March 25, 1884, *The Globe*, March 9, 1886, *Memoirs of William Tilghman*, Handwritten by William Tilghman, Zoe A. Tilghman Handwritten and Typed Research Notes.

16. *Memoirs of William Tilghman*, Handwritten by William Tilghman, Zoe A. Tilghman Handwritten and Typed Research Notes, *Dodge City Globe*, May 25, 1886, *The Sun*, September 9, 1886, *Dodge City Times*, September 23, 1886, *Bill Tilghman: Marshal of the Last Frontier*, pg. 88–89.

17. *Dodge City Times*, November 18, 1886, *Bill Tilghman: Marshal of the Last Frontier*, pg. 89–90, *Memoirs of William Tilghman*, Handwritten by William Tilghman, Zoe A. Tilghman Handwritten and Typed Research Notes.

18. http://genealogytrails.com/kan/allen/history2.html, *Leoti Transcript*, July 5, 1888.

19. *Evening Kansan*, July 6, 1888, *Leoti Transcript*, July 5, 1888, *Alma News*, July 12, 1888, *Fort Scott Daily Monitor*, April 23, 1889.

20. *Grant County Register*, July 14, 1888.

21. *Oklahoma Capital*, April 27, 1888, *Guthrie Democrat*, August 4, 1890, *Marshal of the Last Frontier*, pg. 180–181, *Memoirs of William Tilghman*, Handwritten by William Tilghman, Zoe A. Tilghman Handwritten and Typed Research Notes, *Guthrie Democrat*, July 25, 1890.

22. *Guthrie Democrat*, July 21, 1890, *Memoirs of William Tilghman*, Handwritten by William Tilghman, Zoe A. Tilghman Handwritten and Typed Research Notes.

23. *Chandler News*, October 24, 1891, Zoe A. Tilghman Handwritten and Typed Research Notes.

24. *Jennings Daily News*, April 16, 1931, *Marshal of the Last Frontier*, pg. 186–187, *Memoirs of William Tilghman*, Handwritten by William Tilghman, Zoe A. Tilghman Handwritten and Typed Research Notes.

25. *Perry Daily Times*, November 20, 1893, *Marshal of the Last Frontier*, pg. 180–181, *Memoirs of William Tilghman*, Handwritten by William Tilghman, Zoe A. Tilghman Handwritten and Typed Research Notes.

26. *Marshal of the Last Frontier*, pg. 195–197, *Kingfisher Times*, November 16, 1892.

27. *Marshal of the Last Frontier*, pg. 195–197, *Memoirs of William Tilghman*, Handwritten by William Tilghman, Zoe A. Tilghman Handwritten and Typed Research Notes.

28. *Marshal of the Last Frontier*, pg. 195–197, *Memoirs of William Tilghman*, Handwritten by William Tilghman, Zoe A. Tilghman Handwritten and Typed Research Notes.

29. *Marshal of the Last Frontier*, pg. 195–197, *Memoirs of William Tilghman*, Handwritten by William Tilghman, Zoe A. Tilghman Handwritten and Typed Research Notes.

30. *Marshal of the Last Frontier*, pg. 195–197, *Memoirs of William Tilghman*, Handwritten by William Tilghman, Zoe A. Tilghman Handwritten and Typed Research Notes, *Encyclopedia of Western Lawmen and Outlaws*, pg. 95–97.

31. *Marshal of the Last Frontier*, pg. 195–197, *Memoirs of William Tilghman*, Handwritten by William Tilghman, Zoe A. Tilghman Handwritten and Typed Research Notes, *Encyclopedia of Western Lawmen and Outlaws*, pg. 95–97.

32. *Norman Democrat Topic*, August 27, 1891, *Muskogee Phoenix*, May 28, 1891, *Oklahoma State Capital*, September 19, 1891, *Encyclopedia of Western Lawmen and Outlaws*, pg. 95–97, *Marshal of the Last Frontier*, pg. 188–189.

33. *Marshal of the Last Frontier*, pg. 188–189, Zoe A. Tilghman Handwritten and Typed Research Notes.

34. *Kansas City Times*, October 9, 1893, *Bill Tilghman: Marshal of the Last Frontier*, pg. 102–105, https://encyclopediaofarkansas.net/entries/bill-doolin-1632/.

35. https://www.nps.gov/fosm/learn/historyculture/payment-of-deputy-marshals.htm, *Memoirs of William Tilghman*, Handwritten by William Tilghman, Zoe A. Tilghman Handwritten and Typed Research Notes

36. Zoe A. Tilghman Handwritten and Typed Research Notes.

37. *Oklahoma News*, March 10, 1926, *Oklahoma State Register*, May 20, 1926, Zoe A. Tilghman Handwritten and Typed Research Notes.

38. *Oklahoma News*, April 14, 1926, Zoe A. Tilghman Handwritten and Typed Research Notes.

39. Zoe A. Tilghman Handwritten and Typed Research Notes, *Harlow's Weekly*, April 10, 1926, *Harlow's Weekly*, April 17, 1926.

40. *Harlow's Weekly*, May 8, 1926.

41. https://gateway.okhistory.org/ark:/67531/metadc2017330/, Zoe A. Tilghman Handwritten and Typed Research Notes.

Chapter 3

1. *Chickasha Daily Express*, October 7, 1929, *Verden News*, October 11, 1929.

2. *Chickasha Daily Express*, October 7, 1929, *Verden News*, October 11, 1929.

3. *Chickasha Daily Express*, October 7, 1929, *Verden News*, October 11, 1929.

4. *Chickasha Daily Express*, October 7, 1929, *Verden News*, October 11, 1929.

5. *Oklahoma County News*, December 9, 1927, Zoe A. Tilghman Historical Document Collection.

6. Zoe A. Tilghman Historical Document Collection.

7. Ibid.

8. Zoe A. Tilghman Historical Document Collection, *Verden News*, October 11, 1929, *Cleveland Co. Democrat News*, October 10, 1929.

9. Zoe A. Tilghman Historical Document Collection, *Washington Post*, December 14, 1927, *Blackwell Morning Tribune*, October 29, 1929.

10. *Bartlesville Daily Enterprise*, October 29, 1929, *Verden News*, November 1, 1929.

11. *Bartlesville Daily Enterprise*, October 29, 1929, *Verden News*, November 1, 1929, *Oklahoma News*, October 31, 1929.

12. *Pittsburgh Press*, January 9, 1930, *Cushing Daily Citizen*, January 8, 1930.

13. *Cushing Daily Citizen*, January 8, 1930.

14. Ibid.

15. *Chickasha Star*, January 9, 1930.

16. Ibid.

17. Ibid.

18. *Kenosha Evening News*, January 10, 1930.

19. *Clinton Daily News*, January 14, 1930, *Walters Herald*, March 20, 1930, *Wichita Daily Times*, March 16, 1930.

20. *Wichita Daily Times*, March 16, 1930.

21. Ibid.

22. *Cushing Daily Citizen*, May 24, 1930, *Oklahoma County News*, May 16, 1930.

23. *Oklahoma County News*, May 26, 1930.

24. *Harlow's Weekly*, March 29, 1930.

25. Ibid.

26. Zoe A. Tilghman Handwritten and Typed Research Notes.

27. Zoe A. Tilghman Handwritten and Typed Research Notes, *Memoirs of William Tilghman*, Handwritten by William Tilghman, *Bill Tilghman: Marshal of the Last Frontier*, pg. 120–122.

28. *Memoirs of William Tilghman*, Handwritten by William Tilghman.

29. *Memoirs of William Tilghman*, Handwritten by William Tilghman, *Lost Mines and Buried Treasures of Oklahoma*, pg. 2–6.

30. *Bill Tilghman: Marshal of the Last Frontier*, pg. 121–122, *Encyclopedia of Western Lawmen and Outlaws*, pg. 106–107, *Marshall of the Last Frontier*, pg. 206–207.

31. *Bill Tilghman: Marshal of the Last Frontier*, pg. 121–122, *Encyclopedia of Western Lawmen and Outlaws*, pg. 106–107, *Marshall of the Last Frontier*, pg. 206–207.

32. https://www.usmarshals.gov/who-we-are/history/historical-reading-room/deputies-versus-wild-bunch, US Marshal Service.

33. *Memoirs of William Tilghman*, Handwritten by William Tilghman, *The Encyclopedia of American Crime*, pg. 89–95.

34. *Memoirs of William Tilghman*, Handwritten by William Tilghman, *Tecumseh Republican*, June 15, 1893, *Chronicles of Oklahoma,* Spring 1958, *Three Guardsmen and the Doolin Gang*, pg. 429–445.

35. *Memoirs of William Tilghman*, Handwritten by William Tilghman, *Daily Oklahoman*, June 12, 1970, https://www.usmarshals.gov/who-we-are/history/historical-reading-room/deputies-versus-wild-bunch, https://www.ancestry.com Rose Dunn.

36. *Heck Thomas: Frontier Marshal; The Story of a Real Gunfighter*, pg. 176–177, *Guthrie Daily Leader*, July 13, 1893, *Guthrie Daily Leader*, September 21, 1893.

37. *Heck Thomas: Frontier Marshal; The Story of a Real Gunfighter*, pg. 176–177, *Guthrie Daily Leader*, September 24, 1893, *Oklahoma Times Journal*, November 1, 1893.

38. *Heck Thomas: Frontier Marshal; The Story of a Real Gunfighter*, pg. 177–180, *Memoirs of William Tilghman*, Handwritten by William Tilghman.

39. *Weekly Oklahoma State Capital*, October 7, 1893.

40. *Memoirs of William Tilghman*, Handwritten by William Tilghman, *Heck Thomas: Frontier Marshal; The Story of a Real Gunfighter*, pg. 181–182, *Evening Democrat*, November 14, 1893, *Bill Tilghman: Marshal of the Last Frontier*, pg. 113–115.

41. *Evening Democrat*, November 15, 1893, *Perry Daily Times*, November 24, 1893, *Evening Democrat*, November 4, 1893.

42. *Perry Daily Times*, December 11, 1893, *Guthrie Daily Leader*, December 13, 1893, *Edmond Sun Democrat*, January 5, 1894.

43. *Evening Democrat*, December 14, 1893.

44. *Memoirs of William Tilghman*, Handwritten by William Tilghman, *Evening Democrat*, December 6, 1893, *Perry Daily Times*, December 26, 1893.

45. Zoe A. Tilghman Handwritten and Typed Research Notes, *Vici Beacon*, June 5, 1930.

46. *Memoirs of William Tilghman*, Handwritten by William Tilghman, Zoe A. Tilghman Handwritten and Typed Research Notes.

47. *Memoirs of William Tilghman*, Handwritten by William Tilghman.

48. Ibid.

49. Ibid.

50. Ibid.

51. Ibid.

52. *Memoirs of William Tilghman*, Handwritten by William Tilghman, Zoe A. Tilghman Handwritten and Typed Research Notes.

CHAPTER 4

1. *Memoirs of William Tilghman*, Handwritten by William Tilghman, *Heck Thomas: Frontier Marshal; The Story of a Real Gunfighter*, pg. 151–154.

2. *Memoirs of William Tilghman*, Handwritten by William Tilghman, *Guthrie Daily Leader*, October 24, 1893, *Weekly Oklahoma State Capital,* October 14, 1893.

3. *Memoirs of William Tilghman*, Handwritten by William Tilghman, *Marshal of the Last Frontier* pg. 208–209, *Bill Tilghman: Marshal of the Last Frontier*, pg. 127–128, *Heck Thomas: Frontier Marshal; The Story of a Real Gunfighter*, pg. 151–154.

4. *Memoirs of William Tilghman*, Handwritten by William Tilghman, *Marshal of the Last Frontier* pg. 208–209, *Bill Tilghman: Marshal of the Last Frontier*, pg. 127–128, *Heck Thomas: Frontier Marshal; The Story of a Real Gunfighter*, pg. 151–154.

5. *Memoirs of William Tilghman*, Handwritten by William Tilghman, *Marshal of the Last Frontier* pg. 208–209, *Bill Tilghman: Marshal of the Last Frontier*, pg. 127–128, *Heck Thomas: Frontier Marshal; The Story of a Real Gunfighter*, pg. 151–154.

6. *Memoirs of William Tilghman*, Handwritten by William Tilghman, *Marshal of the Last Frontier* pg. 208–209, *Bill Tilghman: Marshal of the Last Frontier*, pg. 127–128, *Heck Thomas: Frontier Marshal; The Story of a Real Gunfighter*, pg. 151–154.

7. Zoe A. Tilghman Handwritten and Typed Research Notes, *Frederick Leader*, September 22, 1931, *Magnum Daily Star*, July 8, 1931, *Blackwell Journal Tribune*, January 3, 1931, *Daily Oklahoman*, January 3, 1931.

8. Zoe A. Tilghman Handwritten and Typed Research Notes, *Daily Oklahoman*, July 17, 1932, *Seminole Producer*, January 17, 1932, *Harlow's Weekly*, January 3, 1931.

9. *Oklahoma News*, May 21, 1932, *Oklahoma News*, July 25, 1932, *Oklahoma County News*, August 26, 1932, *Cushing Daily Citizen*, August 19, 1932.

10. *Memoirs of William Tilghman*, Handwritten by William Tilghman, Zoe A. Tilghman Handwritten and Typed Research Notes, *Marshal of the Last Frontier,* pg. 207–208.

11. *Memoirs of William Tilghman*, Handwritten by William Tilghman, Zoe A. Tilghman Handwritten and Typed Research Notes, *Chickasaw Chiefton*, June 14, 1894, *Mulhall Enterprise*, June 16, 1894, *Cleveland County Leader*, June 16, 1894.

12. *Memoirs of William Tilghman*, Handwritten by William Tilghman, Zoe A. Tilghman Handwritten and Typed Research Notes, *Chickasaw Chiefton*, June 14, 1894, *Mulhall Enterprise*, June 16, 1894, *Cleveland County Leader*, June 16, 1894.

13. *Memoirs of William Tilghman*, Handwritten by William Tilghman, Zoe A. Tilghman Handwritten and Typed Research Notes.

14. *Memoirs of William Tilghman*, Handwritten by William Tilghman, Zoe A. Tilghman Handwritten and Typed Research Notes, *Vinita Leader*, September 12, 1895, *Arapaho Bee*, September 18, 1895.

15. *Memoirs of William Tilghman*, Handwritten by William Tilghman, Zoe A. Tilghman Handwritten and Typed Research Notes.

16. *Memoirs of William Tilghman*, Handwritten by William Tilghman, Zoe A. Tilghman Handwritten and Typed Research Notes.

17. *Memoirs of William Tilghman*, Handwritten by William Tilghman, Zoe A. Tilghman Handwritten and Typed Research Notes.

18. *Memoirs of William Tilghman*, Handwritten by William Tilghman, Zoe A. Tilghman Handwritten and Typed Research Notes.

19. *Memoirs of William Tilghman*, Handwritten by William Tilghman, Zoe A. Tilghman Handwritten and Typed Research Notes, *Marshal of the Last Frontier* pg. 216–217.

20. *Memoirs of William Tilghman*, Handwritten by William Tilghman, Zoe A. Tilghman Handwritten and Typed Research Notes, *Encyclopedia of Western Lawmen and Outlaws*, pg. 263.

21. *Memoirs of William Tilghman*, Handwritten by William Tilghman, Zoe A. Tilghman Handwritten and Typed Research Notes, *Guthrie Daily Leader*, May 3, 1895, *Oklahoma Daily Star*, May 4, 1895, *Times Democrat*, May 10, 1895.

22. *Memoirs of William Tilghman*, Handwritten by William Tilghman, Zoe A. Tilghman Handwritten and Typed Research Notes, *Oklahoma Daily Star*, May 4, 1895, *Beaver Herald*, May 9, 1895.

23. *Memoirs of William Tilghman*, Handwritten by William Tilghman, Zoe A. Tilghman Handwritten and Typed Research Notes, *Marshal of the Last Frontier*, pg. 217–218.

24. *Memoirs of William Tilghman*, Handwritten by William Tilghman, Zoe A. Tilghman Handwritten and Typed Research Notes.

25. *Memoirs of William Tilghman*, Handwritten by William Tilghman, Zoe A. Tilghman Handwritten and Typed Research Notes.

26. *Memoirs of William Tilghman*, Handwritten by William Tilghman, Zoe A. Tilghman Handwritten and Typed Research Notes, *Weekly Oklahoma State Capital*, January 12, 1896.

27. *Weekly Oklahoma State Capital*, January 16, 1896.

28. Ibid.

29. Ibid.

30. *Bill Tilghman: Marshal of the Last Frontier*, pg. 171–172, *Tecumseh Republican*, March 13, 1896, *Weekly Oklahoma State Capital*, March 16, 1896.

31. *Memoirs of William Tilghman*, Handwritten by William Tilghman, Zoe A. Tilghman Handwritten and Typed Research Notes.

32. *Memoirs of William Tilghman*, Handwritten by William Tilghman, Zoe A. Tilghman Handwritten and Typed Research Notes.

33. *Ponca City Democrat*, December 10, 1896, *Chandler Publicist*, December 11, 1896.

34. *Ponca City Democrat*, December 10, 1896, *Chandler Publicist*, December 11, 1896.

35. *Memoirs of William Tilghman*, Handwritten by William Tilghman, Zoe A. Tilghman Handwritten and Typed Research Notes.

36. *Lamar Republican*, August 21, 1924, *Encyclopedia of Western Lawmen and Outlaws*, pg. 101.
37. *Life Magazine*, May 18, 1959, *Memoirs of William Tilghman*, Handwritten by William Tilghman, Zoe A. Tilghman Handwritten and Typed Research Notes.
38. *Memoirs of William Tilghman*, Handwritten by William Tilghman, Zoe A. Tilghman Handwritten and Typed Research Notes, *Chandler Publicist*, February 24, 1899, *Marshal of the Last Frontier*, pg. 235–237, *Bill Tilghman: Marshal of the Last Frontier*, pg. 174–176.
39. *Memoirs of William Tilghman*, Handwritten by William Tilghman.
40. *Memoirs of William Tilghman*, Handwritten by William Tilghman, Zoe A. Tilghman Handwritten and Typed Research Notes.
41. *Weekly Oklahoma State Capital*, March 31, 1899, *Daily Ardmoreite*, February 8, 1899, *Chandler Publicist*, July 28, 1899.
42. *Memoirs of William Tilghman*, Handwritten by William Tilghman, Zoe A. Tilghman Handwritten and Typed Research Notes, *Chandler News*, April 21, 1899, *Marshal of the Last Frontier*, pg. 235–236, *Chandler Publicist*, February 2, 1899.
43. *Weekly Oklahoma State Capital*, October 14, 1900, *Lincoln County Democrat*, October 18, 1900, *Publicist*, October 19, 1900, *Bill Tilghman: Marshal of the Last Frontier*, pg. 178–179.
44. *Memoirs of William Tilghman*, Handwritten by William Tilghman, Zoe A. Tilghman Handwritten and Typed Research Notes.
45. Zoe A. Tilghman Handwritten and Typed Research Notes.

Chapter 5

1. *Memoirs of William Tilghman*, Handwritten by William Tilghman.
2. *The Publicist*, June 8, 1900, *Chandler News*, January 24, 1901, *The Publicist*, August 17, 1900, *Chandler Publicist*, November 2, 1900.
3. *Memoirs of William Tilghman*, Handwritten by William Tilghman, Zoe A. Tilghman Handwritten and Typed Research Notes, *Stillwater Gazette*, May 16, 1901, *Chandler News*, May 9, 1901.
4. *Memoirs of William Tilghman*, Handwritten by William Tilghman, Zoe A. Tilghman Handwritten and Typed Research Notes, *Stillwater Gazette*, May 16, 1901, *Chandler News*, May 9, 1901.
5. *Norman Transcript*, May 16, 1901.
6. *Memoirs of William Tilghman*, Handwritten by William Tilghman, Zoe A. Tilghman Handwritten and Typed Research Notes, *Jefferson Review*, November 20, 1903, *Marshal of the Last Frontier*, pg. 250–252, *Chandler Publicist*, November 6, 1903, *Chandler Publicist*, November 4, 1903.
7. *Memoirs of William Tilghman*, Handwritten by William Tilghman, Zoe A. Tilghman Handwritten and Typed Research Notes.
8. *Memoirs of William Tilghman*, Handwritten by William Tilghman, Zoe A. Tilghman Handwritten and Typed Research Notes, *Chandler Publicist*, November 6, 1903.

9. *Memoirs of William Tilghman*, Handwritten by William Tilghman, Zoe A. Tilghman Handwritten and Typed Research Notes, *Weekly Oklahoma State Capital*, November 14, 1903, *El Reno Daily American*, November 11, 1903.

10. *Chandler Publicist*, November 18, 1904, *El Reno Weekly Globe*, November 11, 1904, *Shawnee Herald*, November 13, 1904.

11. *Chandler News*, September 18, 1901.

12. *Memoirs of William Tilghman*, Handwritten by William Tilghman, Zoe A. Tilghman Handwritten and Typed Research Notes.

13. *Memoirs of William Tilghman*, Handwritten by William Tilghman, Zoe A. Tilghman Handwritten and Typed Research Notes.

14. *Chandler Publicist*, September 18, 1903.

15. *Chandler Publicist*, September 18, 1903, *Memoirs of William Tilghman*, Handwritten by William Tilghman, Zoe A. Tilghman Handwritten and Typed Research Notes.

16. *Kansas City Star*, April 12, 1931.

17. Ibid.

18. Ibid.

19. *Daily Oklahoman*, June 7, 1932, *Sooner State Press*, February 25, 1933, *Blue Valley Farmer*, February 25, 1903, *Luther Register*, February 23, 1933, Zoe A. Tilghman Handwritten and Typed Research Notes.

20. *Kansas City Star*, February 17, 1933.

21. *Memoirs of William Tilghman*, Handwritten by William Tilghman, Zoe A. Tilghman Handwritten and Typed Research Notes.

22. *Stillwater Gazette*, July 3, 1902, *Stillwater Democrat*, October 9, 1902, *People's Voice*, September 19, 1902, *Marshal of the Last Frontier*, pg. 257–258, *Bill Tilghman: Marshal of the Last Frontier*, pg. 178–179.

23. *Memoirs of William Tilghman*, Handwritten by William Tilghman, Zoe A. Tilghman Handwritten and Typed Research Notes.

24. *Memoirs of William Tilghman*, Handwritten by William Tilghman, Zoe A. Tilghman Handwritten and Typed Research Notes, *The Observer*, January 23, 1902, *Southwest World*, March 29, 1902, *The Observer*, February 8, 1902.

25. *Memoirs of William Tilghman*, Handwritten by William Tilghman, Zoe A. Tilghman Handwritten and Typed Research Notes, *Stroud Sun*, July 17, 1903, *Ripley Times*, June 17, 1903.

26. *Memoirs of William Tilghman*, Handwritten by William Tilghman, Zoe A. Tilghman Handwritten and Typed Research Notes, *Chandler Publicist*, March 9, 1900, *Chandler News*, October 23, 1902, *Chandler News*, October 10, 1901, *Chandler News*, February 25, 1904, *Chandler Tribune*, February 5, 1904.

27. *Memoirs of William Tilghman*, Handwritten by William Tilghman, Zoe A. Tilghman Handwritten and Typed Research Notes, *Chandler Tribune*, August 14, 1903, *Claremore Messenger*, August 28, 1903.

28. *Chandler Publicist*, September 25, 1903.

29. *Memoirs of William Tilghman*, Handwritten by William Tilghman, Zoe A. Tilghman Handwritten and Typed Research Notes, *Chandler Tribune*, December 30, 1904, *Chandler Publicist*, December 30, 1904, *Chandler Daily Publicist*, January 25, 1904.

30. Zoe A. Tilghman Handwritten and Typed Research Notes, *Bill Tilghman: Marshal of the Last Frontier*, pg. 183–184.

31. Zoe A. Tilghman Handwritten and Typed Research Notes, *Bill Tilghman: Marshal of the Last Frontier*, pg. 183–184.

32. *Memoirs of William Tilghman*, Handwritten by William Tilghman, Zoe A. Tilghman Handwritten and Typed Research Notes, Zoe A. Tilghman Historical Document Collection, *Bill Tilghman: Marshal of the Last Frontier*, pg. 183–184, *Marshal of the Last Frontier*, pg. 260–261.

33. *Chandler Daily Publicist*, February 28, 1905, *People's Press*, April 27, 1905, *El Reno Democrat*, March 2, 1905.

34. Zoe A. Tilghman Historical Document Collection.

35. Ibid.

36. *Memoirs of William Tilghman*, Handwritten by William Tilghman, Zoe A. Tilghman Handwritten and Typed Research Notes, *Marshal of the Last Frontier*, pg. 261–262, *Bill Tilghman: Marshal of the Last Frontier*, pg. 184–185.

37. *Memoirs of William Tilghman*, Handwritten by William Tilghman, Zoe A. Tilghman Handwritten and Typed Research Notes, *Marshal of the Last Frontier*, pg. 261–262, *Bill Tilghman: Marshal of the Last Frontier*, pg. 184–185.

38. *Memoirs of William Tilghman*, Handwritten by William Tilghman, Zoe A. Tilghman Handwritten and Typed Research Notes, *Marshal of the Last Frontier*, pg. 261–262, *Bill Tilghman: Marshal of the Last Frontier*, pg. 184–185.

39. *Memoirs of William Tilghman*, Handwritten by William Tilghman, Zoe A. Tilghman Handwritten and Typed Research Notes, *Marshal of the Last Frontier*, pg. 261–262, *Bill Tilghman: Marshal of the Last Frontier*, pg. 184–185, *Chandler Daily Publicist*, February 28, 1905.

40. Zoe A. Tilghman Historical Document Collection, *Memoirs of William Tilghman*, Handwritten by William Tilghman, *Chandler Daily Publicist*, February 28, 1905, *Oklahoma State Register*, March 2, 1905.

41. *Memoirs of William Tilghman*, Handwritten by William Tilghman, Zoe A. Tilghman Handwritten and Typed Research Notes, *Chicago Tribune*, September 29, 1905, https://www.ancestry.com Tench Tilghman.

42. *Daily Oklahoman*, January 29, 1930, *Norman Transcript*, January 28, 1930, *Oklahoma News*, March 18, 1934, *Seminole Producer*, January 17, 1932, *Chickasha Daily Express*, November 22, 1933.

43. Zoe A. Tilghman Handwritten and Typed Research Notes, *Sooner State Press*, April 4, 1931, *Chandler Daily Publicist*, November 2, 1905.

44. *Harlow's Weekly*, November 18, 1933.

45. Zoe A. Tilghman Handwritten and Typed Research Notes, *Weekly State Democrat*, January 25, 1906, *Stroud Messenger*, February 9, 1906, *Funk & Wagnalls New Encyclopedia* Volume 18.

CHAPTER 6

1. *Chandler News*, January 31, 1907.

2. *Oklahoma Weekly Leader*, March 14, 1907, *Chandler Tribune*, March 26, 1907, *Chandler Publicist*, March 29, 1907.

3. *Sparks Review*, April 19, 1907.

4. Ibid.

5. *Chandler Publicist*, January 25, 1907.

6. *Lincoln County Journal/Stroud Star*, June 6, 1907.

7. *Sparks Review*, May 26, 1907, *Chandler Publicist*, May 24, 1907.

8. *Chandler Tribune*, June 4, 1907.

9. Ibid.

10. Ibid.

11. *Chandler Tribune*, July 30, 1907.

12. Ibid.

13. Ibid.

14. Ibid.

15. *Chandler Publicist*, August 23, 1907, *Chandler Tribune*, August 20, 1907.

16. *Chandler Publicist*, September 6, 1907, Zoe A. Tilghman Handwritten and Typed Research Notes.

17. *Chandler Publicist*, September 6, 1907.

18. *Chandler Tribune*, September 10, 1907.

19. Ibid.

20. Ibid.

21. Ibid.

22. Ibid.

23. Ibid.

24. *Daily Oklahoman*, November 17, 1907.

25. *Oklahoma State Capital*, July 4, 1908, *Blackwell Daily News*, June 12, 1908.

26. *Foraker Sun*, October 27, 1911.

27. *Chandler News*, February 6, 1908, *Chandler Tribune*, March 27, 1908, https://www.ancestry.com Dorothy Tilghman.

28. *Shawnee Daily Herald*, June 14, 1908.

29. *Walters Herald*, July 4, 1935, *Grandfield Enterprise*, July 4, 1935, *Harlow's Weekly*, August 20, 1932.

30. *Harlow's Weekly*, August 20, 1932.

31. *Memoirs of William Tilghman*, Handwritten by William Tilghman, Zoe A. Tilghman Handwritten and Typed Research Notes.

32. *Funk & Wagnalls New Encyclopedia* Volume 14.

33. *Perry Republican*, September 10, 1908.

34. *The Independent*, September 3, 1908.

35. *Memoirs of William Tilghman*, Handwritten by William Tilghman, Zoe A. Tilghman Handwritten and Typed Research Notes, *County Democrat*, September 4, 1908, *Chandler News*, March 18, 1909.

36. *Memoirs of William Tilghman*, Handwritten by William Tilghman, Zoe A. Tilghman Handwritten and Typed Research Notes, *Chandler News*, March 18, 1909.

37. *Weekly Oklahoma State Capital,* January 16, 1896, *Memoirs of William Tilghman,* Handwritten by William Tilghman, Zoe A. Tilghman Handwritten and Typed Research Notes.

38. *Weekly Oklahoma State Capital,* January 16, 1896, *Memoirs of William Tilghman,* Handwritten by William Tilghman, Zoe A. Tilghman Handwritten and Typed Research Notes.

39. *Weekly Oklahoma State Capital,* January 16, 1896, *Memoirs of William Tilghman,* Handwritten by William Tilghman, Zoe A. Tilghman Handwritten and Typed Research Notes.

40. *Memoirs of William Tilghman,* Handwritten by William Tilghman, Zoe A. Tilghman Handwritten and Typed Research Notes.

41. *Memoirs of William Tilghman,* Handwritten by William Tilghman, Zoe A. Tilghman Handwritten and Typed Research Notes.

42. *Funk & Wagnalls New Encyclopedia* Volume 7, *Oklahoma State Capital,* April 8, 1909, *Bill Tilghman: Marshal of the Last Frontier,* pg. 191–192.

43. *Memoirs of William Tilghman,* Handwritten by William Tilghman, Zoe A. Tilghman Handwritten and Typed Research Notes.

44. *Shawnee Daily Herald,* March 30, 1909, *The Great Confusion in Indian Affairs: Native Americans and Whites in the Progressive Era, Oklahoma State Capital,* March 30, 1909.

45. *Oklahoma State Capital,* April 3, 1909, *Oklahoma State Capital,* April 16, 1909.

46. *Macon News,* April 15, 1911, *Marshal of the Last Frontier,* pg. 273–274.

47. Zoe A. Tilghman Handwritten and Typed Research Notes, *Miami Daily News Record,* August 2, 1935, *Daily Oklahoman,* August 3, 1935, *Oklahoma News,* August 5, 1935, *Daily Oklahoman,* October 8, 1935, *Oklahoma News,* October 8, 1935.

48. *Oklahoma News,* November 27, 1935.

49. Zoe A. Tilghman Handwritten and Typed Research Notes, *Waurika News Democrat,* November 15, 1935.

50. Zoe A. Tilghman Handwritten and Typed Research Notes, *Waurika News Democrat,* November 15, 1935.

51. *Oklahoma News,* January 28, 1936, *Butler Herald,* January 16, 1936.

52. *Oklahoma News,* February 5, 1936.

53. *Miami Daily News Record,* July 15, 1936, *Oklahoma News,* June 15, 1936.

54. *Daily Oklahoman,* June 16, 1936, Zoe A. Tilghman Handwritten and Typed Research Notes.

55. *Chandler Tribune,* June 24, 1910.

56. Ibid.

57. *Tulsa Post,* January 12, 1911, *Okmulgee Republican,* July 20, 1911, Zoe A. Tilghman Historical Document Collection.

58. *Okmulgee Republican,* July 20, 1911, *Daily Oklahoman,* June 10, 1910, https://www.johnjdwyer.com/post/2017/07/06_Swiping the Seal-Guthrie vs. OKC for State Capital.

59. *Okmulgee Republican,* July 20, 1911.

60. *Chandler Tribune,* July 21, 1911, *Marshal of the Last Frontier,* pg. 194–195.

61. *Chandler Tribune,* July 14, 1911, *Daily Midget,* July 11, 1911.

62. *Memoirs of William Tilghman*, Handwritten by William Tilghman, Zoe A. Tilghman Handwritten and Typed Research Notes, *Chelsea Reporter*, July 27, 1911.

63. *Shawnee News*, August 14, 1911.

64. *Oklahoma City Times*, September 28, 1912, *Oklahoma City Times*, August 1, 1912, *Marshal of the Last Frontier*, pg. 201–202.

65. *Memoirs of William Tilghman*, Handwritten by William Tilghman, Zoe A. Tilghman Handwritten and Typed Research Notes.

Chapter 7

1. *Memoirs of William Tilghman*, Handwritten by William Tilghman, Zoe A. Tilghman Handwritten and Typed Research Notes.

2. *Memoirs of William Tilghman*, Handwritten by William Tilghman, Zoe A. Tilghman Handwritten and Typed Research Notes, *Marshal of the Last Frontier*, pg. 296–298, *Oklahoma News*, October 25, 1912.

3. *Memoirs of William Tilghman*, Handwritten by William Tilghman, Zoe A. Tilghman Handwritten and Typed Research Notes, *Marshal of the Last Frontier*, pg. 299.

4. Zoe A. Tilghman Historical Document Collection, *Meeker Herald*, March 7, 1913.

5. Zoe A. Tilghman Historical Document Collection, *Meeker Herald*, March 7, 1913.

6. *Chandler Tribune*, March 6, 1913, *Marshal of the Last Frontier*, pg. 304–305, *Meeker Herald*, March 7, 1913, *Bartlesville Examiner Enterprise*, March 27, 1913.

7. *Bartlesville Examiner Enterprise*, March 27, 1913.

8. *Enid Morning News*, April 3, 1913, *Daily Armoreite*, March 28, 1913, *Chandler Tribune*, July 24, 1913, *Chandler Tribune*, September 25, 1913.

9. Zoe A. Tilghman Handwritten and Typed Research Notes, *Oklahoma News*, May 14, 1937, *Oklahoma News*, May 23, 1937.

10. Zoe A. Tilghman Handwritten and Typed Research Notes, *Daily Oklahoman*, December 15, 1937.

11. *Bristow Daily Record*, March 5, 1938.

12. Zoe A. Tilghman Handwritten and Typed Research Notes, *Memoirs of William Tilghman*, Handwritten by William Tilghman, *Marshal of the Last Frontier*, pg. 304–305, *Miami Record Herald*, October 31, 1913.

13. *Harlow's Weekly*, March 28, 1914, Zoe A. Tilghman Historical Document Collection.

14. Zoe A. Tilghman Historical Document Collection.

15. Ibid.

16. Ibid.

17. Ibid.

18. Zoe A. Tilghman Handwritten and Typed Research Notes, *Memoirs of William Tilghman*, Handwritten by William Tilghman.

19. *Funk & Wagnalls New Encyclopedia* Volume 16.

20. Zoe A. Tilghman Handwritten and Typed Research Notes, *Memoirs of William Tilghman*, Handwritten by William Tilghman, *Oklahoma City Times*, April 24, 1914.

21. *Morning Examiner*, April 28, 1914.

22. *Funk & Wagnalls New Encyclopedia* Volume 16.

23. Zoe A. Tilghman Handwritten and Typed Research Notes, *Memoirs of William Tilghman*, Handwritten by William Tilghman, *Ellis County Capital*, June 19, 1914, *Collinsville Star*, June 13, 1914.

24. *Democrat and Chronicle*, April 29, 1904, *Saskatoon Daily Star*, December 10, 1913, *Marshal of the Last Frontier*, pg. 310–311.

25. Zoe A. Tilghman Handwritten and Typed Research Notes, *Memoirs of William Tilghman*, Handwritten by William Tilghman, *Muskogee Times*, August 5, 1914, *Westville Record*, July 14, 1914, *Bill Tilghman: Marshal of the Last Frontier*, pg. 206–207, *Tulsa Evening Sun*, July 27, 1914.

26. Zoe A. Tilghman Handwritten and Typed Research Notes, *Memoirs of William Tilghman*, Handwritten by William Tilghman, *Roger Mills Sentinel*, January 22, 1914.

27. *Memoirs of William Tilghman*, Handwritten by William Tilghman, Zoe A. Tilghman Handwritten and Typed Research Notes.

28. *Chandler News*, August 14, 1914.

29. *Daily Oklahoman*, April 22, 1914.

30. Ibid.

31. *Memoirs of William Tilghman*, Handwritten by William Tilghman, Zoe A. Tilghman Handwritten and Typed Research Notes.

32. *Guthrie Daily Leader*, October 27, 1914, *St. Louis Post Dispatch*, May 16, 1914, *Sequoyah County Democrat*, September 4, 1914, *Bill Tilghman: Marshal of the Last Frontier*, pg. 205–207.

33. *Memoirs of William Tilghman*, Handwritten by William Tilghman, Zoe A. Tilghman Handwritten and Typed Research Notes, *Marshal of the Last Frontier*, pg. 206–208.

34. *Muskogee Daily Phoenix*, December 26, 1914.

35. *Memoirs of William Tilghman*, Handwritten by William Tilghman, Zoe A. Tilghman Handwritten and Typed Research Notes, *Lincoln County News*, January 22, 1915, *Daily Oklahoman*, June 13, 1915, *More Oklahoma Renegades*, pg. 94–96, *Chandler News*, January 22, 1915.

36. *Memoirs of William Tilghman*, Handwritten by William Tilghman, Zoe A. Tilghman Handwritten and Typed Research Notes, *Muskogee Daily Phoenix*, December 26, 1914, *Marshal of the Last Frontier*, pg. 317–318.

37. *Lincoln County News*, January 22, 1915, *Chandler News*, January 29, 1915.

38. *Memoirs of William Tilghman*, Handwritten by William Tilghman, Zoe A. Tilghman Handwritten and Typed Research Notes, *Chandler News*, February 5, 1915.

39. Zoe A. Tilghman Historical Document Collection.

40. Ibid.

41. Ibid.

42. *Memoirs of William Tilghman*, Handwritten by William Tilghman, Zoe A. Tilghman Handwritten and Typed Research Notes, *Lincoln County News*, March 12, 1915, *Bill Tilghman: Marshal of the Last Frontier*, pg. 207–209, *Encyclopedia of Western Lawmen and Outlaws*, pg. 291–292.

43. *Muskogee Times Democrat*, March 27, 1915, *Memoirs of William Tilghman*, Handwritten by William Tilghman, Zoe A. Tilghman Handwritten and Typed Research Notes.

44. *Sapulpa Herald*, March 31, 1915, *Bill Tilghman: Marshal of the Last Frontier*, pg. 208–209, *Memoirs of William Tilghman*, Handwritten by William Tilghman, Zoe A. Tilghman Handwritten and Typed Research Notes, *Muskogee Daily Phoenix*, March 28, 1915.

45. *Sapulpa Herald*, March 31, 1915, *Bill Tilghman: Marshal of the Last Frontier*, pg. 208–209, *Memoirs of William Tilghman*, Handwritten by William Tilghman, Zoe A. Tilghman Handwritten and Typed Research Notes, *Muskogee Daily Phoenix*, March 28, 1915.

46. *Memoirs of William Tilghman*, Handwritten by William Tilghman, Zoe A. Tilghman Handwritten and Typed Research Notes.

47. *Chandler Tribune*, May 27, 1915.

48. Ibid.

49. Ibid.

50. *Memoirs of William Tilghman*, Handwritten by William Tilghman, Zoe A. Tilghman Handwritten and Typed Research Notes, *Adair Citizen*, June 3, 1915, *Guthrie Daily Leader*, June 3, 1915, *More Oklahoma Renegades*, pg. 94–96.

51. *Daily Ardmoreite*, July 1, 1915.

52. Ibid.

53. Zoe A. Tilghman Historical Document Collection.

54. Ibid.

55. *Memoirs of William Tilghman*, Handwritten by William Tilghman, Zoe A. Tilghman Handwritten and Typed Research Notes, *Paducah Sun Democrat*, October 6, 1915.

56. Zoe A. Tilghman Historical Document Collection.

57. Ibid.

58. Ibid.

59. Ibid.

60. Zoe A. Tilghman Historical Document Collection, *Bill Tilghman: Marshal of the Last Frontier*, pg. 208–209, *Marshal of the Last Frontier*, pg. 301–302.

CHAPTER 8

1. *Norman Transcript*, July 17, 1939, *Daily Oklahoman*, July 16, 1939.

2. Zoe A. Tilghman Historical Document Collection, Zoe A. Tilghman Handwritten and Typed Research Notes.

3. Zoe A. Tilghman Historical Document Collection, Zoe A. Tilghman Handwritten and Typed Research Notes.

4. Zoe A. Tilghman Historical Document Collection, Zoe A. Tilghman Handwritten and Typed Research Notes, *Memoirs of William Tilghman*, Handwritten by William Tilghman.

5. *Houston Post*, January 31,1916, *Oklahoma News*, January 19, 1916.

6. Zoe A. Tilghman Historical Document Collection, Zoe A. Tilghman Handwritten and Typed Research Notes, *Memoirs of William Tilghman*, Handwritten by William Tilghman, *Daily Oklahoman*, July 20, 1916, *Marshal of the Last Frontier*, pg. 323–324.

7. Zoe A. Tilghman Historical Document Collection, Zoe A. Tilghman Handwritten and Typed Research Notes, *Memoirs of William Tilghman*, Handwritten by William Tilghman.

8. Zoe A. Tilghman Historical Document Collection, Zoe A. Tilghman Handwritten and Typed Research Notes, *Memoirs of William Tilghman*, Handwritten by William Tilghman.

9. Zoe A. Tilghman Historical Document Collection, Zoe A. Tilghman Handwritten and Typed Research Notes, *Memoirs of William Tilghman*, Handwritten by William Tilghman.

10. Zoe A. Tilghman Historical Document Collection, Zoe A. Tilghman Handwritten and Typed Research Notes, *Memoirs of William Tilghman*, Handwritten by William Tilghman.

11. Zoe A. Tilghman Historical Document Collection, Zoe A. Tilghman Handwritten and Typed Research Notes, *Memoirs of William Tilghman*, Handwritten by William Tilghman.

12. Zoe A. Tilghman Historical Document Collections, Zoe A. Tilghman Handwritten and Typed Research Notes, Memoirs of William Tilghman, Handwritten by William Tilghman

13. Zoe A. Tilghman Historical Document Collection, Zoe A. Tilghman Handwritten and Typed Research Notes, *Memoirs of William Tilghman*, Handwritten by William Tilghman, *Marshal of the Last Frontier*, pg. 323–324.

14. Zoe A. Tilghman Historical Document Collection, Zoe A. Tilghman Handwritten and Typed Research Notes, *Memoirs of William Tilghman*, Handwritten by William Tilghman.

15. Zoe A. Tilghman Historical Document Collection, Zoe A. Tilghman Handwritten and Typed Research Notes, *Memoirs of William Tilghman*, Handwritten by William Tilghman.

16. Zoe A. Tilghman Historical Document Collection, Zoe A. Tilghman Handwritten and Typed Research Notes, *Memoirs of William Tilghman*, Handwritten by William Tilghman.

17. Zoe A. Tilghman Historical Document Collection, Zoe A. Tilghman Handwritten and Typed Research Notes, *Memoirs of William Tilghman*, Handwritten by William Tilghman.

18. Zoe A. Tilghman Historical Document Collection, Zoe A. Tilghman Handwritten and Typed Research Notes, *Memoirs of William Tilghman*, Handwritten by William Tilghman, *Marshal of the Last Frontier*, pg. 324–325.

19. Zoe A. Tilghman Historical Document Collection, Zoe A. Tilghman Handwritten and Typed Research Notes, *Memoirs of William Tilghman*, Handwritten by William Tilghman, *Marshal of the Last Frontier*, pg. 323–324.

20. Zoe A. Tilghman Historical Document Collection, Zoe A. Tilghman Handwritten and Typed Research Notes, *Memoirs of William Tilghman*, Handwritten by William Tilghman.

21. Zoe A. Tilghman Historical Document Collection, Zoe A. Tilghman Handwritten and Typed Research Notes, *Memoirs of William Tilghman*, Handwritten by William Tilghman.

22. Zoe A. Tilghman Historical Document Collection, Zoe A. Tilghman Handwritten and Typed Research Notes, *Memoirs of William Tilghman*, Handwritten by William Tilghman.

23. Zoe A. Tilghman Historical Document Collection, Zoe A. Tilghman Handwritten and Typed Research Notes, *Memoirs of William Tilghman*, Handwritten by William Tilghman.

24. Zoe A. Tilghman Historical Document Collection, Zoe A. Tilghman Handwritten and Typed Research Notes, *Memoirs of William Tilghman*, Handwritten by William Tilghman.

25. Zoe A. Tilghman Historical Document Collection, Zoe A. Tilghman Handwritten and Typed Research Notes, *Memoirs of William Tilghman*, Handwritten by William Tilghman.

26. Zoe A. Tilghman Historical Document Collection, Zoe A. Tilghman Handwritten and Typed Research Notes, *Memoirs of William Tilghman*, Handwritten by William Tilghman.

27. Zoe A. Tilghman Historical Document Collections, Zoe A. Tilghman Handwritten and Typed Research Notes, Memoirs of William Tilghman, Handwritten by William Tilghman

28. Zoe A. Tilghman Historical Document Collection, Zoe A. Tilghman Handwritten and Typed Research Notes, *Memoirs of William Tilghman*, Handwritten by William Tilghman.

29. Zoe A. Tilghman Historical Document Collection, Zoe A. Tilghman Handwritten and Typed Research Notes, *Memoirs of William Tilghman*, Handwritten by William Tilghman.

30. Zoe A. Tilghman Historical Document Collection, Zoe A. Tilghman Handwritten and Typed Research Notes, *Memoirs of William Tilghman*, Handwritten by William Tilghman.

31. Zoe A. Tilghman Historical Document Collection, Zoe A. Tilghman Handwritten and Typed Research Notes, *Memoirs of William Tilghman*, Handwritten by William Tilghman.

32. Zoe A. Tilghman Historical Document Collection, Zoe A. Tilghman Handwritten and Typed Research Notes, *Memoirs of William Tilghman*, Handwritten by William Tilghman, *Oklahoma News*, November 17, 1917.

33. Zoe A. Tilghman Historical Document Collection, Zoe A. Tilghman Handwritten and Typed Research Notes, *Memoirs of William Tilghman*, Handwritten by William Tilghman.

34. Zoe A. Tilghman Historical Document Collection, Zoe A. Tilghman Handwritten and Typed Research Notes, *Memoirs of William Tilghman*, Handwritten by William Tilghman.

35. Zoe A. Tilghman Historical Document Collection, Zoe A. Tilghman Handwritten and Typed Research Notes, *Memoirs of William Tilghman*, Handwritten by William Tilghman.

36. Zoe A. Tilghman Handwritten and Typed Research Notes, *Memoirs of William Tilghman*, Handwritten by William Tilghman, *Guthrie Daily Leader*, January 22, 1918, *Harlow's Weekly*, March 6, 1918.

37. Zoe A. Tilghman Handwritten and Typed Research Notes, *Memoirs of William Tilghman*, Handwritten by William Tilghman.

38. *Vinita Leader*, September 5, 1918, *Blackwell Daily World*, September 3, 1918, *Akron Evening News*, July 28, 1919, *Marshal of the Last Frontier*, pg. 329–330.

39. *Daily Oklahoman*, November 30, 1919.

40. Ibid.

41. Zoe A. Tilghman Handwritten and Typed Research Notes, *Memoirs of William Tilghman*, Handwritten by William Tilghman.

42. *Advance Democrat*, September 16, 1920, *Morning Tulsa Daily World*, June 11, 1920.

43. *Morning Tulsa Daily World*, June 11, 1920.

44. Zoe A. Tilghman Handwritten and Typed Research Notes, *Memoirs of William Tilghman*, Handwritten by William Tilghman, *Chandler News*, September 17, 1920, *Oklahoma News*, February 16, 1920, *Oklahoma News*, October 26, 1920, *Marshal of the Last Frontier*, pg. 329–330.

45. Zoe A. Tilghman Historical Document Collection, Zoe A. Tilghman Handwritten and Typed Research Notes, *Memoirs of William Tilghman*, Handwritten by William Tilghman, *Lincoln County Republican*, November 18, 1920.

46. Zoe A. Tilghman Historical Document Collection, Zoe A. Tilghman Handwritten and Typed Research Notes, *Memoirs of William Tilghman*, Handwritten by William Tilghman.

47. Zoe A. Tilghman Handwritten and Typed Research Notes, *Memoirs of William Tilghman*, Handwritten by William Tilghman, *Marshal of the Last Frontier*, pg. 331–334, https://www.okhistory.org/publications/enc/entry.php Ku Klux Klan.

48. https://www.okhistory.org/publications/enc/entry.php Ku Klux Klan, Zoe A. Tilghman Handwritten and Typed Research Notes, *Memoirs of William Tilghman*, Handwritten by William Tilghman, *Bill Tilghman: Marshal of the Last Frontier*, pg. 211–215, *The Headlight*, March 24, 1922.

49. Zoe A. Tilghman Handwritten and Typed Research Notes, *Memoirs of William Tilghman*, Handwritten by William Tilghman.

50. Zoe A. Tilghman Handwritten and Typed Research Notes, *Memoirs of William Tilghman*, Handwritten by William Tilghman, *Oklahoma City Times*, March 3, 1922, *Marshal of the Last Frontier*, pg. 332–333.

51. *Daily Ardmoreite*, March 3, 1922, *Oklahoma City Times*, September 18, 1922.

52. *Ponca City News*, March 3, 1922, *Okmulgee Daily Times*, March 4, 1922, *Ada Weekly News*, September 6, 1922, *Marshal of the Last Frontier*, pg. 335–336, *Muskogee Times Democrat*, May 29, 1922, *Nowata Daily Star*, March 9, 1923.

53. Zoe A. Tilghman Handwritten and Typed Research Notes, *Memoirs of William Tilghman*, Handwritten by William Tilghman, *Marshal of the Last Frontier*, pg. 342–343.

54. *Oklahoma News*, March 2, 1922.

55. Ibid.

56. *Oklahoma Leader*, August 3, 1922, https://shareok.org/handle/11244/4165 A History of the Ku Klux Klan in Oklahoma.

57. Zoe A. Tilghman Handwritten and Typed Research Notes, *Memoirs of William Tilghman*, Handwritten by William Tilghman, *Marshal of the Last Frontier*, pg. 342–343.

58. Zoe A. Tilghman Handwritten and Typed Research Notes.

59. *Harlow's Weekly*, November 4, 1922.

60. Ibid.

61. Zoe A. Tilghman Handwritten and Typed Research Notes, *Memoirs of William Tilghman*, Handwritten by William Tilghman, *Caldwell Messenger*, January 10, 1923.

62. Zoe A. Tilghman Handwritten and Typed Research Notes, *Memoirs of William Tilghman*, Handwritten by William Tilghman, *Albuquerque Journal*, October 15, 1923.

63. *Albuquerque Journal*, October 15, 1923.

64. Ibid.

65. Zoe A. Tilghman Handwritten and Typed Research Notes, *Memoirs of William Tilghman*, Handwritten by William Tilghman, *Alfalfa County* News, November 11, 1923, *Marshal of the Last Frontier*, pg. 344–346.

66. Zoe A. Tilghman Handwritten and Typed Research Notes, *Memoirs of William Tilghman*, Handwritten by William Tilghman, *Bill Tilghman: Marshal of the Last Frontier*, pg. 221–223.

67. *Buffalo Republican*, November 8, 1923.

68. Zoe A. Tilghman Handwritten and Typed Research Notes, *Memoirs of William Tilghman*, Handwritten by William Tilghman, *Bill Tilghman: Marshal of the Last Frontier*, pg. 222–223, Message of Governor Martin E. Trapp State of the State Address.

69. Zoe A. Tilghman Handwritten and Typed Research Notes, *Memoirs of William Tilghman*, Handwritten by William Tilghman, *Bill Tilghman: Marshal of the Last Frontier*, pg. 222–223.

70. Zoe A. Tilghman Handwritten and Typed Research Notes, *Memoirs of William Tilghman*, Handwritten by William Tilghman.

CHAPTER 9

1. Zoe A. Tilghman Handwritten and Typed Research Notes, *Memoirs of William Tilghman*, Handwritten by William Tilghman, *Daily Legal News*, August 22, 1923.

2. *Enid Daily Eagle*, September 3, 1924, *Ada Evening News*, August 12, 1924.

3. Zoe A. Tilghman Handwritten and Typed Research Notes.

4. Ibid.

5. Zoe A. Tilghman Handwritten and Typed Research Notes, *Marshal of the Last Frontier*, pg. 352–353.

6. Zoe A. Tilghman Handwritten and Typed Research Notes, *Memoirs of William Tilghman*, Handwritten by William Tilghman, Zoe A. Tilghman Historical Document Collection.

7. Zoe A. Tilghman Handwritten and Typed Research Notes, *Memoirs of William Tilghman*, Handwritten by William Tilghman, *Weleetka American*, September 18, 1924, *Harlow's Weekly*, October 11, 1924.

8. *Shawnee Morning News*, October 4, 1924.

9. Ibid.

10. Ibid.

11. https://www.law.cornell.edu/wex/mann_act Mann Act.

12. Zoe A. Tilghman Handwritten and Typed Research Notes, *Memoirs of William Tilghman*, Handwritten by William Tilghman, Zoe A. Tilghman Historical Document Collection.

13. Zoe A. Tilghman Handwritten and Typed Research Notes, *Memoirs of William Tilghman*, Handwritten by William Tilghman, Zoe A. Tilghman Historical Document Collection.

14. *Oklahoma News*, October 18, 1924.

15. *Muskogee Daily Phoenix*, October 19, 1924.

16. Zoe A. Tilghman Handwritten and Typed Research Notes.

17. Zoe A. Tilghman Handwritten and Typed Research Notes, *Memoirs of William Tilghman*, Handwritten by William Tilghman, Zoe A. Tilghman Historical Document Collection, *Daily Oklahoman*, October 22, 1924.

18. *Daily Oklahoman*, October 22, 1924.

19. *Daily Ardmoreite*, April 30, 1918, *Madill News*, February 9, 1906.

20. *Madill News*, April 25, 1912, *Red River Farmer*, August 30, 1913, *Madill Record*, May 31, 1917, *Daily Ardmoreite*, August 10, 1917.

21. *Daily Ardmoreite*, July 26, 1920, *Madill Record*, June 24, 1920, *Red River Famer*, December 16, 1920.

22. *Madill Record*, March 22, 1923, *Madill Record*, January 4, 1923, *Madill Record*, February 1, 1923, *Madill Record*, May 3, 1923.

23. *Madill Record*, February 21, 1924, *Madill Record*, March 27, 1924.

24. *Madill Record*, June 26, 1924, *Wewoka Capital Democrat*, June 5, 1924.

25. *Wewoka Capital Democrat*, August 14, 1924.

26. *Shawnee Morning News*, September 13, 1924, *Shawnee Morning News*, October 30, 1924.

27. Zoe A. Tilghman Handwritten and Typed Research Notes, *Memoirs of William Tilghman*, Handwritten by William Tilghman, Zoe A. Tilghman Historical Document Collection, *San Francisco Examiner*, December 14, 1924, *Marshal of the Last Frontier*, pg. 356–357.

28. Zoe A. Tilghman Handwritten and Typed Research Notes, *Memoirs of William Tilghman*, Handwritten by William Tilghman, Zoe A. Tilghman Historical Document Collection, *Marshal of the Last Frontier*, pg. 359–360, *Henryette Daily Free Lance*, November 3, 1924.

29. Zoe A. Tilghman Handwritten and Typed Research Notes, *Memoirs of William Tilghman*, Handwritten by William Tilghman, Zoe A. Tilghman Historical Document Collection, *Daily Oklahoman*, October 22, 1924.

30. *Henryette Daily Free Lance*, November 3, 1924.

31. *Daily Free Weleetka American*, October 23, 1924, *Morning Examiner*, November 11, 1924, *Daily Oklahoman*, November 3, 1924, *Bartlesville Examiner Enterprise*, November 2, 1924, *Madill Record*, November 6, 1924.

32. *Daily Oklahoman*, November 3, 1924.

33. *Daily Oklahoman*, November 3, 1924, *Tulsa World*, November 2, 1924, *Muskogee Daily Phoenix*, November 2, 1924.

34. *Morning Examiner*, November 2, 1924.

35. Ibid.

36. Zoe A. Tilghman Handwritten and Typed Research Notes.

37. Ibid.

38. Ibid.

39. *Daily Ardmoreite*, November 3, 1924.

40. *Daily Oklahoman*, November 3, 1924, *Daily Ardmoreite*, November 3, 1924.

41. Zoe A. Tilghman Handwritten and Typed Research Notes.

42. Ibid.

43. Ibid.

44. *Daily Oklahoman*, November 3, 1924.

45. *Henryette Daily Free Lance*, November 3, 1924.

46. *Muskogee Times*, November 3, 1924.

47. Zoe A. Tilghman Handwritten and Typed Research Notes.

48. Ibid.

49. Ibid.

50. Ibid.

51. *Ardmore Daily Press*, April 29, 1925, *Daily Oklahoman*, November 9, 1924, *Wewoka Capital Democrat*, January 8, 1925.

52. *Morning Examiner*, December 16, 1924, *Nowata Daily Star*, May 21, 1925.

53. *Tulsa Times*, May 22, 1925.

54. Ibid.

55. Ibid.

56. Ibid.

57. Ibid.

58. Ibid.

59. Ibid.

60. *Tulsa Tribune*, May 22, 1925, Zoe A. Tilghman Handwritten and Typed Research Notes, *Marshal of the Last Frontier*, pg. 370–371.

61. *Daily Ardmoreite*, May 26, 1925.

62. *Daily Ardmoreite*, May 26, 1925.

63. *Ardmore Daily Press*, May 26, 1925.

64. *Lawton Constitution*, May 28, 1925, Zoe Tilghman Handwritten and Typed Research Notes, *Marshal of the Last Frontier*, pg. 373-374.

65. Ibid.

66. *Bartlesville Examiner Enterprise*, July 22, 1925.

67. *Henryette Daily Free Lance*, November 13, 1927, *Stillwater Democrat*, April 12, 1928, *Daily Oklahoman*, January 29, 1931.

68. *Cushing Daily Citizen*, July 18, 1932.
69. Ibid.

Chapter 10

1. Zoe A. Tilghman Handwritten and Typed Research Notes, Zoe A. Tilghman Historical Document Collection.
2. Zoe A. Tilghman Handwritten and Typed Research Notes, Zoe A. Tilghman Historical Document Collection.
3. Zoe A. Tilghman Handwritten and Typed Research Notes, Zoe A. Tilghman Historical Document Collection.
4. Zoe A. Tilghman Handwritten and Typed Research Notes, Zoe A. Tilghman Historical Document Collection.
5. Zoe A. Tilghman Handwritten and Typed Research Notes, Zoe A. Tilghman Historical Document Collection.
6. Zoe A. Tilghman Handwritten and Typed Research Notes, Zoe A. Tilghman Historical Document Collection.
7. Zoe A. Tilghman Handwritten and Typed Research Notes, Zoe A. Tilghman Historical Document Collection.
8. Zoe A. Tilghman Handwritten and Typed Research Notes, Zoe A. Tilghman Historical Document Collection.
9. Zoe A. Tilghman Handwritten and Typed Research Notes, Zoe A. Tilghman Historical Document Collection.
10. Zoe A. Tilghman Handwritten and Typed Research Notes, Zoe A. Tilghman Historical Document Collection, *Oklahoma County News*, February 24, 1950, *Ponca City News*, March 23, 1950, *Tulsa Tribune*, April 25, 1960, https://www.ancestry.com Woodrow Tilghman.
11. Zoe A. Tilghman Handwritten and Typed Research Notes, Zoe A. Tilghman Historical Document Collection, *Daily Oklahoman*, https://www.ancestry.com Tench Tilghman.
12. Zoe A. Tilghman Handwritten and Typed Research Notes, Zoe A. Tilghman Historical Document Collection.
13. Zoe A. Tilghman Handwritten and Typed Research Notes, Zoe A. Tilghman Historical Document Collection.
14. https://www.genealogy.com/forum/surnames/topics/parker/14518/ Quanah Parker's Children.
15. Zoe A. Tilghman Handwritten and Typed Research Notes, Zoe A. Tilghman Historical Document Collection.
16. Zoe A. Tilghman Handwritten and Typed Research Notes, Zoe A. Tilghman Historical Document Collection.
17. *Grandfield Enterprise*, July 4, 1935.
18. Zoe A. Tilghman Handwritten and Typed Research Notes, Zoe A. Tilghman Historical Document Collection.
19. Zoe A. Tilghman Handwritten and Typed Research Notes, Zoe A. Tilghman Historical Document Collection.

20. Zoe A. Tilghman Handwritten and Typed Research Notes, Zoe A. Tilghman Historical Document Collection.

21. Zoe A. Tilghman Handwritten and Typed Research Notes, Zoe A. Tilghman Historical Document Collection.

22. Zoe A. Tilghman Handwritten and Typed Research Notes, Zoe A. Tilghman Historical Document Collection.

23. Zoe A. Tilghman Handwritten and Typed Research Notes, Zoe A. Tilghman Historical Document Collection.

24. Zoe A. Tilghman Handwritten and Typed Research Notes, Zoe A. Tilghman Historical Document Collection.

25. Zoe A. Tilghman Handwritten and Typed Research Notes, Zoe A. Tilghman Historical Document Collection.

26. Zoe A. Tilghman Handwritten and Typed Research Notes, Zoe A. Tilghman Historical Document Collection, *Oklahoma News*, December 25, 1938.

27. *Oklahoma News*, December 25, 1938.

28. Ibid.

29. Ibid.

30. Zoe A. Tilghman Handwritten and Typed Research Notes, Zoe A. Tilghman Historical Document Collection, *Oklahoma News*, December 25, 1938.

31. Zoe A. Tilghman Handwritten and Typed Research Notes, Zoe A. Tilghman Historical Document Collection, *Daily Oklahoman*, August 1, 1948.

32. Zoe A. Tilghman Handwritten and Typed Research Notes, Zoe A. Tilghman Historical Document Collection, *Daily Oklahoman*, August 1, 1948.

33. Zoe A. Tilghman Handwritten and Typed Research Notes, Zoe A. Tilghman Historical Document Collection, *Daily Oklahoman*, August 1, 1948.

34. Zoe A. Tilghman Handwritten and Typed Research Notes, Zoe A. Tilghman Historical Document Collection, *Daily Oklahoman*, August 1, 1948.

35. Zoe A. Tilghman Handwritten and Typed Research Notes, Zoe A. Tilghman Historical Document Collection.

36. Zoe A. Tilghman Handwritten and Typed Research Notes, Zoe A. Tilghman Historical Document Collection.

37. Zoe A. Tilghman Handwritten and Typed Research Notes, Zoe A. Tilghman Historical Document Collection.

38. Zoe A. Tilghman Handwritten and Typed Research Notes, Zoe A. Tilghman Historical Document Collection.

39. Zoe A. Tilghman Handwritten and Typed Research Notes, Zoe A. Tilghman Historical Document Collection, *Life Magazine*, May 18, 1959.

40. *Public Opinion*, March 24, 1960.

41. Ibid.

42. *Life Magazine*, May 18, 1959.

43. Ibid.

44. Zoe A. Tilghman Handwritten and Typed Research Notes, Zoe A. Tilghman Historical Document Collection.

45. Zoe A. Tilghman Handwritten and Typed Research Notes, Zoe A. Tilghman Historical Document Collection.

46. Zoe A. Tilghman Handwritten and Typed Research Notes, Zoe A. Tilghman Historical Document Collection.

47. Zoe A. Tilghman Handwritten and Typed Research Notes, Zoe A. Tilghman Historical Document Collection.

48. Zoe A. Tilghman Handwritten and Typed Research Notes, Zoe A. Tilghman Historical Document Collection.

49. Zoe A. Tilghman Handwritten and Typed Research Notes, Zoe A. Tilghman Historical Document Collection.

50. Zoe A. Tilghman Handwritten and Typed Research Notes, Zoe A. Tilghman Historical Document Collection.

51. Zoe A. Tilghman Handwritten and Typed Research Notes, Zoe A. Tilghman Historical Document Collection.

52. Zoe A. Tilghman Handwritten and Typed Research Notes, Zoe A. Tilghman Historical Document Collection.

53. Zoe A. Tilghman Handwritten and Typed Research Notes, Zoe A. Tilghman Historical Document Collection.

54. Zoe A. Tilghman Handwritten and Typed Research Notes, Zoe A. Tilghman Historical Document Collection.

55. *Lincoln County News*, June 18, 1964, *Daily Oklahoman*, June 15, 1964, *Tulsa World*, June 15, 1964.

Bibliography

Books

Butler, Ken More. *Oklahoma Renegades*. New Orleans: Pelican Publishing, 2007.

DeArment, Robert K. *Bat Masterson: The Man and the Legend*. Norman: University of Oklahoma, 1979.

Enss, Chris, and Howard Kazanjian. *Thunder over the Prairie: The True Story of a Murder and Manhunt by the Greatest Posse of All Time*. Guilford, CT: TwoDot Books, 2009.

Gaines, Craig. *Lost Mines and Buried Treasures of Oklahoma*. Hendersonville, TN: Goldminds Publishing, 2013.

Holm, Tom. *The Great Confusion in Indian Affairs: Native Americans and Whites in the Progressive Era*. Austin: University of Texas Press, 2005.

Miller, Floyd. *Bill Tilghman: Marshal of the Last Frontier*. Garden City, NY: Doubleday & Company, Inc., 1968.

Miller, Nyle H., and Joseph W. Snell. *Great Gunfighters of the Kansas Cowtowns, 1867–1886*. Lincoln: University of Nebraska Press Lincoln, 1963.

Nash, Jay Robert. *Encyclopedia of Western Lawmen and Outlaws*. New York, NY: Paragon House, 1992.

Rutter, Michael. *Bedside Book of Bad Girls: Outlaw Women of the American West*. Helena, MT: FarCountry Press, 2008.

Shirley, Glenn. *Heck Thomas: Frontier Marshal. The Story of a Real Gunfighter*. Philadelphia, PA: Chilton Company, 1962.

Sifakis, Carl. *The Encyclopedia of American Crime*. New York: Smithmark Publishing, 1982.

Tilghman, Zoe. *Marshal of the Last Frontier*. Norman, OK: Arthur H. Clark Company, 1949.

———. *Outlaw Days: A True History of Early-Day Oklahoma Characters*. Oklahoma City, OK: Harlow Publishing Company, 1926.

Wright, Robert M. *Dodge City: The Cowboy Capital and the Great Southwest*. Wichita, KS: Wichita Eagle, 1913.

Young, Fredric R. *Dodge City: Up through a Century in Story and Pictures*. Dodge City, KS: Boot Hill Museum, 1972.

Historical Archives, Magazines, and Pamphlets

Funk & Wagnalls New Encyclopedia: Volume 7, pg. 132-133; Volume 14, pg. 398-399; Volume 16, pg. 229-237; Volume 18, pg. 129–132.

Leslie McRill. *Chronicles of Oklahoma, Spring 1958: Three Guardsmen and the Doolin Gang.*

Life Magazine, Vol. 46, No. 20, May 18, 1959.

Memoirs of William Tilghman, Handwritten by William Tilghman. Western History Collections, University of Oklahoma.

Message of Governor Martin E. Trapp. State of the State Address 1923-1927, pg. 43–46.

Social Science Quarterly, Vol. 49, No. 4, March 1969. "The Fight for Prohibition in Oklahoma Territory," pg. 876–885.

Zoe A. Tilghman. Handwritten and Typed Research Notes Re: Bill Tilghman. Life and Career of Marshal Tilghman/Collection Maintained by the Tilghmans' granddaughter, Suzie Baerst.

Zoe A. Tilghman. Historical Document Collection. Oklahoma Historical Society/ University of Oklahoma.

Newspapers

Ada Evening News, Ada, Oklahoma, August 12, 1924.

Ada Weekly News, Ada, Oklahoma, July 6, 1922.

Adair Citizen, Adair, Oklahoma, June 3, 1915.

Advance Democrat, Stillwater, Oklahoma, September 16, 1920.

Akron Evening News, Akron, Ohio, July 23, 1919.

Albuquerque Journal, Albuquerque, New Mexico, October 15, 1923.

Alfalfa County News, Cherokee, Oklahoma, November 9, 1923.

Alma News, Alma, Georgia, July 12, 1888.

Arapaho Bee, Arapaho, Oklahoma, September 13, 1895.

Ardmore Daily Press, Ardmore, Oklahoma, April 29, 1925; May 26, 1925.

Atchison Weekly Patriot, Atchison, Kansas, February 23, 1878; October 23, 1878; January 4, 1879.

Atoka County Jeffersonian, Atoka, Oklahoma, June 11, 1925.

Bartlesville Daily Enterprise, Bartlesville, Oklahoma, March 27, 1913; April 27, 1914; October 29, 1929.

Bartlesville Examiner Enterprise, Bartlesville, Oklahoma, November 2, 1924; July 22, 1925.

Beaver Herald, Beaver, Oklahoma, May 9, 1895.

Belleville Telescope, Belleville, Kansas, August 29, 1895.

Blackwell Daily News, Blackwell, Oklahoma, June 12, 1908; September 13, 1918.

Blackwell Morning Tribune, Blackwell, Oklahoma, October 28, 1924; October 29, 1929; January 3, 1931.

Blue Valley Farmer, Oklahoma City, Oklahoma.

Bristow Daily Record, Bristow, Oklahoma, March 5, 1938.

Buffalo Republican, Buffalo, Oklahoma, November 8, 1923.

Butler Herald, Butler, Oklahoma, January 16, 1936.

Butte Miner, Butte, Montana, August 24, 1895.

Caldwell Messenger, Caldwell, Kansas, January 10, 1923.

Chandler Daily Publicist, Chandler, Oklahoma, September 16, 1903; February 27, 1905; February 28, 1905; March 27, 1905; April 27, 1905; November 7, 1905.

Chandler News, Chandler, Oklahoma, October 24, 1891; April 21, 1899; November 2, 1900; January 24, 1901; May 9, 1901; May 23, 1901; October 10, 1901; October 23, 1902; February 25, 1904; January 31, 1907; February 2, 1908; March 18, 1909; August 14, 1914; January 22, 1915; January 29, 1915; February 5, 1915; September 17, 1920.

Chandler Publicist, Chandler, Oklahoma, December 11, 1896; February 24, 1899; July 28, 1899; March 9, 1900; November 2, 1900; January 10, 1902; September 18, 1903; September 25, 1903; November 4, 1903; November 6, 1903; January 25, 1904; November 18, 1904; December 30, 1904; February 23, 1905; April 27, 1905; January 25, 1907; March 29, 1907; May 24, 1907; August 9, 1907; August 23, 1907; September 6, 1907.

Chandler Times, Chandler, Oklahoma, March 6, 1913.

Chandler Tribune, Chandler, Oklahoma, August 14, 1903; February 5, 1904; December 30, 1904; September 29, 1905; March 26, 1907; June 4, 1907; July 30, 1907; August 20, 1907; September 10, 1907; March 27, 1908; June 24, 1910; June 21, 1911; July 14, 1911; July 24, 1913; September 25, 1913; May 27, 1915.

Chelsea Reporter, Chelsea, Oklahoma, July 27, 1911.

Chicago Chronicle, Chicago, Illinois, August 22, 1895.

Chickasha Chiefton, Chickasha, Oklahoma, June 14, 1894.

Chickasha Daily Express, Chickasha, Oklahoma, October 7, 1929; November 22, 1933.

Chickasha Star, Chickasha, Oklahoma, January 9, 1930.

Cimarron News, Boise City, Oklahoma, August 27, 1908.

Claremore Messenger, Claremore, Oklahoma, August 28, 1903.

Cleveland Co. Democrat News, Norman, Oklahoma, October 10, 1929.

Cleveland County Leader, Norman, Oklahoma, June 16, 1894.

Clinton Daily News, Clinton, Oklahoma, January 14, 1930.

*Collinsville Sta*r, Collinsville, Oklahoma, June 13, 1914.

County Democrat, Tecumseh, Oklahoma, September 4, 1908.

Cushing Daily Citizen, Cushing, Oklahoma, May 19, 1910; January 8, 1930; May 24, 1930; July 18, 1932; August 19, 1932.

Daily Ardmoreite, Ardmore, Oklahoma, February 8, 1899; March 28, 1913; July 1, 1915; August 10, 1917; April 30, 1918; July 26, 1920; March 3, 1922; November 3, 1924; May 26, 1925.

Daily Legal News, Oklahoma City, Oklahoma, August 23, 1923.

Daily Midget, Kingfisher, Oklahoma, July 17, 1911.

Daily Oklahoman, Oklahoma City, Oklahoma, November 17, 1907; June 10, 1910; April 22, 1914; June 13, 1915; July 20, 1916; November 30, 1919; March 31, 1924; October 18, 1924; October 22, 1924; November 3, 1924; November 4, 1924; November 9, 1924; May 23, 1925; January 29, 1930; January 3, 1931; July 7, 1932; July 17, 1932; July 16, 1939; July 12, 1970; August 3, 1935; October 8, 1935; June 16, 1936; December 15, 1937; April 29, 1945; August 1, 1948; February 2, 1950; June 15, 1964.

The Democrat, Wichita, Kansas, April 5, 1884.

Democrat and Chronicle, Rochester, New York, April 29, 1904.

Dodge City Democrat, Dodge City, Kansas, August 16, 1884.
Dodge City Globe, Dodge City, Kansas, February 1, 1878; February 5, 1878; April 23, 1878; January 7, 1879; April 3, 1883; March 25, 1884; July 15, 1884; March 31, 1885; October 20, 1885; May 25, 1886.
Dodge City Kansas Cowboy, Dodge City, Kansas, August 9, 1884, August 29, 1884.
Dodge City Times, Dodge City, Kansas, July 10, 1884; May 6, 1877; February 16, 1878; October 12, 1878; September 23, 1886; November 18, 1886; December 26, 1889.
Drumright Evening Derrick, Drumright, Oklahoma, October 23, 1924.
Duncan Banner, Duncan, Oklahoma, May 29, 1985.
Edmond Sun Democrat, Edmond, Oklahoma, January 5, 1894.
El Reno Daily American, El Reno, Oklahoma, November 7, 1903.
El Reno Democrat, El Reno, Oklahoma, March 2, 1905.
El Reno Weekly Globe, El Reno, Oklahoma, November 11, 1904.
Ellis County Capital, Arnett, Oklahoma, June 19, 1914.
Emporia Ledger, Emporia, Kansas, December 5, 1878.
Enid Daily Eagle, Enid, Oklahoma, September 3, 1924.
Enid Morning News, Enid, Oklahoma, April 3, 1913.
Evening Democrat, Perry, Oklahoma, November 4, 1893; November 14, 1893; November 15, 1893; December 6, 1893.
Evening Kansan, Newton, Kansas, July 6, 1888.
Florence Bulletin, Florence, Kansas, February 7, 1924.
Foraker Sun, Foraker, Oklahoma, April 27, 1911.
Ford County Globe, Dodge City, Kansas, October 29, 1878; July 15, 1884.
Fort Scott Daily Monitor, Bourbon, Kansas, April 23, 1889.
Frederick Leader, Frederick, Oklahoma, November 4, 1924; September 22, 1931.
Garden City Herald, Garden City, Kansas, May 5, 1883.
The Globe, Portis, Kansas, May 6, 1884; March 9, 1886.
Grandfield Enterprise, Grandfield, Oklahoma, July 4, 1935.
Grant County Register, Ulysses, Kansas, July 14, 1888.
Great Bend Register, Great Bend, Kansas, January 31, 1878.
Guthrie Daily Leader, Guthrie, Oklahoma, July 13, 1893; September 21, 1893; September 24, 1893; October 24, 1893; December 13, 1893; May 3, 1895; October 27, 1914; June 3, 1915; January 22, 1918; November 3, 1924.
Guthrie Democrat, Guthrie, Oklahoma, July 21, 1890; July 25, 1890; July 29, 1890; August 4, 1890.
Harlow's Weekly, Oklahoma City, Oklahoma, March 28, 1914; March 6, 1918; November 4, 1922; October 11, 1924; April 10, 1926; April 17, 1926; May 8, 1926; March 29, 1930; January 3, 1931; August 20, 1932; November 18, 1933.
Hays City Sentinel, Hays, Kansas, April 27, 1878.
The Headlight, Augusta, Oklahoma, March 24, 1922.
Henryetta Daily Free Lance, Henryetta, Oklahoma, November 3, 1924; November 11, 1927.
Hooker Advance, Hooker, Oklahoma, October 19, 1923.
Houston Post, Houston, Texas, January 31, 1916.
The Independent, Cashion, Oklahoma, September 3, 1908.

Jefferson Review, Jefferson, Oklahoma, November 20, 1903.
Jennings Daily News, Jennings, Louisiana, April 16, 1931.
Journal Democrat, Dodge City, Kansas, March 29, 1884; April 5, 1884; October 17, 1885.
Kansas Cowboy, Dodge City, Kansas, August 23, 1884.
Kansas City Star, Kansas City, Missouri, October 9, 1893.
Kansas City Times, Kansas City, Missouri, April 10, 1931; February 17, 1933.
Kenosha Evening News, Kenosha, Wisconsin, January 10, 1930.
Kingfisher Times, Kingfisher, Oklahoma, November 16, 1892; November16, 1893.
Larmar Republican, Larmar, Missouri, August 21, 1924.
Lawton Constitution, Lawton, Oklahoma, May 25, 1925; July 11, 1930.
Leoti Transcript, Leoti, Kansas, July 5, 1888.
Lincoln County Democrat and Telegram, Chandler, Oklahoma, October 18, 1900.
Lincoln County Journal/Stroud Star, Stroud, Oklahoma, June 6, 1907.
Lincoln County News, Chandler, Oklahoma, January 22, 1915; March 12, 1915; June 18, 1964.
Lincoln County Republican, Chandler, Oklahoma, November 18, 1920.
Luther Register News, Luther, Oklahoma, November 1, 1929; February 23, 1933.
Macon News, Macon, Georgia, April 15, 1911.
Madill News, Madill, Oklahoma, February 9, 1906.
Madill Record, Madill, Oklahoma, May 31, 1917; June 24, 1920; January 4, 1923; February 1, 1923; March 22, 1923; May 3, 1923; February 21, 1924; March 27, 1924; June 26, 1924; November 6, 1924.
Magnum Daily Star, Magnum, Oklahoma, July 8, 1931.
Meeker Herald, Meeker, Oklahoma, March 7, 1913.
Miami Daily News Record, Miami, Oklahoma, August 2, 1935; July 15, 1936.
Miami Record Herald, Miami, Oklahoma, October 31, 1913.
Morning Examiner, Bartlesville, Oklahoma, April 28, 1914; November 2, 1924; November 11, 1924; December 16, 1924.
Morning Tulsa Daily World, Tulsa, Oklahoma, June 11, 1920.
Mulhall Enterprise, Mulhall, Oklahoma, June 16, 1894.
Muskogee Daily Phoenix, Muskogee, Oklahoma, December 26, 1914; March 28, 1915; October 19, 1924; November 2, 1924.
Muskogee Phoenix, Muskogee, Oklahoma, May 28, 1891.
Muskogee Times, Muskogee, Oklahoma, August 5, 1914; March 27, 1915.
Muskogee Times Democrat, Muskogee, Oklahoma, May 29, 1922; November 3, 1924.
Norman Democrat Topic, Norman, Oklahoma, August 27, 1891.
Norman Transcript, Norman, Oklahoma, May 16, 1901; January 28, 1930; July 17, 1939.
Nowata Daily Star, Nowata, Oklahoma, March 9, 1923; May 21, 1925.
Observer, Guthrie, Oklahoma, January 23, 1902; February 8, 1902.
The Oklahoman, Oklahoma City, Oklahoma, August 9, 1936.
Oklahoma City News, Oklahoma City, Oklahoma, September 28, 1912.
Oklahoma City Times, Oklahoma City, Oklahoma, August 1, 1912; September 28, 1912; April 24, 1914; March 3, 1922; September 18, 1922; November 6, 1922.
Oklahoma County News, Jones, Oklahoma, December 9, 1927; May 16, 1930; August 26, 1932; May 14, 1937; May 23, 1937; February 24, 1950.

Oklahoma Daily Star, Oklahoma City, Oklahoma, May 4, 1895.
Oklahoma Leader, Guthrie, Oklahoma, December 30, 1915; August 2, 1922; August 3, 1922.
Oklahoma News, Oklahoma City, Oklahoma, October 25, 1912; July 30, 1914; January 19, 1916; November 17, 1917; February 16, 1920; October 26, 1920; March 2, 1922; October 18, 1924; March 10, 1926; April 19, 1926; October 31, 1929; May 26, 1930; May 21, 1932; July 25, 1932; March 18, 1934; August 5, 1935; October 8, 1935; November 27, 1935; January 28, 1936; February 5, 1936; June 15, 1936; December 25, 1938.
Oklahoma State Capital, Guthrie, Oklahoma, January 12, 1896; March 31, 1899; September 25, 1900; October 14, 1900; July 4, 1908; March 30, 1909; April 3, 1909; April 8, 1909; April 16, 1909.
Oklahoma State Register, Guthrie, Oklahoma, March 2, 1905; April 20, 1905; May 20, 1926.
Oklahoma Times Journal, Oklahoma City, Oklahoma, November 1, 1893.
Oklahoma Weekly Leader, Oklahoma City, Oklahoma, March 14, 1907.
Okmulgee Daily Times, Okmulgee, Oklahoma, March 4, 1922; October 13, 1925.
Okmulgee Republican, Okmulgee, Oklahoma, July 20, 1911.
Oswego Independent, Oswego, Kansas, October 26, 1878.
Paducah Sun Democrat, Paducah, Kentucky, October 6, 1915.
People's Press, Perkins, Oklahoma, April 27, 1905.
People's Voice, Norman, Oklahoma, September 19, 1902.
Perry Daily Times, Perry, Oklahoma, November 20, 1893; November 24, 1893; December 11, 1893; December 26, 1893.
Perry Democrat, Perry, Oklahoma, September 12, 1895.
Perry Republican, Perry, Oklahoma, September 10, 1908; September 18, 1908.
Pittsburgh Press, Pittsburgh, Pennsylvania, January 9, 1930.
Ponca City Democrat, Ponca City, Oklahoma, December 10, 1896.
Ponca City News, Ponca City, Oklahoma, March 3, 1922; March 23, 1950.
Pond Creek Daily Vidette, Pond Creek, Oklahoma, July 18, 1903.
The Publicist, Chandler, Oklahoma, June 8, 1900; August 17, 1900; October 19, 1900.
Public Opinion, Chambersburg, Pennsylvania, March 24, 1960.
Red River Farmer, Madill, Oklahoma, August 30, 1913; December 16, 1920.
Ripley Times, Ripley, Oklahoma, July 17, 1903.
Roger Mills Sentinel, Cheyenne, Oklahoma, January 22, 1914.
Salt Lake Telegram, Salt Lake, Utah, October 13, 1923.
San Francisco Examiner, San Francisco, California, December 14, 1924.
Sapulpa Herald, Sapulpa, Oklahoma, March 31, 1915.
Saskatoon Daily Star, Saskatoon, Saskatchewan, Canada, December 10, 1913.
Seminole Producer, Seminole, Oklahoma, January 17, 1932.
Sequoyah County Democrat, Sallisaw, Oklahoma, September 4, 1914.
Shawnee Daily Herald, Shawnee, Oklahoma, June 14, 1908; March 30, 1909.
Shawnee Herald, Shawnee, Oklahoma, November 13, 1904.
Shawnee Morning News, Shawnee, Oklahoma, August 24, 1924; September 13, 1924; October 4, 1924; October 30, 1924; November 4, 1924.

Shawnee News, Shawnee, Oklahoma, August 14, 1911.

Sioux City Journal, Sioux City, Iowa, November 4, 1923.

Sooner State Press, Norman, Oklahoma, April 4, 1931; October 1, 1932; February 25, 1933.

Southern Kansas Gazette, Augusta, Kansas, October 17, 1878.

Southwest World, Guthrie, Oklahoma, March 29, 1902.

Sparks Review, Sparks, Oklahoma, April 19, 1907; May 26, 1907.

St. Louis Post Dispatch, St. Louis, Missouri, October 3, 1913; March 1, 1914; May 16, 1914.

Stillwater Gazette, Stillwater, Oklahoma, May 16, 1901; July 3, 1902; October 9, 1902; August 14, 1914.

Stroud Messenger, Stroud, Oklahoma, February 9, 1906.

Stroud Sun, Stroud, Oklahoma, July 17, 1903.

Sumner County Press, Wellington, Kansas, October 24, 1878.

The Sun, Dodge City, Kansas, September 9, 1886.

Taloga Advocate, Taloga, Oklahoma, September 7, 1895.

Tecumseh Republican, Tecumseh, Oklahoma, March 13, 1893; June 15, 1893.

Times Democrat, Pawnee, Oklahoma, May 10, 1895.

Tulsa Evening Sun, Tulsa, Oklahoma, July 27, 1914.

Tulsa Post, Tulsa, Oklahoma, January 12, 1911.

Tulsa Tribune, Tulsa, Oklahoma, November 7, 1924; May 22, 1925; April 25, 1960.

Tulsa World, Tulsa, Oklahoma, November 2, 1924; June 15, 1964.

Verden News, Verden, Oklahoma, October 11, 1929; November 1, 1929.

Vici Beacon, Vici, Oklahoma, June 5, 1930.

Vinita Leader, Vinita, Oklahoma, September 12, 1895; September 5, 1918.

Walters Herald, Walters, Oklahoma, March 20, 1930; July 4, 1935.

Washington Post, Washington, DC, December 14, 1927.

Washington Times, Washington, DC, December 14, 1927.

Waurika News Democrat, Waurika, Oklahoma, November 15, 1935.

Weekly Commonwealth, Topeka, Kansas, July 26, 1872.

Weekly Oklahoma State Capital, Guthrie, Oklahoma, April 27, 1888; September 19, 1891; October 7, 1893; October 14, 1893; January 16, 1896; March 16, 1896; November 14, 1903.

Weekly State Democrat, Lawton, Oklahoma, January 25, 1906.

Weleetka American, Weleetka, Oklahoma, September 18, 1924; October 23, 1924.

Wellston News, Wellston, Oklahoma, May 26, 1905.

Westville Record, Westville, Oklahoma, July 14, 1914.

Wewoka Capital Democrat, Wewoka, Oklahoma, June 5, 1924; January 8, 1925; August 14, 1924; October 23, 1924; May 28, 1925.

Wichita Daily Times, Wichita Falls, Texas, March 16, 1930.

Winfield Courier, Winfield, Kansas, February 7, 1878.

Websites

http://genealogytrails.com/kan/allen/history2.html

About the Authors

Howard Kazanjian is a film producer renowned for his work on the Star Wars films and the Indiana Jones movies. Kazanjian is a published nonfiction author, focusing on the factual Old West of US history. In 2021, he published his memoir *Howard Kazanjian: A Producer's Life*. He lives in San Marino, California.

Chris Enss is a *New York Times*–best-selling author who has been writing about women of the Old West for more than thirty years. She has penned more than fifty published books on the subject. Her work has been honored with nine Will Rogers Medallion Awards, two Elmer Kelton Book Awards, an Oklahoma Center for the Book Award, three *Foreword Review* Magazine Book Awards, the Laura Downing Journalism Award, three Western Writers of America Spur Finalist Awards, and a WILLA Award from Women Writing the West for Best Scholarly Nonfiction Book. Enss's most recent works are *The Widowed Ones: Beyond the Battle of the Little Bighorn*, *Along Came a Cowgirl: Daring and Iconic Cowgirls of Rodeos and Wild West Shows*, and *Straight Lady: The Life and Times of Margaret Dumont, "The Fifth Marx Brother."*